Virtual and Augmented Reality in English Language Arts Education

Virtual and Augmented Reality in English Language Arts Education

Edited by
Clarice M. Moran and Mary F. Rice

LEXINGTON BOOKS
Lanham • Boulder • New York • London

Published by Lexington Books
An imprint of The Rowman & Littlefield Publishing Group, Inc.
4501 Forbes Boulevard, Suite 200, Lanham, Maryland 20706
www.rowman.com

6 Tinworth Street, London SE11 5AL, United Kingdom

British Library Cataloguing in Publication Information Available

Library of Congress Cataloging-in-Publication Data

Names: Moran, Clarice M., 1964- editor. | Rice, Mary, 1980- editor.
Title: Virtual and augmented reality in English language arts education / Edited by Clarice M. Moran and Mary Rice.
Description: Lanham : Lexington Books, [2021] | Includes bibliographical references and index.
Identifiers: LCCN 2020051086 (print) | LCCN 2020051087 (ebook) | ISBN 9781793629852 (Cloth : acid-free paper) | ISBN 9781793629869 (eBook)
Subjects: LCSH: Language arts—Computer-assisted instruction. | Virtual reality in education.
Classification: LCC LB1576.7 .V57 2021 (print) | LCC LB1576.7 (ebook) | DDC 372.6—dc23
LC record available at https://lccn.loc.gov/2020051086
LC ebook record available at https://lccn.loc.gov/2020051087

Contents

List of Tables and Figures

TABLES

FIGURES

Introduction

Teachers have been asked to do *virtually everything*—plan fantastic educational lessons, manage behavior, use technologies to engage and promote learning, assess and report to stakeholders, build strong relationships, advocate for students, keep family secrets, and more. However, as technologies have progressed and become more widely available, and as the COVID-19 pandemic set in, teachers are now being asked to do *everything, virtually*. This book was born from this shift in paradigms. It is both story and vision, and it is about how English language arts (ELA) teachers are learning to do everything virtually—through virtual and augmented reality technologies.

Virtual realities are digital worlds that users completely immerse themselves in to interact with materials, objects, and other users. By contrast, *augmented realities* blend virtual reality and so-called real life. Virtual reality (VR) and augmented reality (AR) share the goal of immersing users in content. For many, *virtual reality* or *augmented reality* are terms that conjure images from *The Matrix*, where Keanu Reeves's character Neo works to escape the agents. Or, they may trigger memories of the paralyzed soldier, Jake, lying in a pod, interacting virtually with the inhabitants of Pandora in *Avatar*. These science fiction explorations imply that inhabiting other worlds with only our minds is dystopic and is likely to lead to ruin. Contrary to these images, VR/AR applications in education can support civilization rather than destroying it. For example, VR/AR have been used successfully in psychological rehabilitation; they have also been adopted as aids for understanding the human body (Székely & Satava, 1999).

Such technologies also sponsor and support identities. Sherry Turkle (2011) originally suggested that Internet technologies would allow users to hide their identities and be *anyone*, maybe even be *everyone* they wanted. This might be true for some. However, it is more common that advanced technologies do not give us new identities as much as they reinforce or extend the ones we already have (Ellwell, 2014). For teacher education, this is a vital proposition—the mission is not to make teachers different people when they teach with VR/AR or other advanced technologies. Instead the mission is to help them be the strongest version of the best parts of themselves as teachers that they can be (Craig, 2013; Rice, 2019).

Historically, the use of VR/AR in education has been dominated by Science Technology Engineering, and Mathematics (STEM) disciplines (Helsel, 1992). This may have been for a variety of reasons, including the possibility that VR/AR is associated with coding, which requires preparation in STEM. Initial VR/AR programmers and designers would have been more familiar with content in these fields; they may have even felt the need for STEM learning with VR/AR technology was more pressing for political reasons, and, therefore, they were more likely to produce STEM-related educational resources. Even so, the humanities were not forgotten. There are many existing and emerging VR/AR resources for ELA teachers who want to take their students into the Tudor England of Shakespeare or other worlds that support adolescent literature. Bringing VR/AR into the ELA classroom does not mean completely abandoning traditional methods. ELA teachers still can prepare students for strong rhetorical debate and discussion. They can play creatively with conceptions of hybridity and remix. VR/AR can support and enhance the secondary ELA curriculum.

At the moment, VR/AR applications are fairly benign and nonconfrontational. They provide teachers and students with an opportunity to visit museums, tour virtual historic sites, and investigate the inner workings of the human body. However, the future of VR/AR may lie in the work associated with the Stanford University Virtual Human Interaction Lab. There, the gentle and safe aspects of VR are disrupted by explorations of racism and empathy (Roswell et al., 2020). Imagine, for instance, seeing the world through the eyes of an African American in the Jim Crow South or experiencing life as a Jew with a star in a ghetto in Nazi Germany. These immersive, emotional experiences likely would alarm some stakeholders and result in tensions about the realness of reality. They may create the same deep, emotional responses that an affecting piece of literature does. It is only a matter of time before tensions about the nature of reality and its place in schools arise.

Accessibility to VR/AR is improving as affordable devices and mobile apps increase. While educators in STEM fields have a head start in using VR/AR for classroom learning, we offer this volume as an opportunity for ELA teachers to advance in this area. Many ELA teachers simply do not know how to incorporate VR/AR into the curriculum, and they are largely unaware of the potential of VR/AR tools for teaching literary works, supporting writing instruction, enriching discussion, and advancing interdisciplinary learning experiences. They may have even tried before and found that resources were scarce, and there was a general sense that VR/AR was not for them.

This book is offered as a preliminary guide and resource to the emerging possibilities of VR/AR. The chapters here explore the use of VR/AR in secondary ELA classrooms and provide a roadmap for those who want to understand VR/AR better, as well as see concrete examples of how these technologies have been used in ELA classrooms. The book is divided into three sections: The first section begins with an overview of previous research and offers readers ways to conceptualize the use of VR/AR in ELA teaching. The second section contains examples of practical uses of VR/AR in traditional classrooms through literature teaching, virtual field trips, and the use of VR goggles to promote writing development. The third part of the book focuses on interdisciplinary work in ELA teaching. Topics include geolocation and bomb-making. After all, ELA is a discipline that can accommodate interdisciplinary integration well (Davis, 1999).

We believe that education is at the edge of a new beginning. Teaching and learning, online experiences, and digital tools are shifting. We see that ELA teachers are devoted to learning new ways to teach with advanced technologies, and VR/AR are poised to take their place alongside traditional methods. We are grateful for the opportunity to offer this book as a resource for taking on these new challenges, for embracing these destinies, and even for making new worlds—actual, augmented, and virtual.

Clarice M. Moran, PhD, Appalachian State University, Boone, NC
Mary F. Rice, PhD, University of New Mexico, Albuquerque, NM

REFERENCES

Craig, C. J. (2013). Teacher education and the best-loved self. *Asia Pacific Journal of Education*, *33*(3), 261–272.

Davis, M. (1999). Design's inherent interdisciplinarity: The arts in integrated curricula. *Arts Education Policy Review*, *101*(1), 8–13.

Elwell, J. S. (2014). The transmediated self: Life between the digital and the analog. *Convergence*, *20*(2), 233–249.

Helsel, S. (1992). Virtual reality and education. *Educational Technology*, *32*(5), 38–42.

Rice, M. (2019). Projections of identity: How technological devices become us and why it matters in ELA teacher education. *Ubiquity*, *6*(1), 22–40.

Roswell, R. O., Cogburn, C. D., Tocco, J., Martinez, J., Bangeranye, C., Bailenson, J. N., Wright, M., Mieres, J. H., & Smith, L. (2020). Cultivating empathy through virtual reality. *Academic Medicine*. doi: https://10.1097/ACM.0000000000003615.

Turkle, S. (2011). *Life on the screen*. Simon and Schuster.

Székely, G., & Satava, R. M. (1999). Where are we going? Virtual reality in medicine. *BMJ, 319*, 1305–1307.

Part 1

OVERVIEW AND RESEARCH

HOW CAN VIRTUAL AND AUGMENTED REALITIES SUPPORT TEACHER LEARNING?

Chapter 1

A Review of the Literature on Virtual Reality

A New Frontier for English Language Arts Teaching

Paige Jacobson

The spirit and power of education resides in its teachers. Education progresses because of the teachers who run their classrooms with a fervor to teach their content, reach their students, and share their love for learning that made them become teachers in the first place. Teachers continue to push the envelope when it comes to creating engaging lessons that they regularly revise to reflect their students and the world around them, thus making the students' learning more relevant, meaningful, and long-lasting. Teachers seek out new ideas, methods, and technologies to incorporate into their classrooms because they want to provide their students with the best education, to equip them with the skills and knowledge to navigate and participate in their local and global communities. And teachers know that the art of teaching is intricately intertwined with learning—both student learning and their own. Teachers learn and should always be learning—about pedagogy, about their subject, about their students, and about their world—alongside their students (Demirel & Akkoyunlu, 2017).

Teachers strive to be flexible and adaptive inside and outside of the classroom (Vaughn & Parsons, 2013). When schools implement new initiatives, curricula, or technology, teachers are often quick to adapt them into their teaching practice, despite their own hesitations (Rice, 2019). From overhead projectors to document cameras to smart boards, from different Learning Management Systems, digital platforms, websites, and apps, teachers are no strangers to taking on new technology for the benefit of their students, especially in this age where the rate of technological development is exponentially increasing. Even though it can feel overwhelming to try to keep up, by their own agency teachers still research advancements and learn about the latest pedagogical methods or emergent technology. Many teachers are already using multiple technologies on a daily basis. While education as an institution is slow to take on new technologies, teachers readily respond and adapt to the shifting technological landscape around them. And when teachers expand their skill sets and tool kits, they are pioneers whose explorations into this shifting landscape pave the way for all future students and teachers alike.

One of the technologies that has come to prominence in recent years is virtual reality (VR) and augmented reality (AR). Like most new technologies, VR and AR have been slow to be adopted in educational realms, particularly in primary and secondary school. Moreover, they have been adopted faster in Science Technology Engineering and Mathematics (STEM) fields. Yet, VR and AR are slowly but surely making their way into the humanities, where there is so much untapped potential, particularly in English Language Arts (ELA). The purpose of this chapter is to provide a review of the literature on VR and AR, discuss how VR specifically has been used in education, shed light on its use and great potential in ELA, and provide a foundation from which to start a journey into this new frontier of ELA teaching.

A BIT OF BACKGROUND ABOUT
AUGMENTED AND VIRTUAL REALITY

VR, as we know it, came about in the 1960s as a way to simulate interaction with the real world via technology that engages multiple senses (Freina & Ott, 2015). As the technology and the field of VR grew, distinctions between different types of VR naturally came about and continue to evolve. VR can be categorized both according to the levels of immersion and the degree of technology used. AR is perhaps a rung below VR, as it "adds on to" or "improves" the user's real physical environment through technology but does not seek to transport and immerse the user in a completely different virtual setting. Gandolfi (2018) points out that one easily understandable example of AR is a hologram or, from a more modern context, Snapchat filters or Pokemon appearing on location, for instance, when playing the popular mobile game *Pokémon Go*. VR, on the other hand, seeks to portray a completely alternate reality, but users may or may not feel like they are actually "there," depending on the technology involved. According to Freina and Ott (2015), non-immersive VR is when the user is situated in a 3D environment which he or she can manipulate through tools like a keyboard, mouse, controller, or joystick (usually associated with a computer or a console) but does not feel wholly immersed or "there" in the VR environment.

Immersive VR, then, is when the user feels "physically present in a non-physical world" through various stimuli that affect the senses in a way that feels authentic and real (Freina & Ott, 2015, p. 134). Whereas non-immersive VR mostly comes in the form of video game-like "virtual" worlds in which the user interacts with the environment through an avatar, immersive VR typically requires the use of more distinct technology in the form of some sort of headset, goggles, and "data gloves" or "data suits" which allow users to interact with his or her 3D environment (Moore, 1995, p. 92). Though full immersion means stimulation of all of the senses, usually in "immersive virtual reality rooms" with stereoscopic sound and the simulated ability to touch virtual objects through technology that works with vibration and motion, most immersive VR devices typically only involve sight and hearing (Dede, 2009, p. 66). As development in the realm of VR technology has grown, this deliberate focus on just these two senses has allowed VR devices to be made less expensive and more accessible to the public. AR, especially, is widely being used via mobile apps by the general public, and though it has great potential benefit in education, its potential lies in "supporting informal learning and cooperative thinking" (Gandolfi, 2018, p. 546). On the other hand, VR has huge potential to engage and motivate people to learn, support different learning styles (such as visual, auditory, or kinesthetic), help users overcome real-world challenges, and expose them to novel perspectives, so it is only natural that VR is being utilized as an educational tool in many domains (Freina & Ott, 2015; Gandolfi, 2018). See table 1.1 for a breakdown between AR, non-immersive VR, and immersive VR.

VR has been and continues to be used in an array of fields, such as computer science, engineering, mathematics, medicine, social sciences, decision sciences, materials sciences, physics, neuroscience, and nursing; and it is also making its way into the humanities in fields such as theater and journalism. VR is also used in vocational and training settings where potentially hazardous situations are offset by the use of the technology. Other motivations for using VR in these and other areas include overcoming the limits of time (e.g., exploring different historical time periods), physical space (e.g., exploring different geographical or universal locations), and even ethics (e.g., experimenting with ethical dilemmas in a simulated environment). Furthermore, studies have shown that use of VR in education has led to increased time-on-task, enjoyment, and motivation, as well as deeper learning and long-term retention of material (Kavanagh et al., 2017).

Although VR has shown such promise in these areas, it has seen limited use in the field of primary and secondary education—particularly in ELA. Instead, it is used more in higher education (Kavanagh et al., 2017). This

Table 1.1 Technological Capabilities, Limitations, and Potential of Virtual Reality

AR	Non-immersive VR	Immersive VR
• Adds on to the user's real physical environment • Does not seek to transport the user in a completely different setting • E.g., a hologram or Snapchat filter • Widely used by the general public via mobile apps • Potential in education is in promoting informal learning, cooperation, and engagement	• User is situated in a 3D environment which can be manipulated through tools like a keyboard, mouse, controller, or joystick • User does not feel wholly immersed or "there" in the VR environment • Mostly comes in the form of video game-like "virtual" worlds • User interacts with the environment through an avatar • Potential in education is in engagement and motivating learning, supporting different learning styles, helping users overcome real-world challenges, and exposing users to new perspectives	• User feels physically present in the virtual world through stimuli that affect the senses • Focuses mostly on senses of sight and sound • Typically requires use of hardware such as a headset, goggles, data gloves, etc. • Complete and full immersion: stimulation of all the senses • Potential in education is in engagement and motivating learning, supporting different learning styles, helping users overcome real-world challenges, and exposing users to new perspectives

area is ripe for exploration, especially since immersion through VR can, as proposed by Dede (2009), enhance education by enabling multiple perspectives, situating learning in meaningful and authentic contexts, and promoting learning transfer to new applications. From the standpoint of an ELA teacher, these benefits are greatly conducive to the overarching goals of the subject, no matter the grade level. When teachers explore texts with our students ("texts" being anything from which meaning can be constructed, e.g., a book, poem, short story, article, movie, video, song, rap, artwork, dance, game), one of the inherent goals is to expose them to new and other perspectives that expand and possibly challenge their worldview. From these texts and with guidance, students can connect to the universal and transcendent themes within them, ultimately constructing, tearing down, and reconstructing their own beliefs and ways of being in the world. And perhaps the ultimate goal as ELA teachers is to foster the ability of students to apply what they have learned—knowledge about the germane themes they have encountered in texts, specific skills or strategies relevant to the "reading" of these texts, the ability to express their knowledge and understanding through speech and writing—to all areas of their experience in the real world, on an individual, social, professional, and interpersonal level. Gadelha (2018) discusses how VR has the potential to engage students in a way that mirrors Dede's (2018) proposals for the technology: it allows students to "experience new things to deepen their knowledge and broaden their horizons," to connect with the material on an individualized level, and to demonstrate their "newly acquired or effectively reinforced skills" on new applications (Gadelha, 2018, p. 42).

Despite the limited research on the potential of VR in ELA, it is fairly easy to extrapolate from the research that *is* out there what the benefits and challenges to incorporating VR in the ELA classroom may be. Outlined below is some information on the technology; general findings about VR and its uses in education, in the classroom, and in ELA specifically; and its potential challenges to adopting it in the classroom.

THE TECHNOLOGY

Multiple options exist for the adoption of VR technology in the classroom, especially since the production of cheaper headsets and devices has become more commonplace as the field of VR has developed. Of course, each school is different and has idiosyncratic needs, capabilities, funds, support, and intention for use, so finding the right VR system depends on these factors. Among the most popular VR devices that are used across libraries are the HTC VIVE, Oculus Rift, and Google Cardboard (Pope, 2018). According to Pope (2018), in a report on VR and AR in libraries, these three devices are the most popular for specific reasons relating to affordability, accessibility, and quality. The Oculus Rift was the first "affordable fully immersive virtual reality headset that was available on the market" (pp. 8–9), and it is still considered one of the best VR devices out there. The appeal of the HTC VIVE has surpassed that of the Oculus Rift in recent years because it is also more reasonably priced, easier to access, and has better optic and motion sensing (Pope, 2018).

Yet there is one more VR device being used in libraries, schools, and other settings that sits apart from the others due to its affordability and accessibility that surpasses that of both the Oculus Rift and the HTC VIVE: Google Cardboard. Google Cardboard is a device made out of cardboard and lenses that fits over a smartphone and works with apps that can be downloaded to the user's phone to give the user the sense of another reality. Google even provides instructions to construct such a device with cardboard from home, as opposed to buying their premade versions, thus increasing accessibility of the device by making it virtually free (you can access these instructions at the following link: https://vr.google.com/cardboard/get-cardboard/). Though Google Cardboard is limited depending on the current level of smartphone technology associated with AR and VR apps (and some argue it is not "true" VR because of these limitations), its benefits in terms of affordability and accessibility has made it a key purveyor of the VR experience to the eager public, especially when it comes to educational opportunities. To pair with Google Cardboard, Google created an app called Google Expeditions that enables users to experience distant and significant sites like the Great Wall of China, Mars, the moon, and more, and which also offers training to help teachers lead these virtual field trips (https:// www.google.com/edu/expeditions/). And since Google Cardboard has seen such success, Google created Google Daydream (https://vr.google.com/ daydream/), an improved, updated version of Google Cardboard that uses a clicker and a certain type of smart device with better optics (Pope, 2018). However, Google Daydream was discontinued in 2019 because of a lack of broad consumer and developer adoption, though the Daydream app and store is still available to users. Table 1.2 shows the price ranges of a few immersive VR devices and shares helpful links to find more information about them.

However, there is still limited availability of educational apps because of the time it takes to create them and because schools and libraries are often slower to adopt trends like VR technology (Pope, 2018). Nonetheless, the use of VR in education is growing daily, especially because VR offers so much possibility for exploration, such as taking "virtual field trips" to museums, historical and archaeological sites, and other important places ripe for study, such as rain forests, coral reefs, outer space, and so on (Ray & Deb, 2016, p. 69). These and other apps have a clear connection with education, and they can also be used for research, collaboration, simulations, and creating projects.

Table 1.2   VR Devices Available

VR Device	Significance	Price Range	Helpful Links
Oculus Rift	First affordable immersive VR on the market	$399–$599	https://www.oculus.com/rift/
HTC VIVE	Better optic and motion sensing than Oculus Rift	$549–$1,199	https://www.vive.com/us/
Google Cardboard	Highly accessible and affordable. Made out of cardboard and lenses that fit over a smartphone	Free–$39.95	https://arvr.google.com/cardboard/https://vr.google.com/cardboard/get-cardboard/
Google Daydream	Improved and updated version of Google Cardboard that uses a clicker and smart device with better optics	$79–$99	https://arvr.google.com/daydream/

Other devices: Microsoft HoloLens, Google Glass, 360 degree video cameras, PlayStation VR, etc.

VIRTUAL REALITY IN EDUCATION

The typical view of a classroom is one in which the teacher is standing in front of the students at the board, disseminating information that the students are expected to absorb and regurgitate. Of course, that may seem harsh, and not all classrooms are like this. But this sort of teaching approach is largely prescriptive in nature and creates a distance from practical learning, "which results in a lack of deep and robust understanding of the subject matter" (Ray & Deb, 2016, p. 68). In addition, this model focuses more on lower levels of thinking, such as simply remembering certain facts and bits of discrete knowledge, rather than on higher levels of thinking that encourage the application of knowledge, analysis, synthesis, evaluation, and creation, according to Bloom's Taxonomy. Ray and Deb (2016) discuss how these teaching methods "are inherently static in nature" and require "little or no student interaction" (p. 68). Consequently, students are easily distracted and learning is less easily assimilated. In their study, they found that students using VR (more specifically, Google Cardboard) had a significant increase in academic performance and interest in the classroom (Ray & Deb, 2016). These findings are corroborated in many other studies that saw higher performance when students used VR, such as in Zantua's (2017) study on using Google Cardboard in a sixth-grade social studies class. Moreover, Winn (1993) proposed that such artificial environments like VR allow students to "construct anything they want" ("Learning by Constructing Knowledge," para. 15), which is not possible using traditional teaching strategies, and it is this capacity to allow students to "construct knowledge from direct experience" ("VR Applications in Education section," para. 3) that makes using technology like VR "superior" ("Learning by Constructing Knowledge," para. 15) to other pedagogical methods. If students are not taught or given the opportunity to construct knowledge and see the results of their ideas, choices, and actions through experimentation and play, then it can be argued that they are remaining in the stages of lower-order thinking (Hanson & Shelton, 2008). Many education systems and classroom teachers are moving away from focusing on these lower-order thinking skills, such as rote memorization, and toward higher-order thinking skills, such as analysis, critical thinking, and problem-solving. As such, this focus on the lower levels of Bloom's Taxonomy is no longer acceptable in today's education, as students' success now often depends on "their ability to envision and manipulate abstract multidimensional information spaces" (Hanson & Shelton, 2008, p. 119). And on a broader level, students are taught to think conceptually and hypothetically; it is easier to do this—to conceive of possible solutions, scenarios, results—if one has the freedom and space to explore and experiment, like one does in a VR platform.

Furthermore, learning occurs more easily when students are offered the opportunity to interact with others, experiment with questions and possibilities, work on an authentic issue or project, apply what they have learned to a new situation, be creative, and construct meaning—and VR can help this to happen. Despite the large amount of time since his research, Winn (1993) makes a salient point—the capability of VR to immerse the user in a different, ideally authentic experience that promotes collaboration is a factor unique to VR: "it alone allows a synthetic experience to capture the essence of what it really means for a person to come to know the world" ("VR Applications in Education," para. 2). However, Whitelock et al. (1996) note that VR has been used for "drill and practice" exercises in "previous VR training environments" (p. 3) which, though sometimes helpful and necessary, by their nature fall into the realm of lower levels of thinking. In a study done on different forms of pedagogy that used VR in the classroom, Johnston et al. (2018) found that though VR is most often used in classrooms that employed experiential learning, VR has also been used in classrooms that follow discovery learning, situated cognition, constructivism, and direct instruction. This direct instruction model is based on behaviorism, a theory which posits that learning occurs when subjects are conditioned by stimulus and response (Johnston et al., 2018). According to Engelmann (2008, as cited in Johnston et al., 2018), in this framework, focus is on cultivating knowledge or a skill through tutorials, paced and repetitive instruction, and "drill, practice, reward, and recognition for accomplishment" (p. 423) to incite learning. For example, Johnston et al. (2018) mention House of Languages as a program where students learn vocabulary and pronunciation by speaking the vocabulary word aloud. If the student correctly pronounces the word, then they receive auditory and visual reinforcement in the form of cheers and stars and sparkles around the word. The researchers note that the goal of House of Languages is to develop the user's familiarity with and usage of vocabulary, which is a "limited skill or knowledge set" (Johnston et al., p. 423) that is relatively low on Bloom's Taxonomy. However, even the incorporation of VR in direct instruction offered visual and kinesthetic support for students as they were learning the vocabulary. In House of Languages, users can explore an environment like a kitchen or playroom, point to an object, and learn the word for that object in the language they are studying. In this way, VR naturally enhanced direct instruction to support learners through discovery (Johnston et al., 2018).

VR can be used effectively to help students think on many levels and demonstrate their learning through recitation, application, analysis, synthesis, evaluation, and creation. To help students think on deeper levels of understanding, Whitelock et al. (1996) advise that it is necessary for educators to understand what elements of VR encourage students to become engaged in "sense making" (pp. 2–3) activities and conceptual learning wherein they are required to explain and extrapolate their learning, rather than simply displaying knowledge and executing tasks. They propose that in order to encourage conceptual and implicit thinking—that is, "the ability to perform tasks consistent with an improved understanding"—the VR experience should foster autonomy and interaction (Whitelock et al., 1996, p. 7). Hanson and Shelton (2008) affirm this in their findings. They lay out three criteria for artificial, virtual environments to be well designed and encourage the sort of learning that we want students to be engaged in. In such an environment, students "experience high levels of presence," the environment is interactive, and it is also autonomous (Hanson & Shelton, 2008, p. 119). When these criteria are met, students are able to see relationships between causes and effects, and they can more easily assess, evaluate, and make connections between discrete bits of information because they are not in a "decontextualized, non-immersive setting" (Hanson & Shelton, 2008, p. 119).

These factors—autonomy, interaction, and continual construction of knowledge—are key components to the theory of constructivism (Vygotsky, 1978). According to constructivist theory, knowledge is constructed by the learner and is built upon with each new piece of information. Proponents of constructivism believe that the learner's environment has a potentially strong effect on his or her learning, and education should be "experimental and experiential" (Kavanagh et al., 2017, p. 95). Because VR lends itself to experimentation, creating experiences, and deriving meaning from those experiences, it can be used as a tool in a classroom that adopts a constructivist approach to teaching and learning. These novel experiences with virtual environments and VR technology, coupled with the advent and ubiquitous use of the Internet, challenge our concept of reality and our place in it, so we as a society have felt the need to "redefine ideas according to the new cultural perspectives provided by these developments" (Moore, 1995, p. 96). If a classroom is one in which the students are guided by the teacher to cocreate meaning, grapple with complex ideas and open-ended questions, and build upon prior knowledge to cultivate new insight and skills, then use of VR fits well in that classroom because it naturally focuses on "the ways in which knowledge is created and negotiated in virtual environments" and how social learning occurs in these environments (Moore, 1995, p. 97). And social learning naturally fosters communication and collaboration, which Kavanagh et al. (2017) found to be a common motivator for incorporating VR into the classroom. Though communication limitations between users of VR exist (depending on the type of VR), VR also has potential to break down communication barriers between users; and when students feel comfortable and communication is free-flowing, then the classroom environment is likely to be more healthy and conducive to learning.

Within this sort of collaborative, experimental, autonomous environment, students may experience increased motivation to participate in learning rather than when they are taught with traditional methods. In Kavanagh et al.'s (2017) survey on VR in education, many educators cited this as being among their top reasons for incorporating VR into their pedagogy. According to a study by Huang et al. (2010, as cited in Kavanagh et al., 2017), students have a tendency to learn better when they are more motivated, students are more motivated by 3D technology and applications than 2D technology and applications, and the consistent use of VR can not only improve motivation but also long-term retention of knowledge. Furthermore, many participants in the survey cited "deeper learning" as their motivation for using VR due to VR's potential to allow students to be able to "explore, immerse, and infer their own meaning from their experiences" (Kavanagh et al., 2017, p. 98). Lastly, many authors in the survey mentioned "personalized learning" as their motivation for using VR (Kavanagh et al., 2017, p. 97). This notion that VR can allow lessons to be tailored to individual students' needs is particularly relevant today, as differentiation is becoming standard practice within classrooms. Lessons in VR can allow students to learn at their own pace, and they can potentially change along with the students' abilities, slowing down and revisiting content or speeding up and offering a new challenge as necessary.

Moore (1995) discussed applications of VR in education and the value of its use to the development of its user. To illustrate how VR can serve as a training grounds to practice a task that would otherwise be difficult due to the level of safety, distance, or cost, Moore (1995) noted that repairs to the Hubble Telescope, for example, were first practiced in a VR simulation before the real repairs were done in space. Similarly, medical professionals use VR to promote rehabilitation and practice their techniques in high-pressure situations, which can then be transferred to patients in the real world, and potentially save lives due to this previous experience. Kavanagh et al. (2017) also noted that VR can be used to provide access to limited resources—that is, "any thing which is in high demand and/or limited supply" (pp. 93–94)—and can be used for distance learning, which is being used in increasing amounts across the globe for reasons such as providing students with more flexibility to work at their own pace and develop their autonomy, sustaining the consistency of education during environmental pressures like a pandemic. Other situations in which VR is helpful for education are when it is used to manipulate the typical laws of nature so that other laws or elements come to the forefront in "what if" scenarios typical of science. Winn (1993) argued that people learn through firsthand experience in their daily lives, and VR furnishes firsthand experiences that are designed to help students learn material through this potential for manipulation. He concludes that though students may be capable of mastering concepts, VR "provides a route to success for children who might otherwise fail in our education system" because it allows them immediate experience with these concepts via the "symbol systems" of each subject (Winn, 1993, "Summary and Conclusion," para. 2). This ability to manipulate the virtual world can be taken even further by actually *creating* and experiencing virtual worlds, which allows for construction of knowledge through a virtual experience.

And though many of these aforementioned examples are based in professional and scientific fields, it is not hard to think of scenarios in which VR can be used to successful ends in an ELA classroom. David et al. (2008) explored how new classroom space with dedicated advanced technology encouraged students to "think about the writing process, engage in self-directed learning, and participate more in collaborative learning that reflects the practical applications of writing they will need outside of the classroom" (p. 18). Their study did not research VR specifically, but adoption of VR in the classroom can easily offer students a unique way to develop their writing. For example, students can practice, revise, edit, and experiment with their writing in a virtual environment before sending off the final product to be assessed. If their writing is a narrative, they can create the world of that narrative and experiment with the conditions therein to produce a world that best fits their vision and purposes for writing. This could also offer students an interesting avenue from which to receive feedback, and affording students such agency "can expand the scope of peer-tutoring and creative storytelling," which we will explore in more detail later in this chapter (Gandolfi, 2018, p. 552). Essentially, when used in education, VR provides an opportunity for its user to be immersed in either realistic or novel and abstract environments, allowing him or her to experience, interact with, manipulate, and discover virtual or digital knowledge which can then be related to real-world concepts and understandings; from this, the user's knowledge base and personal experience grows, which is the ultimate goal of education (Moore, 1995).

One way in which VR seems to be an effective tool is when it is used in project-based learning (PBL), an approach to learning in which students work on projects. This project-based approach encourages students to learn a concept through work and experimentation, with varying levels of teacher guidance. PBL has great potential for independent, group, and peer-mentored learning in an authentic way that appeals to students (Morales et al., 2012). In a study on PBL and VR, Morales et al. (2012) found that among the different social interactions in the class encouraged by the PBL model, "play" (p. 799) was among the primary interactions and served to generate ideas and creativity. We will explore this capability of VR to foster creativity in further detail later, but it is interesting to note that since the combination of PBL and VR can feel like play and encourage students to be creative—something many students feel they struggle with—it has great potential to bring an element of fun and engagement into the classroom that might otherwise have been lacking. That being said, VR does not need to be used in combination with PBL to feel like play: it naturally lends itself to "gamification" and "game-based learning"—"the application of game-mechanics and/or other game-like elements to non-gaming situations"—which "usually . . . increase student motivation, engagement and enjoyment of the learning experience" (Kavanagh et al., 2017, p. 95).

Similarly, PBL and VR encourage peer-mentoring and collaboration, which fit well within the constructivist approach because they become key parts of the "knowledge-building community of practice" (Morales et al., 2012, p. 799). To demonstrate this, Morales et al. (2012) share a transcription of a conversation between a student struggling to depict the reflection of trees in water in his VR simulation and a more knowledgeable, experienced student trying to help him. After toying with the camera, pressing various buttons, and many patient explanations from both students of what the desired effect is and what certain manipulations do, the students eventually succeeded in creating the right effect and demonstrated that VR cultivates peer-mentorship and that "expertise on particular topics, not seniority or status," leads to "effective mentoring" (Morales et al., 2012, p. 799). This may knock down some barriers to effective problem-solving and tutoring because the problem becomes collective when more experienced students *want* to help their less experienced peers, rather than when mentors are assigned to partners because of their older age even though they might not be interested in their partner's problem. This personal interest contributes to students enhancing learning in the classroom alongside the teacher. The same mentor from the above example used the Internet to not only develop his own knowledge of VR from social media and social networking sites like blogs, forums, and YouTube videos, but he also used that knowledge to mentor his peers on their class projects as well as in the global Blender community (Morales et al., 2012).

Morales et al. (2012) also posit that PBL with VR can lead to a deeper understanding of the content and help students explore possibilities for the most effective and efficient solutions to their problems. When one student who was failing math class used VR to explore the concepts he was having difficulty with—such as surface area, density, volume, and perimeter—he was able to see them in a new way, and his grade improved. Another student took her project in a different direction and rendered her family's farm with accurate scales, ratios, and proportions to figure out the best way to rearrange the buildings to maximize efficiency and productivity. This simulation allowed this student—and her parents—to experiment with different possibilities without wasting time, energy, and money on actually rearranging the farm without knowing the full effect of the rearrangement. In the end of the study, Morales et al. found that both the students' teachers and parents noticed that the students developed in terms of their social capacity and their academic ability. There was overall growth in the students' senses of maturity, self-sufficiency, leadership, mentoring ability, responsibility, public speaking, creativity, self-confidence, belonging, organization, and professionalism. The students also grew in their academics, such as in their reading, critical thinking, and problem-solving skills; in their understanding of math and science concepts; in their oral and written language ability; and in their ability to transfer between subjects, to question, and to use logic (Morales et al., 2012).

This significant growth in multiple areas afforded by the combination of PBL and VR is why schools like Washington Leadership Academy (WLA)— also known as "High-Tech Hogwarts"—are emerging (McKibben & Davis, 2019, p. 48). At WLA, which serves 99 percent students of color, students engage in a curriculum that is both personalized and highly technologically advanced: they are required to take computer science classes to help them "gain the foundational skills they need to break into careers like coding and other tech-related fields," and are offered courses that "match their interests," such as virtual reality, arts-based computer science, DJing and music production, advanced coding, and robotics (McKibben & Davis, 2019, pp. 51–52). The curriculum is focused on PBL and "design thinking," pushing students to be innovators and creators instead of consumers (McKibben & Davis, 2019, p. 51). And VR is a cornerstone of this curriculum: students at WLA have developed and coded VR experiences that range from harrowing to thrilling. One module students created follows the story of a migrant traveling from Guatemala to Texas; another allows users to experience a private Prince concert front and center (McKibben & Davis, 2019). WLA also partners with CommonLit, an education platform that provides texts and resources aligned to the Common Core Language Arts curriculum, in an effort to ensure that student learning is personalized and that students are advancing based on competency (McKibben & Davis, 2019). WLA's test results in math and ELA compared to those of surrounding charter schools suggest that this fresh take on education is a thriving success.

Ultimately, this research into VR in PBL indicates that the combination of both fosters an engaging, student-driven environment in which the students' learning and skill development is communal and authentic. By creating advanced VR projects in Morales et al.'s (2012) study, students were able to delve into academic content in a way that was individualized to their needs and interests and more meaningful to them, in addition to developing technology literacy skills beyond that typically learned in a computer class. Because their projects were "confined" to VR, they were learning and practicing skills in a sort of "risk-free" trial grounds that they felt comfortable to experiment and even fail in. And, in such a collaborative setting with the help of like-minded peers, the students felt faced with not so much of a problem as with a challenge. Because of this mindset brought on by the PBL environment, the students developed and used valuable social skills in the classroom that are applicable in the larger global community, especially as it is becoming more and more normal to work with advanced technology like VR and to be able to connect with people effectively and productively on multiple platforms.

VIRTUAL REALITY IN THE CLASSROOM

The potential of VR as a tool in education is very high. As we saw from Morales et al.'s (2012) study, VR can be used to great effect to develop students' social and academic skills when it is used in conjunction with PBL. In this sort of setting, learning is student-driven rather than transmitted by the teacher, so the teacher's role is more to ensure that the students "maintain appropriate behavior, be productive in projects, share knowledge with each other, and present projects to visitors" (Morales et al., 2012, p. 803). The teacher is a guide to facilitate the open and collaborative classroom. He or she makes sure that the students are using their time efficiently, that he or she is fostering relationships between students who would most benefit from mentorship from specific peers, and that, perhaps, he or she is providing structure for students who may flounder in a more open and self-directed environment. In discussing good teaching practices that should be implemented to successfully promote a technology-enhanced classroom, David et al. (2008) recall the seven hallmarks of effective classroom instruction as noted by Chickering and Gamson (1991, as cited in David et al., 2008). Good teaching practice contains many of the following characteristics.

- student-faculty contact
- cooperation among students
- active learning
- giving prompt feedback
- time on task
- high expectations
- respect for diverse talents and ways of learning

When adopting VR in the classroom, teachers should keep these tenets in mind, especially if the class is engaged in student-driven PBL because of the greater potential for the class to fall into disorder and for the students to find PBL less beneficial with a detached teacher who has a low sense of responsibility.

In the same vein, and as Whitelock et al. (1996) point out, VR should be implemented in a way that actively encourages learning beyond simple, rudimentary levels. Kavanagh et al. (2017) report that students generally feel a stronger sense of engagement and motivation to participate in the lesson if VR is incorporated, which in itself is preferable to them being passive participants in class, but this isn't necessarily a given in all cases in which VR is used; rather, it's about *how* the teacher incorporates VR into the content or lesson. This means that VR's adoption in the classroom should be because the teacher sees potential beyond just engagement and interest of the students and beyond just the fact that it is "the new normal" since modern students may be less excited by such technology than they have potentially previously encountered, and this can weaken the learning process rather than empower it (Gandolfi, 2018; Kavanagh et al., 2017). Like Whitelock et al. (1996), Gandolfi (2018) also advises that when teachers use VR in the classroom, they should do so in a way that encourages autonomy and individual agency within a constructivist framework in order to maximize the potential for growth and learning.

In order for VR to become a generally viable tool, however, teachers claim they need more technical support and professional development. It is important for the teacher to have an understanding of the VR systems being used, as it won't always be the case that each class has an adequate number of students with sufficient expertise to be able to teach the rest of the students and work on their own projects at the same time. Ritz and Buss (2016, as cited in Gandolfi, 2018) suggest becoming familiar with the technology before teaching it, and Cabero and Barroso (2016, as cited in Gandolfi, 2018) recommend maintaining a "proper awareness of how to combine content and technology" and a "previous competence about tools and software adopted" (p. 550). This is easier said than done, however, because teachers need adequate support from their administration, which needs adequate support from the school district. If the support is there, then the teacher is confronted with weighing the priorities between creating an ideal learning environment for the students based on instructional design and learning objectives and creating an environment based on the available resources and technological constraints (Hanson & Shelton, 2008). Naturally, the type of technology involved often depends on factors outside of the teacher's control, and these drive what the lesson may look like, but as with any new tool, resource, or technology, it is up to the teacher to determine how best to incorporate it into his or her lesson for the best learning outcome for the students. As Hanson and Shelton (2008) pointed out, regardless of these instructional and design challenges, incorporation of VR into a lesson supports learning by making it experiential and personal.

In addition to considering what specific VR technology aligns with a teacher's or school's resources and means, other factors to consider when incorporating VR into the classroom include specific goals, objectives, and assessments; where the VR technology fits within the general curriculum (as there are usually already-existing materials, texts, and equipment to support the curricular goals); and the teacher's philosophy of teaching and learning (Johnston et al., 2018). In regard to the latter, Johnston et al. (2018) compiled a helpful list of VR technologies and programs according to different types of pedagogy so that educators can research and decide which program would best suit their and their students' needs, though they note that "the VR applications reviewed" did not include "extended curriculum materials"; designers of VR programs, therefore, could make their program more accessible and applicable to educators if they communicate the pedagogical foundations within the program and develop guidelines for curricular use (Johnston et al., 2018, p. 431).

Many of the programs reviewed by Johnston et al. (2018) provide opportunities for the users to take virtual field trips that can complement a lesson or unit of study. While not all courses allow for physical field trips due to financial or time constraints, it's safe to say that almost all subjects and content areas can be enhanced through some sort of excursion outside of the classroom or the bounds of the traditional lesson format because they provide an experiential approach to learning. Traditional field trips are included, or at least considered to be included, in the general curriculum because they reinforce what is learned in class, offer opportunities to learn new information, and foster interest and engagement. If teachers want to enhance what they are teaching to students but don't have the financial resources, virtual field trips are a new and steady trend that offer the benefit of a comparatively cheaper way to do this. When teachers find a suitable program that fits with their pedagogy and has a spot within the curriculum, and when they become familiar with the technology themselves to adequately facilitate a virtual field trip, VR can enrich students' learning and illuminate course content. Lisichenko (2015) wrote how VR has been used in explorations of geography like national parks, deserts, and the Amazon rainforest to enhance "geographic literacy" (p. 160), along with excursions via Google Earth and other VR physical geography apps. On top of learning about the geography of an area, students can be encouraged to think critically and discuss topics relevant to the site with peers in a different country. For example, in a program called Bosnia Virtual Field Trip, students are exposed to the physical geography of Bosnia and have the opportunity to discuss "relevant topics between U.S. and Bosnian students" (Crampton, 1999, as cited in Lisichenko, 2015, p. 160). Students can also explore landmarks and places with significant historical or cultural backgrounds, such as the National World War II Museum, the focus of which can be on D-Day, the Holocaust, the impacts of science and technology during this time period, or on specific populations of people during the war (e.g., African Americans and Latino Americans; Lisichenko, 2015).

With VR, studies of history and architecture can be enhanced because it helps students think critically about the history that they are being taught and allows them to freely move around the space they have learned about in class and to autonomously learn about the elements of the environment and architecture as if they were really there. In this virtual space—standing at the foot of the pyramids at Giza, for example, or on the floor of the Roman senate—students may better understand how events fit together in the context of history because through their experience, they can comprehend that the events and people in history were *real* and not so far removed (Craddock, 2018). In addition, because they can control their pace and make decisions about what they want to pay particular attention to, students may be more engaged than in a traditional lesson.

And VR programs can help students take this learning experience further: students can also work productively toward solving problems and simulating what would happen if they made certain decisions in the virtual space. In a three-year study, Frontera (2009) had 13-year-old students design structures based on their knowledge of the architecture they interacted with in their virtual environment, and the students learned about the history of architecture in the process. In one project, students had to restore a Romanesque church to its original appearance using the existing remains in the simulation; in another, students were tasked with constructing a Gothic temple on their own from scratch, choosing the style, form, and dimensions. The technology used was non-immersive VR, but the results of the study supported the proposition that incorporation of advanced technology into the classroom can allow for more meaningful experiences and foster autonomy and collaboration. Assessment of the students' work showed high levels of student performance, and Frontera (2009) attributes this to multiple advantages of working with VR: all students started at the same level of understanding the technology; students were able to monitor their own progress during the process of using the new software; the learning process caused immediate satisfaction, which increased student interest and motivation; the work was challenging but not excessively difficult; and it allowed for more autonomy while the teacher acted as a guide and adviser. The students in this study expressed high levels of satisfaction. They particularly appreciated that this methodology afforded them more learning that they felt was practical; they valued the opportunity to both collaborate and be autonomous, and they felt that their learning was fun.

VR field trips are beneficial not only because they can be accessible to all students, but also because they "provide a stepping stool for the students who have the least access to print text in English, travel, and technology," including English language learners (ELLs) (Craddock, 2018, p. 7). For these students, VR can help them concentrate on the content that is visually right in front of them and not be stressed about decoding and processing

(Craddock, 2018). Craddock (2018) noted that while observing ELLs learn about the parts of the cell, the students struggled processing not only vocabulary words like *mitochondria, endoplasmic reticulum,* and *ribosomes,* but also the metaphors we frequently use to make these terms comprehensible, such as *powerhouse, highway,* and *control center.* However, using VR to illustrate that cells make up the human body and placing students *inside* a cell via VR technology makes the language component less important to their understanding because they can better understand both the idea of the cell and that different parts of it have different functions (Craddock, 2018). By decreasing this area of cognitive load, students are better able to learn the content.

Bonner and Reinders (2018) also describe different ways AR and VR can be used to foster engagement and learning for second language learners, and each activity they describe comes with helpful information that decreases the haziness surrounding implementing AR and VR in the classroom. For each activity, they provide a brief overview of the aims, amount of class time, and the resources necessary for implementation in the classroom—including the AR or VR programs being used—before describing what the activity would look like in a lesson plan. Many of the aims of these activities would transfer well to an ELA classroom because they focus on things like vocabulary, grammar, speaking skills, listening comprehension, using descriptive language, and so on. For example, in an activity on presentation practice using a VR headset like the HTC VIVE, Oculus GO, or Google Cardboard, students can practice giving presentations in a less intimidating way while still in front of actual audiences. First, they shadow the speech given by a different presenter by trying to copy their gestures, making eye contact, and then they transfer these exercises to practicing their own presentations (Bonner & Reinders, 2018).

Such activities can facilitate more speaking and listening practice for students, one of the core standards of ELA (which is often overshadowed by the reading and writing standards), and potentially decrease performance anxiety. A study done on virtual reality exposure therapy (VRET) revealed that VR can help reduce speaking anxiety, especially when the anxiety levels were high (Stupar-Rutenfrans et al., 2017). Similarly, a pilot study on the effectiveness of virtual reality therapy (VRT) found that VR can be used to reduce test anxiety and improve the performance of students who have it (North et al., 2004). Craddock (2018) also points out how VR literally eliminates distractions for students who have attention deficit disorder, anxiety disorders, or impulsivity. Moreover, Gandolfi (2018) and Ghanouni et al. (2018) have noted positive effects of using VR to help students with special needs such as autism spectrum disorder. As educators become increasingly aware of the different needs of their students, new strategies for support, such as VR, should be considered.

VIRTUAL REALITY IN ENGLISH LANGUAGE ARTS

The research about VR in the ELA classroom is relatively limited, but it is gaining momentum as scholars and educators seek to learn more about the benefits of incorporating VR into the ELA curriculum and how to implement it. The benefits that VR provides in terms of promoting collaboration, inquiry, critical thinking, social interaction, responsibility, leadership skills, autonomy, interest, motivation, and engagement all can be applied to its potential use in ELA. And using VR can make concepts learned in ELA more comprehensible to students and help them develop skills related to reading, writing, and speaking and listening. Pilgrim and Pilgrim (2016) discussed how VR tools can be used by an ELA teacher to support student learning by providing students with visual and experiential scaffolding, specifically by building background knowledge through explorations via Google Cardboard. Before jumping into a text or topic, students should often be given background knowledge to help situate their understanding and make the subsequent learning more comprehensible and meaningful: while students who have prior knowledge can problem-solve more effectively, focus on what is most important in a lesson, and ask questions that are more relevant to the topic, students who do not have prior knowledge often struggle to differentiate between what information is most and least important to know (Pilgrim & Pilgrim, 2016). In addition, the teacher should aim to activate prior learning or experiences that students may have had because drawing on students' previous knowledge helps build their understanding for the coming lesson. VR tools like Google Cardboard and Expeditions can be used to activate students' prior knowledge and build background in a way that is particularly engaging, and doing so increases comprehension and retention (Pilgrim & Pilgrim, 2016).

Moran and Woodall's (2019) study highlights these findings and illuminates the success and ease of using VR in the ELA classroom. In an effort to enhance the ELA curriculum and students' literacy skills, as well as deepen their students' experience with texts, Moran and Woodall (2019) integrated Google Cardboards and two Google Expeditions modules into Woodall's unit on *To Kill a Mockingbird* (Lee, 1960) with her eighth-grade honors students. Instead of building context and background knowledge with historical texts describing what it was like during the Great Depression in the American South—physically, economically, socially—and asking students to "imagine what it's like in the Great Depression," Moran and Woodall (2019, p. 91) wanted to provide students with a deeper understanding of the setting of *To Kill a Mockingbird* and help them connect to the text and history on a more personal level. To prepare students to explore the world of *To Kill a Mockingbird* through VR, Moran and Woodall first had the students download apps and play around with using the Google Cardboard devices; doing so allowed students to experience the novelty of and become familiar with using VR so that later when they used it more purposefully to engage in the content of the unit, the novelty and unfamiliarity would not pose any barriers to deep learning. In a later lesson, the class discussed the importance of understanding the setting and time period of a text in relation to its themes and messages, and then the moment arrived: students downloaded the Google Expeditions app and viewed "The Great Depression" and the "Mattox Family Home at the Henry Ford Museum" expeditions (Moran & Woodall, 2019, p. 92).

As they "walked" around in a VR Dust Bowl, a Hooverville, and the house of the impoverished Mattox family, students related their real-time experiences in VR with the setting and context of *To Kill a Mockingbird*. The students worked in pairs, so while one student used the VR to explore and recount his or her experience, the other student took down notes. After both students experienced each role, the pair discussed "the power of setting, moving beyond where and when a story takes place to the way setting affects our view of events and can even create bias" (Moran & Woodall, 2019, p. 92). With their new heightened understanding, the students chose a scene in *To Kill a Mockingbird* and then wrote an adaptation of that scene in a completely different setting to explore how this change would affect the events (and possibly the message) of the novel. This type of creative narrative exercise is one of the mainstays of the Georgia Milestones Assessment System, the mandated standardized test for Georgia students. Though students are tasked with and complete such exercises in most ELA classes, Moran and Woodall (2019) express that incorporating VR into the activity helped students experience the setting of the novel on a deeper level:

VR was the portal through which the students were able to learn about a new semiotic domain, connect with each other, and pave the way for future explorations into the role of setting, time, and place in literature. It enhanced the literacy experiences of the students by helping them to think critically about the impact of setting on the novel's events. (p. 93)

Upon surveying the students about their experience using VR and how it affected their understanding of *To Kill a Mockingbird*, the authors found that the students' responses were overwhelmingly positive. The students reported that the immersion of the experience made them feel like they had traveled back in time, and it helped them better understand the setting and time period of the novel— and that the characters felt more human and "real" because of it (Moran & Woodall, 2019, p. 93). However, there were some hitches in the overall experience. A few students complained about having to hold up the Google Cardboard device for an extended period of time and wished for a strap so the device could be secured to their head. Some students had phones larger than six inches, making it difficult for them to use the Google Cardboard device since its current design only accommodates phones six inches or less. And other students mentioned that the VR experience made them motion sick; Moran and Woodall (2019) encouraged these students to stay seated and rotate their heads slowly when using the device, and to take frequent breaks as needed. These sorts of challenges will be discussed in further detail later on in the chapter, but that being said, the integration of VR into the study of *To Kill a Mockingbird* undoubtedly enhanced the students' understanding of both the setting of the novel *and* how setting, time period, and place affect stories on a fundamental level. This understanding was reflected in the rich and vivid writing that the students produced after their experiences with VR, leading Moran and Woodall (2019) to conclude that using VR in the ELA classroom can simultaneously enhance the curriculum and the lives of the students.

Likewise, in their study on introducing students to Shakespeare's *A Midsummer Night's Dream* via multimodal instruction when participating in learning stations, Harvey et al. (2020) found that providing students with the opportunity to use technology such as VR, QR codes, videos, websites, and smartphone apps alongside traditional print materials like scholarly articles led to increased engagement, collaboration, and immersion (both in terms of using immersive VR technology and being immersed in the content). And though traditional print media and teaching methods are undoubtedly valuable, it is becoming increasingly important to incorporate multimodal texts and instruction into the classroom, as students are developing alongside these modalities and new ways of interacting with the world. When their interactions with various forms of digital media are driven by inquiry, collaboration, and problem-solving, students are likely to grow in their abilities to read, write, speak, and more (Lenters, 2016, and Wiseman et al., 2017, as cited in Harvey et al., 2020). Furthermore, the ability to engage with these multimodal technologies and texts at learning stations with clear and distinct objectives provided students with a refreshing sense of agency and the ability to develop their autonomy. Interestingly, station 1, at which students used two Oculus Go VR devices to explore the Globe Theater, saw the most autonomy from the students; after initial guidance from the teachers on how to use the VR headset, students then "trained themselves" so that station 1 "practically ran itself," while other stations with less technology saw students needing more attention, assistance, and redirection from the teachers (Harvey et al., 2020, p. 564). This speaks to the students' desire to use multimodal texts and technologies that they may already use outside of the classroom in order to engage with literary content—which in Shakespeare's case may be old, but not outdated (Harvey et al., 2020). The lively discussions and rich written reflections that emerged from stations with high technology usage revealed that students made cross-curricular connections between Shakespeare and previously read texts, as well as connections between their unique understandings of themselves and the world and the "timeless truths of humanity" of Shakespeare's canon (Harvey et al., 2020, pp. 566–567).

Moran and Woodall (2019) demonstrated that on a fundamental level, VR can increase engagement and provide opportunities to deepen understanding of background knowledge and the importance of setting, and Harvey et al. (2020) illustrated how that deep understanding derives from the experiential nature of using VR and other multimodalities alongside traditional ELA content. Pilgrim and Pilgrim (2016) explained that ELA teachers can capitalize on this potential of VR and use it to build opportunities for experiential learning, which ultimately enables students to develop their own opinions of a newly learned concept because they are able to interact with and experience it directly. This allows for more room to support varying viewpoints and perspectives, which is key to creating a healthy classroom environment in which students feel comfortable, safe, and free to be themselves as they learn and grow. This visual, experiential nature of VR, combined with its capacity to increase interest by building background knowledge and fostering connections, leads to more motivation to learn. For ELA teachers interested in incorporating VR into their classroom but unsure of where to start, Pilgrim and Pilgrim (2016) provided a helpful chart of websites and apps with associated descriptions to help teachers determine which resource would be best suited to their content and classroom, and Moran and Woodall (2019) provided a list of tips for teachers who are interested in using VR with their students to study literature.

One of the earlier studies of VR in ELA—in which students learned about VR and either interacted with the virtual world using a "wand" or experienced it further by building their own virtual worlds—revealed positive outcomes (Kumar & Bristor, 1999, p. 48). The results of the informal VR project suggest that through building their own virtual worlds, students learn because they must first study a concept in order to decide how to represent it, they must plan how to create it via speaking and writing activities, they must model what their plan will look like, and they must discuss how objects are supposed to interact with each other in their world, which leads to them experiencing their world and performing assigned tasks within it (Kumar & Bristor, 1999). Kumar and Bristor (1999) also suggested that the students who created worlds learned more than those who only interacted with them, though both sets of students learned more than those taught in a conventional manner. VR has the potential to foster creativity by requiring students to consider the possibilities within certain limitations of whatever program they are working in. This is corroborated by Lin et al. (2017), who also found that incorporating VR into the curriculum allows students to explore beyond their comfort zones and fosters creativity, motivation, and leadership skills.

Yet while emphasis on increasing motivation in the classroom via technology like VR is substantial, attention to cultivating creativity in students through the use of VR is notably lacking. For this reason, and because research into VR applications in ELA is less common than in science education, Patera et al. (2008) sought to explore how to use VR to promote imagination and creativity, as opposed to more technical skills like spelling and grammar, in an ELA classroom. They designed a virtual reality environment (VRE) in order to create an immersive and shared experience so that students could collaborate and experience a world together, simultaneously, and to make the experience more vivid, real, engaging, and inspiring. The "semi-immersive collaborative VRE," called the "Magic Cottage," used a projection system to present the environment while the user stood in front of the projection screen wearing Crystal Eyes stereo goggles with an "active stereo CRT projector" behind him or her; the user used a joystick to navigate through the world (Patera et al., 2008, "3.2 The Technology"). And while only one student was able to navigate at a time, in this study the other students gathered around the user so that they could collaborate together and vocally guide the student using the joystick, thus enhancing the sense of "being a member of an exploration team" on a journey (Patera et al., 2008, "3.2 The Technology"). The VRE was designed as a way to inspire students to write their own stories by using the setting of the Magic Cottage as a starting point (Patera et al., 2008). Aimed at primary school students, the setting emulated that of a fairy tale. And while there were some "unusual" and "out of place" objects around the environment to provoke questions and foster imagination (e.g., spiders and coins in a chest, a diary, a strange bottle in a closet, a tiny bed next to a normal-sized bed), the VRE did not include puzzles, prompts, or any animated characters (Patera et al., 2008, "2.2 Imaginative Writing," para. 6). By offering a simple, imagined setting, the Magic Cottage fostered free exploration and interaction with virtual objects in the hopes of cultivating creativity.

In exploring the world of the Magic Cottage, groups of students naturally developed an oral narrative by collaborating on ideas, thoughts, and questions (Patera et al., 2008). For example, if a student asked, "Whose house is this?" the other students would chime in to express their ideas, which would then trigger new comments and questions (Patera et al., 2008, "4.5 Observations"). Interestingly, only a few of these verbal ideas made it into the students' writing assignments after the VRE experience; Patera et al. (2008) therefore suggest further research into how oral narration can be effectively transferred to writing. Upon evaluation of the study, the authors found that while the

VRE fostered engagement and positivity throughout—from both students and teachers—the levels of creativity of students who experienced the Magic Cottage versus those who did not were not necessarily amplified. This does not mean, however, that using VRE has no effect on creativity: Patera et al. (2008) point out potential flaws in their research methods, such as small numbers of participants in the study, individual differences in the pupils, overly sensitive assessment criteria designated by the Scotland government (where the study took place), and the current educational system's general misunderstanding about the nature of imaginative writing. "Imaginative writing" has at least three different skills involved: "creativity . . . , retrieving and restructuring that material for the purposes of writing, and language skills" (Patera et al., 2008, "Conclusions and Future Work," para. 5). As such, they suggest that alongside offering a vivid experience to encourage imagination, teachers should offer opportunities to promote memory skills and some kind of planning or structure so that students can express their imaginations clearly. While students were engaged in and stimulated by the VRE, some were not able to internalize it and express their experience in their writing. Since the students were provided with a vivid setting already, Patera et al. (2008) suggest that a VRE may be a good tool to use in order to lay the foundation, or jumping-off point, of a creative space, and this would then allow for more focused practice on the other stages of imaginative writing (i.e., retrieving, planning, writing, revising) rather than brainstorming.

In addition, Patera et al. (2008) call attention to Robertson and Good's (2003) study in which the participants successfully made and tested out creative decisions in a way that was largely independent from other criteria like language skills. Robertson and Good (2003) created a VRE called *Ghostwriter* to simulate a computer game called *Unreal* in which two avatars, controlled by students, and one "role-play leader" (p. 5) interact. The creative stories of students who wrote during normal classroom conditions were compared to stories created by students who engaged in the VRE of *Ghostwriter*. What Robertson and Good (2003) found was indicative of the capacity of VR to cultivate creativity and other ELA skills: "the stories written after the virtual role-play contained more indications of characters' relationships, particularly as portrayed through dialogue, than did normal classroom stories" (pp. 5–6).

This conclusion is supported by Mirzaei et al.'s (2019) study, in which the authors explored the use of VR to encourage users to collaborate and cocreate meaningful stories. Mirzaei et al. (2019) found that the study's participants—all intermediate English learners—delved deep into their story creation "by adding 'meta-explanations' about the characters' feelings and mental states" (p. 298). The VR story creation platform allowed users to build upon each others' ideas, shift between alternate perspectives, and think critically and creatively when it came to moving the story forward.

In this collaborative setting, Mirzaei et al. (2019) observed the participants attempt to navigate how to make the story realistic and meaningful. The following includes a few things Mirzaei et al. (2019) heard the participants say while working through cocreating their characters and stories: "I don't think she should be kind to him because he was so mean to her," "If I were her, I would leave him," "I think she felt heartbroken, but not angry," and so on (p. 302). Because they were able to express their thoughts about the characters and the story with their peers *and* visualize their thoughts in the VR platform, participants were able to exercise their creative juices and build stories in a safe and collaborative environment that naturally stimulated creativity (Mizraei et al., 2019).

As ELA teachers in this day and age, finding time to make room for personal and creative writing in the classroom is becoming increasingly difficult amidst more stringent curriculum standards and a heightened focus on testing. But it is important to not let these types of writing fall by the wayside, as they play an invaluable role in personal development. Children, and even adults, make sense of the world and their place in it through the stories they create; Engel (1999, as cited in Robertson & Good, 2003) argued that "the stories we tell ourselves, aloud or silently, play a vital role in shaping what we feel, think, and know about our lives" (p. 6). And creating narratives is a thought process that also helps us understand not only ourselves, but other people, human intentions, and the results of human behavior (Bruner, 1986, as cited in Robertson & Good, 2003). Furthermore, imaginative writing helps writers take on others' perspectives, which is a key goal of the ELA classroom.

One way that students take on others' perspectives is through characterization, which is essential to stories of any kind because it is the characters who make the stories seem real, even in magical and fantastical worlds (Ellis & Friel, 1998, as cited in Robertson & Good, 2003). Characterization is essentially being able to describe a person or being, either directly or indirectly, and distinguish numerous characteristics that make up who they are, distinct from all others. In order to successfully characterize another person or character, real or fictional, one needs a well-developed sense of empathy, and the development of empathy is not something that is often *explicitly* taught in schools, though many educators and school systems are now recognizing the importance of social-emotional learning and implementing it into their pedagogical mission, and many ELA teachers naturally teach about the virtues of empathy, kindness, integrity, in their literature studies. Numerous studies have shown that VR has the potential to develop its users' senses of empathy, and if we want to help students with their characterization skills to create more authentic stories with which they and others can grapple with their experiences in the world—and if we want our students to be mentally healthy people—this new advancement is something to seriously consider.

In one study using video recordings and Google Cardboard, participants experienced a scenario in which one of their classmates was having a party after school, but the student using the Google Cardboard was not invited, even after hearing the party host make a concession to have one more person over (Berg et al., 2016). The aim of this study by Berg et al. (2016) was to illustrate how VR can be used to raise awareness about the social dynamics surrounding bullying and "ambiguous social situations" ("Choice of Terminology")—so called since bullying is a complex dynamic—and increase empathy for others. Berg et al. (2016) noted that in a discussion after this project was presented to an audience, the discussion lasted longer than the presentation itself due to the huge amount of feedback and different perspectives the audience members provided on the subject, even taking it beyond the school environment. This study supports Bailey and Bailenson's (2017) understanding that VR can "act as a safe environment for individuals to practice their social cognition skills without major social repercussions" (p. 108); for example, VR can provide a simulation in which adolescents and teens can practice how to effectively handle a situation in which they notice someone else being bullied without having to worry about having the bullying turn on them if they act in such a way that escalates the situation.

The capability of VR to allow its users to take on the perspective of someone else is documented in other studies, as well. Bertrand et al. (2018) write that the ability of immersive simulations to "displace the first-person point of view" (p. 10) makes it easier to take on a different perspective and role-play being in that person's experience. And both immersive and non-immersive VR have been correlated to having positive empathic responses from users, especially if the perspective is in first person, as opposed to third person (Bertrand et al., 2018). Research has shown that VR can reduce implicit race bias when adult users embodied an avatar of a different race (Peck et al., 2013, as cited in Bailey & Bailenson, 2017). Ahn et al. (2013) also explored how immersive virtual environment technology (IVET) can enable users to better take on the perspectives of others, which may lead to a heightened sense of concern, a feeling of presence, and more motivation to help. Ahn et al. (2013) researched whether simulating red-green colorblindness—where a person is not able to perceive differences between red and green—would promote more empathy for people with disabilities perceptual differences compared to other perspective-taking activities where participants had to imagine what it would be like to be colorblind. In all three experiments, they found participants had increased empathy (Ahn et al., 2013). For a more comprehensive exploration into the possibilities of VR fostering empathy, see Bertrand et al. (2018).

Beyond acting as a potential environment to improve empathy and social perspective taking (SPT) capacities, VR may also be used to train people in conflict resolution, especially if it is complemented by trainings in the real world, as previously illustrated when discussing the potential for teens to experiment with dealing with bullying (Gehlbach et al., 2015). While this capability may have further implications for use in schools in general, these sorts of conflict resolution activities can also help ELA students resolve the conflicts between characters in their stories. One large issue with personal and narrative writing is that without proper instruction and structure, students do not know how to apply their imaginations and creative skills to the form of a story, especially when the teacher's overzealous focus on language skills like spelling, grammar, and punctuation deters students from writing due to stress and fear of making mistakes (Robertson & Good, 2003). While undoubtedly important, the development of these skills has its place; when attempting to foster children's natural ability to weave imaginative stories and transfer that creativity in a structured form in their writing, ELA teachers should consider lightening up on the focus of these surface features so as to not decrease children's enthusiasm for creating stories (Robertson & Good, 2003).

Robertson and Good (2003) sought to explore how participating in a VRE as a prewriting activity could affect the characterization in the children's imaginative writing. Before detailing their study, they describe the writing preparation activities, based on Graves's (1983, as cited in Robertson & Good, 2003) process approach to writing, that were the foundation of their work. This process approach is based on the idea that children want to express themselves; as such, it specifies that children should

- write regularly and frequently
- decide that they want to write
- draft and redraft their work
- discuss it with their teacher and peers
- have an opportunity to publish it

(Graves, 1983, as cited in Robertson & Good, 2003)

The students should have control over their writing—which fosters motivation and a sense of ownership and pride—while the teacher's role is to model good writing and offer guidance and assistance when necessary. Before they write, however, students need to prepare and plan their stories; Robertson and Good (2003) relay that drama is considered to be a good preparation activity because participants need to imagine that the story is really happening and apply what they know about real life to this imaginary world, ultimately creating an interactive and immediate experience that can be translated to a story (Neelands, 1998 and Booth, 1994, as cited in Robertson & Good, 2003).

Robertson and Good (2003) used their VRE *Ghostwriter* as the writing preparation activity, which included elements of drama, to help motivate students' writing. In this simulation, pairs of students experienced the activity together, taking on roles of different characters of the story as they are led by someone else who takes on the role of the role-play leader who makes decisions throughout the story. "The storyline," according to Robertson and Good (2003), "was designed to encourage participants to think deeply about moral issues, and empathise with others" (p. 12). The environment they created challenged participants with moral conundrums so that they were forced to make decisions that would impact the other characters; this structure ultimately succeeded in having participants take on the role of a different person, form relationships with other characters, make difficult decisions that have effects on others, and learn about the effects of these decisions (Robertson & Good, 2003). By comparing the stories between students who did and did not participate in the VRE, Robertson and Good (2003) found that using *Ghostwriter* led to higher-quality characterization in terms of relationships between characters, especially through the use of dialogue, though it did not have any significant effects in terms of personality of the characters or mood in the stories. These findings indicated that using VR as a way to cultivate more ELA skills like characterization can be effective.

Moreover, and as previously discussed, VR like *Ghostwriter* has shown great potential to act as a motivating factor to get students engaged—in this case in the writing process. All of the participants of Robertson and Good's (2003) study expressed positive opinions of the program, most often commenting that they enjoyed communicating with their peers as they played, both in real life and in messages they were able to type. The teacher in this study reported a similar assessment from a more objective perspective: the game had elements of a story—surprise, characterization, decision-making, suspense—that made it exciting to engage in, and even students who were notably unenthusiastic about writing were more willing to slowly type their messages to their partners. Furthermore, participating in *Ghostwriter* seemed to motivate students and show them that they were able to produce quality writing, "[P]upils with lower levels of literacy seemed to surpass their normal performance" in both the role-playing activity, which required reading and writing, and in their stories after the activity (Robertson & Good, 2003, p. 26). Other students who had exhibited challenging behaviors also demonstrated positive effects from the activity (Robertson & Good, 2003).

The implication that engaging with digital media and VR motivates reluctant writers is echoed by Xu et al. (2011). Xu et al. (2011) performed a study based on how virtual worlds like *Second Life*—a non-immersive VRE in which people taking on the form of 3D avatars can interact, communicate, and build worlds—can affect writing self-efficacy and flow, and they also discuss numerous other benefits to digital storytelling. First and foremost, because digital storytelling can help students express their thoughts and ideas, students were more likely to actively participate in the lesson, leading to more student-centered learning (Xu et al., 2011). Xu et al. (2011) also discussed how digital storytelling can improve writing skills, critical thinking skills, and media literacy. In one study by Ballast et al. (2008, as cited in Xu et al., 2011), sixth graders who engaged with creating a digital story more carefully edited and revised their stories (editing for word choice, rearranging sentences, removing sentences altogether, etc.) than a control group who simply checked for spelling errors and word count. And Warburton and Perez (2009, as cited in Xu et al., 2011) reviewed how *Second Life* in particular helps the user visualize objects or ideas that he or she cannot see in real life and enriches the experience by including a variety of interactions and feeding the sense of being immersed in the digital environment.

In their study, Xu et al. (2011) found that between a group of students who used *Second Life* to create digital stories and a group of students who wrote their stories offline using Windows Movie Maker, the former group had significantly higher scores in terms of self-efficacy and writing flow. Xu et al. attribute this to the fact that a virtual environment like *Second Life* can provide participants with a challenge in terms of their skill level in playing the game, which increases motivation and engagement in the activity of digital storytelling. In addition, the students can see their stories evolve in real time, so it is easier to spot problems and make revisions as necessary. This ability, combined with their heightened sense of immersion, effectively led to more flow in the students' writing (Xu et al., 2011). And while *Second Life* is non-immersive, the implications of Xu et al.'s (2011) study are fairly conclusive: VR can provide an open-ended learning environment that provides room for students to interact without limitations such as time and space, ultimately stimulating their imaginations and encouraging creative writing because they can visualize the stories they imagine and realistically enact their stories in a clearly structured way.

Madigan (2018) discussed programs that can be used in the ELA classroom to promote writing, as well as other activities and skills related to ELA, highlighting Google Expeditions and Google Spotlight Stories (https://atap .google.com/spotlight-stories/) in particular. Google Spotlight Stories are VR short stories that Madigan (2018) described as "visually stunning" stories that will effectively engage students and which can be used for analyzing visual elements, characters, and themes (p. 56). Google Spotlight Stories can also be used to stimulate the students' own writing: the high level of immersion, control, and choice allows students to intensely experience a story and help them "build their own settings and descriptions," use sensory detail to develop the mood and tone, and make their stories come to life (Madigan, 2018, p. 56). The short stories are available in different formats in addition to VR mode (used with VR goggles), allowing for potential discussions about the differences between each mode and how that affects the viewer

(Madigan, 2018). Each VR story comes with articles that can complement the learning. Madigan (2018) provided creative ideas for using the stories in the ELA classroom, especially ideas that inspire writing activities (such as "diary entries, setting and character descriptions, reviews, poetry, interviews, scripts and essays"), as well as activities that explore elements of storytelling, genre, visual literacy, and filmmaking (Madigan, 2018, p. 56).

Madigan (2018) provided two examples of stories available from Google Spotlight Stories that students can experience through both film and VR, and she delineates clear possibilities for focus throughout each short story: from previewing and making predictions about the film and VR to reading and discussing certain topics relevant to the film, to analyzing the story's construction, to creating storyboards for different scenes and from different viewpoints, to adding dialogue to different scenes and discussing those rhetorical choices, to writing an authentic review of the film, to composing tweets and creating news articles, to comparing and contrasting similar stories and films, and to thinking about genre conventions, Madigan (2018) provided great insight into how to get started using these easy-to-access resources. In addition, Madigan (2018) suggested Google Stories' Story Development Kit to assist teachers and students with making their own Google Stories, as well as the site "Taster" and the online gallery Sketchfab. Taster, a sister site to the BBC, allows the BBC to share and showcase new ideas and technologies which can be easily coupled with ELA lessons. Sketchfab houses a wide variety of 3D and VR content, and on it students can explore real and imagined objects, which could be a helpful way in to creating a story because it can build students' attention to detail and improve this often lackluster component of student writing. And of course, all of these platforms allow for increased immersion, leading to more student choice and interaction (Madigan, 2018).

And while the existing literature on VR in the ELA classroom seems to focus on writing, there is naturally potential for VR in terms of reading, as well. Webb (2012) compiled a book based on many teachers' and researchers' use of virtual worlds and VR in their middle school, high school, and college classes while exploring canonical texts. One chapter explores a range of "immersive" (though not in the sense of using immersive VR technology and gear) literary worlds, such as *Dungeons and Dragons*, *World of Warcraft*, *EverQuest*, and even *Grand Theft Auto* (Webb, 2012, p. xi). Ironically, students already play many of these games (or games that are similarly literature-heavy) without quite realizing they are engaging in literary texts and using skills they learn and develop in ELA. That being said, it is easy to understand the connections between participating in highly engaging literary worlds and in the ELA classroom. For example, many people have heard of the popular role-playing game (RPG) *World of Warcraft* (WoW). Though WoW is similar to *Second Life* in that it is an engaging role-playing platform and both games are non-immersive, WoW is different in that there is a set storyline that users, also occupying avatars like in *Second Life*, can choose to interact with. Users can go on quests or explore the world to their heart's content in a very rewarding and engaging experience. Because of its high levels of engagement and sheer amount of content, WoW is played at home by millions of players, and it is recently being used in schools for its educational potential. McCrea (2012) writes about an educator in New York named Peggy Sheehy who noticed the educational value in WoW, including "learning folklore through literature, vocabulary building, and socialization and digital literacy skills" (p. 23). Sheehy and other staff members cofounded a club that uses WoW for educational purposes and blends the game with common core standards, focusing on (but not limited to) ELA. In one project, students were reading *The Hobbit* in class and on their own time, and Sheehy tasked them with looking for similarities between Bilbo Baggins and their own WoW characters. (*Beowulf* was the next text they would use in conjunction with WoW.) The students also wrote short stories based on their own characters' exploits and adventures (McCrea, 2012). According to Sheehy, "This allows them to get engaged with the character and the book, learn vocabulary, and relate the experience to their own lives," while also bringing language to students who do not want to read because the game is replete with lore and text to guide users on their adventures (McCrea, 2012, p. 25).

At another school, Lucas Gillespie taught a WoW elective class that also fit into the Language Arts schedule (McCrea, 2012). Each lesson was broken down into "quests" that corresponded with the curriculum, and students received experience points and badges for their achievements. The quests were also designed to be authentic in nature so that students would be even more engaged by interacting with the real world. For example, one quest "instructs students to use the internet to read the mission statements of several large corporations and apply that understanding to develop mission statements for their individual player guilds in WoW" (McCrea, 2012, p. 26). In their mission statements, students included information about why their guild exists and its key goals, similar to the mission statements they saw in real life (McCrea, 2012). In addition, Gillespie also had his students engage in writing activities in which he informally noticed growth in terms of their writing, vocabulary, and sentence structure on formative assessments—and these students were taking their learning and growth into their regular ELA classes (McCrea, 2012). From these sorts of explorations into using non-immersive virtual worlds to improve ELA-specific skills like reading comprehension and writing, it is fairly easy to extrapolate how immersive VR can do the same—or potentially even better due to VR's increased immersion and levels of heightened engagement of the senses.

Indeed, though it is lower-immersion than VR, AR has been used in conjunction with books in an effort to increase the reading engagement of students and lessen the poor reading performance and general disinterest in reading across Europe in recent years (Meletiou-Mavrotheris et al., 2020). *The Living Book—Augmenting Reading for Life* project has recently been implemented in six countries with high proportions of "low-achievers"—Cyprus, Estonia, Italy, Romania, Portugal, and the UK—in an effort to increase young people's (specifically ages 9–15) motivation to read, decrease the number of "low achievers" in the EU, and boost their competency in terms of digital skills, learning how to learn, critical thinking, cooperative skills, and so on (Meletiou-Mavrotheris et al., 2020, p. 57). Foundational to the *Living Book* project are studies that found that combining AR with books created an interactive and engaging way to enhance teaching and foster learning. The typical experience of reading can be enlivened with sounds, 2D and 3D illustrations, and even tactile activities via the use of mobile devices (Meletiou-Mavrotheris et al., 2020). Meletiou-Mavrotheris et al. (2020) report that of the few but growing number of studies on the impact of AR books on student learning outcomes, most of them indicate "numerous positive attributes that have the potential to enhance both formal and informal student learning" (p. 59). These benefits include an increase in motivation, engagement, interest, and fun; an improvement in story comprehension, understanding of concepts, and development of contextual awareness, critical thinking, and problem-solving skills; and a range of affordances and accessibility for all students, including those with reading difficulties, emotional and behavioral difficulties, low motivation, different learning styles and preferences, and so forth (Meletiou-Mavrotheris et al., 2020). And while Meletiou-Mavrotheris et al. do point out limitations and potential challenges of incorporating new technology like AR, it is clear that the use of AR and VR in ELA and other areas is going to become more commonplace because of their great potential benefits to students.

With true AR and VR on the rise and more and more research into VR in education (and specifically in ELA) being produced, it is important to shape new lessons and curriculum that incorporate these technologies according to standards that truly embrace constructive learning, as opposed to simply including them "just because" they are the new fad in education. McCrea (2012) notes that Gillespie advises that before incorporating gaming and gamification—and, by extension, virtual worlds and AR and VR technologies—into classroom instruction, educators should "first examine the cognitive processes and decision-making that take place" (p. 27) during the users' experience, and then find a way to incorporate that entire experience into the curriculum. Likewise, Meletiou-Mavrotheris et al. (2020) also cautioned educators to be aware of the potential pitfall of "technological determinism" (Wyatt, 2008, as cited in Meletiou-Mavrotheris et al., 2020, p. 61)—essentially using technology just for the sake of using technology. In order to avoid this pitfall, educators must make sure they are implementing the technology primarily to cultivate meaningful learning for their students (Meletiou-Mavrotheris et al., 2020). Marsh and Yamada-Rice (2018) outlined five principles to serve as guidelines to incorporating AR and VR into the ELA curriculum in meaningful ways. The use of AR and VR in the classroom:

1. "needs to lead to literacy experiences that are rich, meaningful, and build on the affordances of the technology" (Marsh & Yamada-Rice, 2018, p. 48). By this, Marsh and Yamada-Rice meant that the focus should always remain on learning, rather than on the new technology. This idea is in accord with many of the voices heard previously in the section "VR in the Classroom."

2. "should enable children to engage in playful approaches to learning in which meaning and affect are key" (Marsh & Yamada-Rice, 2018, p. 48). Essentially, AR and VR should not *only* foster fun and exciting feelings for students, though these are, of course, conducive to a healthy classroom; through play and experiential learning, AR and VR should also help students explore other emotions such as anger, fear, suspense, and curiosity, because these are also important for their learning and the development of their emotional well-being.

3. "should lead to productive as well as consumptive practices" (Marsh & Yamada-Rice, 2018, p. 49). While AR and VR apps and programs allow for new experiences and explorations in different environments that would otherwise not be possible—and this is no doubt beneficial—educators should also consider ways to use AR and VR technologies in such a way that helps students be creative and produce their own work, like narratives and stories.

4. "should foster the development of critical literacy skills" (Marsh & Yamada-Rice, 2018, p. 49). AR and VR have great potential to foster curiosity, critical thinking, and inquiry skills in their users and should be used to encourage these skills. For example, while exploring the "Deforestation in Brazil" expedition by Google Expeditions, students should consider questions that get at the causes and results of deforestation, such as "What are the implications for wildlife and humans of what is happening?" (Marsh & Yamada-Rice, 2018, p. 49).

5. "should build on children's encounters with these technologies outside of the classroom" (Marsh & Yamada-Rice, 2018, p. 49). Many students already experience AR and VR technologies outside of the classroom, most commonly on smartphone apps. These experiences should be

acknowledged within the classroom to build on students' outside knowledge and experiences to support their in-class learning.

Ultimately, despite the limited research of AR and VR in the ELA classroom, what is out there indicates great potential for fostering learning in a modern day and age. VR offers a way for teachers to provide visual and experiential scaffolding by building background knowledge and cultivating reading comprehension. The engagement it offers helps develop students' sense of empathy, which not only translates to more creativity, detailed descriptions, and complex characterization in their writing, but also encourages students to be more empathetic and understanding inside and outside of the classroom. And by offering fun and exciting ways to learn through authentic experiences, VR increases long-term retention and motivates students to keep learning, growing, and bettering themselves—which is one of the ultimate goals and most rewarding of outcomes for an ELA teacher.

POTENTIAL CHALLENGES

While the benefits of AR and VR are numerous, they do not come without potential challenges that should be considered. In a study by Petersen and Stricker (2015, as cited in Kurilovas, 2016), the findings indicated that though AR has been around for at least twenty years, one barrier to its ubiquitous use in education is that—in addition to the limitations of creating ergonomic technology—creating AR (and, naturally, VR) environments for education can be time-consuming. However, AR is purported to have a more long-standing impact on society (and possibly education) because it is more readily available and easier to create than VR (Pope, 2018). On the other hand, such an infusion of AR into daily life (via smartphone apps) may cause people to become overwhelmed and uninterested in exploring new AR apps and technologies that may be better in terms of technological capability or educational opportunity, and there is the potential for students to feel "cognitive overload" (Gandolfi, 2018; Meletiou-Mavrotheris et al., 2020; Pope, 2018). In addition, AR is limited in its accessibility because it primarily focuses on the sense of sight, though there are efforts being made to create apps and technology that can communicate touch, taste, and smell. That being said, due to the current nature of the technology at hand, this limitation of AR is something to keep in mind when considering some of the challenges or disadvantages for this population.

VR, too, has these challenges, though less so than AR because it focuses on more of the user's senses. However, people who are sight- and hearing-impaired are not able to be fully immerse in the VR experience, and the devices may not have been properly designed for people with physical disabilities even though VR has been touted as having great potential for use special education classrooms (Gandolfi, 2018, p. 552). And VR comes with other challenges that AR does not. For instance, accessing multiple headsets that use more sophisticated technology than Google Cardboard can be an expensive barrier to using them in schools, as this hardware can often be "beyond student or institutional budgets" (Ray & Deb, 2016, p. 68). There are other considerations teachers have to take into account: some students may not be able to afford smartphones or may be embarrassed if their smartphone is an older model or has a cracked screen (which also may prevent them from using it with Google Cardboard). As such, Bonner and Reinders (2018) suggest that when incorporating VR in the classroom, teachers provide non-VR alternatives for these students, potentially by sharing their own VR experience with the whole class via a projector or television. Another possibility is to group students who have sufficient devices with those who do not, making sure to collect this data before the actual activity and keep it in confidence so as to not lead to any discomfort or allow for any bullying. Moran and Woodall (2019) mention that in their study of using Google Cardboard with Woodall's eight-grade class, Woodall knew beforehand that some of her students did not have smartphones, so she had students who "'forgot' to bring their phones to school" (pp. 91–92) pair with students who had their phone handy so no one would be embarrassed. This careful consideration about what method and phrasing to employ in these delicate scenarios is up to each teacher, as he or she knows his or her students best.

Pope (2018) posits that another downside to immersive VR with headsets is that the users are not able to directly interact with one another, which can make many of the benefits of VR—such as collaboration and users having similar experiences—more difficult for teachers to facilitate. However, in programs that do allow for interaction, other potential risks exist. If the virtual space is not monitored or designated to only allow participation by certain users, like a classroom teacher and students, then "harassers can enter another person's personal space and . . . make it difficult or even impossible for that person to retaliate . . . without quitting the space altogether," depending on the VR environment (Bonner & Reinders, 2018, p. 50). These free agents or unruly users can also destroy creations made in the VR space if the program does not have certain protections in place, so if the class is using a program or platform open to anyone, the teacher should monitor the students' interactions and carefully consider the pros and cons of using that platform (Bonners & Reinders, 2018).

Another potential challenge is that because VR's use in primary and secondary education is still in its initial stages, there is limited information out there on how to consistently incorporate VR in an ELA classroom. If ELA teachers are using VR in a creative capacity—that is, their students are potentially creating their own environments—then the teachers need adequate training and knowledge of how to do that themselves. This hurdle can be intimidating to overcome, as these sorts of programs can be complex and often "require advanced knowledge in order to create a virtual environment" (Pope, 2018, p. 24). Gandolfi (2018) mentioned that teacher preparation (or lack thereof) is one of the barriers to implementation of AR or VR into the classroom because teachers are not ready "to deal with technical problems and usability concerns" (p. 550). Kavanagh et al. (2017) echo this sentiment. Not only do teachers need to be trained when a new technology is incorporated in the school, they note, but each teacher may require more or less training depending on his or her degree of experience with the technology. And when they are trained, teachers need to spend time training the students how to use the new technology, which may detract from teaching the content—though the potential benefits after this groundwork is laid can be well worth it (Kavanagh et al., 2017).

In addition, teachers should also be aware of other elements of AR and VR that need to be considered before implementation, such as the potential physical side effects like nausea and imbalance, as well as ethical issues that deal with copyright, privacy, and unappropriated content (Gandolfi, 2018). In terms of the physical side effects, some argue that along with VR comes safety concerns because being fully immersed in another environment requires the separation of one's senses from the physical world. Videos showcasing people using VR headsets often show these people falling down or walking into walls or furniture because their senses are obscured. This may lead to a sense of disorientation and instability, causing balance issues and possibly nausea; or it follows that the user is less able to perceive the outside environment and thus walks into things he or she would otherwise navigate around. Zantua (2017) noted that in a study on the learning outcomes and student reactions after using Google Cardboard and Google Expeditions, some participants mentioned feeling motion sick after their experience, which may be attributed to the use of the "built-in accelerometer of mobile phones that causes headaches or motion sickness" (p. 9). Even so, the study found that student test scores increased after students participated in the Google Expeditions with Google Cardboard, and students reported an overall positive experience; Zantua (2017) concluded that Google Cardboard could be used to great effect in building upon student learning in a constructivist approach. As with any new product or technology, the user needs to be aware of the potential side effects, especially, in this case, if he or she is particularly susceptible to vertigo and imbalance. In addition, these effects can be mitigated if the application is rendered in higher quality (Theodorakopoulos et al., 2017).

As for privacy issues, teachers and other users should be aware that since AR and VR is such a burgeoning area, smartphone apps are popping up that may access the user's locations, microphone, camera, browser history, or other sensitive information depending on the permissions granted when installing the app (Bonner & Reinders, 2018). Bonner and Reinders (2018) expla that while some apps may only collect this data for ad purposes, there may be more "nefarious" apps out there, so it is important to be sure the app is verified as educational and sound before asking students to install it (p. 50). Google Cardboard and Google Expeditions have partnered with institutions like the Smithsonian, the Wildlife Conservation Trust, and the Royal Collection Trust to keep the quality of the content high and educational in nature (Craddock, 2018). Another consideration is the cost of apps, which may be free at first but then have limitations that prevent their continued use in the classroom, such as built-in subscription fees after a certain amount of time or new costs if the developers need revenue to keep their app going or if they foresee more profit after they have established a larger user base (Bonner & Reinders, 2018).

In Kavanagh et al.'s (2017) review of the problems of VR in education as noted by other researchers, many researchers report challenges with hardware and software usability issues. They noted that while sometimes the issue faced was related to the user's lack of training, many of the issues stemmed from the inherent difficulties within the systems themselves, leading to problems with clarity, navigation, readability, and so on. These issues and other issues that are difficult to home in on can actually lead to a *lack* of engagement, even though engagement is often cited as a motivation for incorporating VR into the classroom. As mentioned earlier, the novelty factor of incorporating VR may be helpful for kindling engagement, but this should not be relied on as the sole means to engage students in the content or lesson. Furthermore, this should not be the only reason why VR is used in the classroom, "as poor educational design (even within VR) can still result in a lack of engagement" (Kavanagh et al., 2017, p. 103).

More awareness of all of these challenges and elements of VR leads to more effective teaching of this new approach to learning. Yet the lack of simple and sufficient guiding materials for ELA teachers can make the implementation of this technology difficult, and this can also lead to negative feelings toward incorporating VR into the classroom. These may include fear, intimidation, anxiety, and impatience. However, VR can be used to great effect in an ELA class. As with any new technology, the benefits of pioneering it can outweigh the challenges that come along with it; while AR and VR have their share of potential challenges, there is little doubt that they will be worthy challenges to tackle considering the great promise that using VR in the ELA classroom holds.

REFERENCES

Ahn, S.J., Le, A.M.T., & Bailenson, J.N. (2013). The effect of embodied experiences on self-other merging, attitude, and helping behavior. *Media Psychology, 16*(1), 7–38. https://vhil.stanford.edu/pubs/2013/the-effect-of-embodied-experiences-on-self-other-merging-attitude-and-helping-behavior/

Bailey, J.O., & Bailenson, J.N. (2017). Considering virtual reality in children's lives. *Journal of Children and Media, 11*(1), 107–113.

Berg, K., Larsson, M., Lindh, F., Remertz, P., & Soderstrom, B. (Contributors). (2016). Different perspectives: An immersive experience using 360° video and Google Cardboard. *Proceedings of SIDeR'16 — student interaction design research conference*, Malmo University, Sweden.

Bertrand, P., Guegan, J., Robieux, L., McCall, C.A., & Zenasni, F. (2018). Learning empathy through virtual reality: Multiple strategies for learning empathy-related abilities using body ownership illusions in embodied virtual reality. *Frontiers in Robotics and AI, 5*(26). DOI: 10.3389/frobt.2018.00026.

Bonner, E., & Reinders, H. (2018). Augmented and virtual reality in the language classroom: Practical ideas. *Teaching English with Technology, 18*(3), 33–53.

Craddock, I. M. (2018). Immersive virtual reality, Google Expeditions, and English language learning. *Library Technology Reports, 4*(7), 7–9.

David, D., Keaton, R., Morris, R., Murphy, J., & Stapley, I. (2008). A space for writing: Developmental writing instruction in a technology-enhanced classroom. *Research and Teaching in Developmental Education, 24*(2), 15–26.

Dede, C. (2009). Immersive interfaces for engagement and learning. *Science, 323*(5910), 66–69.

Demirel, M., & Akkoyunlu, B. (2017). Prospective teachers' lifelong learning tendencies and information literacy self-efficacy. *Educational Research and Reviews, 12*(6), 329–337.

Freina, L. F., & Ott, M. O. (2015). A literature review on immersive virtual reality in education: State of the art and perspectives. *Elearning & Software for Education, 1*, 133–141.

Frontera, E. B. (2009). Teaching students to build historical buildings in virtual reality: A didactic strategy for learning history of art in secondary education. *Themes in Science and Technology Education, 2*(1–2), 165–184.

Gadelha, R. (2018). Revolutionizing education: The promise of virtual reality. *Childhood Education, 94*(1), 40–43.

Gandolfi, E. (2018). Virtual reality and augmented reality. In Kennedy, K. & Ferdig, R.E. (Eds.), *Handbook of research on k-12 online and blended learning* (2nd ed., pp. 545–561). ETC Press.

Gehlbach, H., Marietta, G., King, A., Karutz, C., Bailenson, J.N. & Dede, C. (2015). Many ways to walk a mile in another's moccasins: Type of social perspective taking and its effect on negotiation outcomes. *Computers in Human Behavior, 52*, 523–532.

Ghanouni, P., Jarus, T., Zwicker, J. G., Lucyshyn, J., Mow, K., & Ledingham, A. (2018). Social stories for children with autism spectrum disorder: Validating the content of a virtual reality program. *Journal of Autism and Developmental Disorders, 49*(2), 660–668.

Hanson, K., & Shelton, B. E. (2008). Design and development of virtual reality: Analysis of challenges faced by educators. *Journal of Educational Technology & Society, 11*(1), 118–131.

Harvey, M., Deuel, A., & Marlatt, R. (2020). "To be, or not to be": Modernizing Shakespeare with multimodal learning stations. *Journal of Adolescent & Adult Literacy, 63*(5), 559–568.

Johnston, E., Olivas, G., Steele, P., Smith, C., & Bailey, L. (2018). Exploring pedagogical foundations of existing virtual reality educational applications: A content analysis study. *Journal of Educational Technology Systems, 46*(4), 414–439.

Kavanagh, S., Luxton-Reilly, A., Wuensche, B., & Plimmer, B. (2017). A systematic review of virtual reality in education. *Themes In Science & Technology Education, 10*(2), 85–119.

Kumar, D., & Bristor, V. J. (1999). Integrating science and language arts through technology-based macro contexts. *Educational Review, 51*(1), 41–53.

Kurilovas, E. (2016). Evaluation of quality and personalisation of VR/AR/MR learning systems. *Behaviour & Information Technology, 35*(11), 998–1007.

Lin, M. T., Wang, J., Kuo, H., & Luo, Y. (2017). A study on the effect of virtual reality 3D exploratory education on students' creativity and leadership. *EURASIA Journal of Mathematics, Science & Technology Education, 13*(7), 3151–3161.

Lisichenko, R. (2015). Issues surrounding the use of virtual reality in geographic education. *The Geography Teacher 12*(4), 159–166.

Madigan, P. (2018). A spotlight on virtual reality in the English classroom. *METAphor*, (2), 56–58.

Marsh, J., & Yamada-Rice, D. (2018). Using augmented and virtual reality in the language arts curriculum. *Language Arts, 96*(1), 47–50.

McCrea, B. (2012). WoWing language arts: Schools across the country are mapping their curriculum to the fantasy RPG World of Warcraft, proving that students can learn a surprising amount from dwarves, elves, and orcs. *T H E Journal (Technological Horizons in Education), 39*(7), 24–27.

McKibben, S., & Davis, K. (2019). Making magic at "High-Tech Hogwarts." *Educational Leadership, 76*(5), 48–53.

Meletiou-Mavrotheris, M., Charalambous, C., Mavrou, K., Dimopoulos, C., Anastasi, P., Lasica, I.-E., Stylianidou, N., & Vasou, C. (2020). Empowering teachers to augment students' reading experience: *The Living Book* project approach. In T. Prodromou (Ed.), *Augmented reality in educational settings* (pp. 56–79). Brill | Sense.

Mirzaei, M. S., Zhang, Q., Meshgi, K., & Nishida, T. (2019). Collaborative learning through story envisioning in virtual reality. In F. Meunier, J. Van de Vyver, L. Bradley & S. Thouësny (Eds.), *CALL and complexity — short papers from EUROCALL 2019* (pp. 297–303). Research-publishing.net.

Moore, P. (1995). Learning and teaching in virtual worlds: Implications for virtual reality in education. *Australian Journal of Educational Technology, 11*(2), 91–102. DOI: 10.14742/ajet.2078

Morales, T. M., Bang, E., & Andre, T. (2013). A one-year case study: Understanding the rich potential of project-based learning in a virtual reality class for high school students. *Journal of Science Education and Technology, 22*(5), 791–806. https://doi.org/10.1007/s10956-012-9431-7

Moran, C. M., & Woodall, M. K. (2019). "It was like I was there": Inspiring engagement through virtual reality. *English Journal, 109*(1), 90–96.

North, M. M., North, S. M., & Crunk, J. (2004). Virtual reality combats test anxiety: A case study report. *Studies in Health Technologies and Informatics, 98*(12), 278–280.

Patera, M., Draper, S., & Naef, M. (2008). Exploring "Magic Cottage": A virtual reality environment for stimulating children's imaginative writing. *Interactive Learning Environments, 16*(3), 245–263. https://doi.org/10.1080/10494820802114093

Pilgrim, J. M., & Pilgrim, J. (2016). The use of virtual reality tools in the reading-language arts classroom. *Texas Journal of Literacy Education, 4*(2), 90–97. https://eric.ed.gov/contentdelivery/servlet/ERICServlet?accno=EJ1121641

Pope, H. (2018). Virtual and augmented reality in libraries. *Library Technology Reports, 54*(6), 1–25.

Ray, A. B., & Deb, S. (Contributors). (2016). Smartphone based virtual reality systems in classroom teaching — A study on the effects of learning outcome. *2016 IEEE Eighth International Conference on Technology for Education (T4E), Technology for Education (T4E), 2016 IEEE Eighth International Conference on, T4E*, 68–71. https://doi.org/10.1109/T4E.2016.022

Rice, M. (2019). Projections of identity: How technological devices become us and why it matters in ELA teacher education. *Ubiquity, 6*(1), 22–40.

Robertson, J. & Good, J. (2003). Using a collaborative virtual role-play environment to foster characterisation in stories. *Journal of Interactive Learning Research, 14*(1), 5–29. Association for the Advancement of Computing in Education (AACE). https://www.learntechlib.org/primary/p/17802/

Stupar-Rutenfrans, S., Ketelaars, L. E. H., & van Gisbergen, M. (2017). Beat the fear of public speaking: Mobile 360° video virtual reality exposure training in the home environment reduces public speaking anxiety. *Cyberpsychology, Behavior, and Social Networking, 20*(10). https://doi.org/10.1089/cyber.2017.0174

Theodorakopoulos, M. et al. (2017). Personalized augmented reality experiences in museums using Google cardboards. *2017 12th International Workshop on Semantic and Social Media Adaptation and Personalization (SMAP), Semantic and Social Media Adaptation and Personalization (SMAP), 2017 12th International Workshop On*, 95–100. https://doi.org/10.1109/SMAP.2017.8022676

Vaughn, M., & Parsons, S.A. (2013). Adaptive teachers as innovators: Instructional adaptations opening spaces for enhanced literacy learning. *Language Arts, 91*(2), 81–93.

Vygotsky, L.S. (1978). *Mind in society: The development of higher psychological processes*. Harvard University Press.

Webb, A. (2012). *Teaching literature in virtual worlds : Immersive learning in English studies*. Routledge.

Whitelock, D., Brna, P. & Holland, S. (1996). What is the value of virtual reality for conceptual learning? Towards a theoretical framework. *Proceedings of EuroAIED*, Lisbon.

Winn, W. (1993). *A conceptual basis for education applications of virtual reality*. Human Interface Technology Laboratory, University of Washington. Retrieved from http://www.hitl.washington.edu/research/learning_center/winn/winn-paper .html~

Xu, Y., Park, H., & Baek, Y. (2011). A new approach toward digital storytelling: An activity focused on writing self-efficacy in a virtual learning environment. *Journal of Educational Technology & Society, 14*(4), 181–191.

Zantua, O. L. S. (2017). Utilization of virtual reality content in grade 6 social studies using affordable virtual reality technology. *Asia Pacific Journal of Multidisciplinary Research, 5*(2.2), 1–10.

Chapter 2

VR Immersion in the ELA Classroom

Supporting the Professional Development of Novice Teachers

Christine Chang, Elisabeth Etopio,
Erin Kearney, and David Mawer

Using virtual reality (VR) in teacher education is a new practice that holds great potential in terms of the experiences it can afford teacher candidates and the teacher educators who work with them (Brown, 1999; Dieker et al., 2014). This chapter first describes a specific use of VR in the teacher education program in which the coauthors work and then presents data and analyses emerging from initial research into this program's use of VR. Based on these descriptions and analyses, we make the broader case that there are several fruitful purposes of VR in teacher education and other forms of professional development.

THE CHALLENGES OF OBSERVATION IN PRESERVICE TEACHER EDUCATION

Several challenges led our teacher education program to turn to VR as an option for complementing the valuable in-person observation experiences that novice teachers undergo. First, although numerous and varied clinical experiences already take place in our program, it is never possible to predict exactly what preservice teachers will see when they perform observations in area schools. While certain elements of instruction—supporting emergent multilinguals in an English language arts (ELA) class—are ones we hoped that preservice teachers would observe, these opportunities might not surface on days the novice teachers visit classrooms or be common in the classrooms they observe in the first place. A related concern was that even when such opportunities are available, novices may not notice them. The benefit of a teacher educator's cues to direct a novice's gaze would address this challenge, but teacher educators are rarely alongside teacher candidates during classroom observations. Furthermore, we often wonder about the vantage point from which teacher candidates observe. If one of the goals of field observations is to help novices notice salient features of the classroom environment and significant instructional moments as a more expert teacher does, viewing in a relatively detached fashion, usually from the back of the classroom, does not make for easy entry into the teacher's perspective. Also, importantly, we have grappled with the challenge of better connecting teacher candidates' observations in schools and the insights gained from these with the work they eventually do in classrooms as student teachers and eventually as teachers of record.

As a response to these potential challenges, the advent of VR has provided alternative "modes of access to relevant phenomena" (Goodwin, 1994, p. 628) and offers additional, supplementary means for preservice teachers to both experience and gain knowledge of "core" practices (Grossman, 2011) of teaching before entering into the field as student teachers. Purposefully designed VR environments furnish opportunities for preservice teachers to observe and reflect upon the professional practice of teachers before stepping foot into the classroom. In addition, as VR environments are removed from the vulnerable population of school-age children, preservice teachers are provided with a "soft failure" environment in which they may "try out different actions, reflect on the consequences of actions taken, and then press reset and try a different set of actions" (Brown, 1999, p. 316). Of course, as Brown (1999) suggests, VR environments are not meant to replace the traditional clinical experience of student teaching. Instead, VR is regarded as a tool that mirrors the realities of professional practice and provides formidable access to the "core practices cycle" (Lampert et al., 2013) as discussed below as a means of socializing preservice teachers into the professional community of teaching. For these reasons and others, we began to explore the opportunities that VR might offer to address some of the challenges we faced in providing a clinically rich, intentional observational experience for novice teachers and in facilitating the movement from observation to classroom practice.

To this end, we have engaged in design of VR immersive experiences and shifts to our teacher education pedagogy. Focusing first on the ways VR designs offer opportunities for observation and reflection on teaching practice, we have embarked on research that asks:

1. What do preservice teachers notice about teaching practice and how do they make sense of VR observations of instructional practice in immediate post-viewing discussion and exercises?

2. What perceptions to preservice teachers have of the VR segments and of the use of VR in teacher education?

These guiding questions direct our ongoing design and research efforts and have shaped our approach to analysis. Analysis involved (1) coding transcripts of group discussions and responses to reflection questions and application exercises completed by preservice teachers participating in VR sessions and (2) analyzing survey responses.

A FRAMEWORK FOR REIMAGINING OBSERVATION

When we embarked on making shifts in our teacher education program, VR represented a technological innovation for us as we reconsidered the observational experiences of our preservice teachers, but we were also engaged simultaneously in reimagining our teacher education pedagogy. This reshaping was anchored in a theory of professional vision (Goodwin, 1994) and an accompanying theory of core practices (Grossman, 2011). According to Goodwin, all professions have their own view of the world, quite different from that of the layperson; a perception that is constituted by discipline-internal processes, practices, and tools, and one that is necessarily learned through socialization (e.g., Lave & Wenger, 1991). Accordingly, Goodwin (1994) suggests that "all vision is perspectival and lodged within endogenous communities of practice" (p. 606). In our professional communities, writes Goodwin (1994), "discursive practices are used by members of a profession to shape events in the domains subject to their professional scrutiny" (p. 606). In the world of teaching, the classroom constitutes a significant domain of scrutiny, as are the learning experiences and spaces within teacher education programs, as these are primary venues through which novices are socialized into historically constructed instructional practices.

At present, certain instructional practices are being proposed as "core" (Grossman, 2011) within and across various disciplines of teaching (e.g., math, science, literacy, world languages). In turn, a "core practices cycle" (Lampert et al., 2013) of inquiry and enactment has grown increasingly pervasive within teacher education scholarship and practice (see figure 2.1). Within this cycle, novice teachers first come to perceive and name instructional practices and their subcomponents, as they also discuss and consider the unique situational realizations of any instructional practice. As teacher candidates and teacher educators engage in dialogue around particular representations of teaching practice (e.g., video recordings of teaching, lessons modeled by teacher educators, curricular or instructional documents), the process of observation and analysis involves movement back and forth between

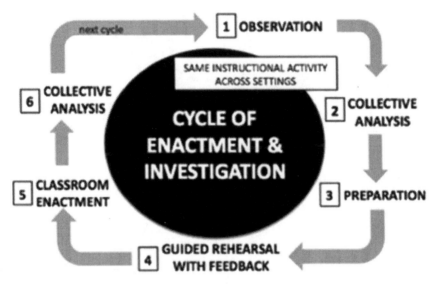

Figure 2.1   Core Practices Cycle in Teacher Education (Lampert et al., 2013, p. 223).

a perceptual level (i.e., What do you notice? What else might you attend to? Have you noticed X?) and discussion of a range of interpretations (How was instruction happening? What were the contributions from and impacts on students? How were teachers and students relating to each other? What learning unfolded, and how do we know?). Following these phases of dialogic inquiry, core practices cycle theory posits that teachers move into a phase of enactment. In this stage, they rehearse practices, based on the common understandings of complex instructional practice and common terminology they have developed collaboratively in the inquiry stage. Novice teachers internalize and animate these practices through coached rehearsals and ever more independent enactments (as in the clinical experiences afforded by student teaching).

What the core practices cycle and much scholarship identifying core practices does not heavily emphasize is that instructional practices and interactions in classrooms are always embedded in particular school and classroom cultures, situated in particular relationships of teacher and students, shaped by the contours of a day or a moment and the unique histories and subjectivities of the teacher and students in the classroom. Sidelining the situatedness of practice risks stripping complex social interactions of their humanity and may perpetuate hegemonic and prescriptive views of teaching and learning, ones based in whiteness and counter to social and educational justice (Daniels & Varghese, 2019; Philip et al., 2019). Although it can be useful to focus attention on practice (what teachers and learners are doing and how and when and what it might lead to in terms of learning), this process must always be conscious of the network of human relations and historical power relations in which any teaching-learning interaction is situated. A focus on relationships in teaching and learning interactions, embedded in robust foundations course-work of a broader teacher education program, represents a more critical dimension of the dialogue that can occur during the investigation and enact-ment phases of a core practices cycle; that is, a core practices approach need not put practice over people. To date, we simply have not often seen such a balance struck. However, some recent scholarship (Fredericks & Peercy, 2020; Peercy et al., 2019) seeks to reconcile a core practices approach with the humanizing, critical, and linguistically and culturally sustaining pedago-gies needed to teach language minoritized youth and to frame novice teacher learning.

The type of instructional practices we have focused on in our VR designs—those that relate to culturally and linguistically sustaining (Paris & Alim, 2017) and translingual (Celic & Seltzer, 2013) pedagogies—explicitly aim to better connect instructional practices with the relationships of teachers and students and to facilitate development of a critical stance toward core practices. We recognize, moreover, that certain instructional practices that figure in our VR designs—namely, the Sheltered Instructional Observational Protocol (SIOP) strategies—are typical of but not unproblematic in the classroom environment (Crawford & Reyes, 2015); observing SIOP practices offers opportunity for familiarizing novice teachers with this widely used instructional approach, while our collaborative deconstructions and analyses of practice allow us to critically examine and reimagine alternatives to these practices. SIOP specially targets English Language Learners (ELLs) and consists of eight components:

- Lesson Preparation
- Building Background
- Comprehensible Input
- Strategies
- Interaction
- Practice/Application
- Lesson Delivery
- Review & Assessment

(Center for Applied Linguistics, 2018)

VR, furthermore, may be especially well suited to facilitating the type of perspective-shifting that can lead to more critical and context-grounded con-sideration of practice and more direct engagement around new teachers' own positions, interpretive frames and perspectives as they observe and eventually enact professional practice.

KEY FEATURES OF IMMERSIVE VR ENVIRONMENTS AND AFFORDANCES FOR TEACHER LEARNING

According to Dede, Jacobson and Richards (2017), VR:

> interfaces provide sensory immersion, at present focusing on visual and audio stimuli with some haptic (touch) interfaces. The participant can turn and move as they do in the real world, and the digital setting responds to maintain the illusion of presence of one's body in a simulated setting. (p. 3)

VR, then, is defined as a computer simulation of real or imagined physical contexts, creating an immersive environment that allows users to disconnect from their actual surroundings and gain a sense of embodiment, which is to feel presence in a simulated environment. Three key features of VR are generally recognized to be immersion, presence, and interactivity. What immersion, presence, and interactivity qualities of VR create is a potential for embodied learning, or "how our bodies and our environments are related to cognitive processes" and in service of learning of various types (Skulmowski & Rey, 2018). While the nature of bodily interaction and the nature of tasks vary widely when we design VR environments for learning, the VR designs in our study promote and facilitate a particular type of embodied learning: embodied perspective-taking. Lindgren (2012) writes that the term *perspective*

> is frequently used to refer not only to what is visible, but the thinking and feeling that are behind these perceptions. People discuss perspectives primarily as originating from people, people who are making decisions about what to look at and judgements about what they see. To adopt another perspective involves, at least to a certain extent, the integration of these decisions and judgements into one's own understanding of a domain. (p. 1130)

Lindgren's (2012) study demonstrated the ability to immerse learners in expert perspectives through VR and in doing so to induce greater attentional focus and more successful task performance than a comparison group that did not experience first-person, expert perspective.

In the case of teacher learning, VR designs, then, can facilitate experiences from a first-person point of view or from many alternative points of view (students, co-teachers, aerial disembodied viewpoint), achieving the perceptual dimensions of perspective-taking in many possible ways. Perspective-taking theory would privilege adoption of the expert vantage point when the learning goal for preservice teachers is to access the perceptual and attentional but also decision-making perspectives that expert teachers enact. The particular stretches of immersion are inherently selective; viewers cannot be immersed in VR for long periods for safety reasons, but the need to be selective also prompts intentional design decision-making for those producing VR segments. There is the need and opportunity to choose how to represent teaching practice in VR environments, and the effect of these choices is that preservice teachers' attention and noticing is initially focused by virtue of the segment content and design itself. Perspective, then, is already being shaped by the design of the VR teacher learning tool.

While immersed in VR, preservice teachers may notice features of classroom interaction, student attributes and behaviors, and collaborations among teaching professionals in the room in ways that detached observation at the back of a classroom, for example, would not. Given that the observations are not of events unfolding in real time, there is opportunity for multiple viewings with multiple rounds of noticing and critical engagement. VR immersions can be designed such that the immersive experience includes cues (in the form of words, arrows, circles or other highlighting tools on the screen) to even further direct novice teachers' gaze and noticing. Yet, even when the designs simply immerse viewers, immediate post-viewing analytic and reflective discussion of the experience can build novice understandings of expert perspective and practice in ways that traditional observation simply cannot. The conversations that occur after being immersed in VR, when intentionally guided by teacher educators, are likely to be more focused on particular elements of practice and classroom interaction and more grounded in the fine details of practice as opposed to general impressions of preservice teachers. At the same time, the post-viewing dialogue is also a space to engage directly with the existence of many perspectives and experiences of classroom events and teaching and learning interactions. That is, immersion in VR and engagement in thoughtfully supported post-viewing dialogue can also promote reflection and make space for engagement with subjectivities in a way that is different from other 2D representations of teaching (e.g., video). VR makes it possible for preservice teachers and their teacher educators to focus on who the classroom teachers are in the VR segments, who the students are, how they relate to each other and, significantly, how to engage with questions about how their own subjectivities and histories frame and shape the way they teach. In this way, VR allows for the trying on of different perspectives while also critically engaging with our own, especially in significant moments of professional becoming, as is the case in teacher preparation programs.

Methodology

Research Design

Design-based research (DBR) is simultaneously a method and a theory of how educational change takes place. DBR provides opportunities to test innovative instructional approaches and particular tools through "continuous cycles of design, enactment, analysis, and redesign" (The Design-Based Research Collective, 2003, p. 5). In this methodological approach, iterative designs draw from and inform ongoing refinement of theory. Theoretical "conjectures" (Sandoval, 2004) about the nature of teaching and learning are tested and developed through cycles of designing, analyzing/ reflecting and redesigning, often in a participatory fashion, involving stakeholders from the educational setting in question. The research process, including generation of empirical evidence and continuous theory-building is embedded in a teaching and learning context. Bell (2004) identified several strengths of this approach:

> What is gained in design-based research by analytically interpreting and privileging the social worlds constructed by children and teachers? I can foresee three beneficial consequences of giving a significant degree of epistemic authority during research to the microcultures of the participants: (a) as a way of promoting the local appropriation of designs by microcultures (perhaps even through participatory design), (b) as an analytical way to compare the constituted activities of school with reference communities to better understand how they can be better articulated, and (c) as a means of understanding the limitations of a particular theoretical projection about human learning or activity. (p. 248)

In alignment with the benefits Bell (2004) identifies, the project we describe is part of an effort to transform teacher education practices and culture at a particular school of education. The design iterations tested at this site also help us to understand more about the context and teacher education practices enacted there, including the group of preservice teachers, the field experience requirement and observation more specifically. Study of this single learning ecology (Cobb et al., 2003) stands to inform practices in other teacher education settings and the theorizing of teacher education more broadly, especially with regard to development of professional vision, facilitating observation through a core practices approach, and engaging preservice teachers in discussions of practice that are both analytic and reflective.

Participants and Context

Design-based approaches to educational research strongly emphasize the importance of deeply knowing and describing the local context in which the design is being implemented and tested. In our case, a set of various stakeholder groups converged to form a microculture around preservice teacher education and VR-based observation activities. Participants included fifty-five preservice teachers across primary and secondary level preparations, representing a range of disciplinary areas (i.e., ELA, social studies, science, math, ELL, music), teacher educator-researchers, and an ELA teacher working in a local high school who assisted with creation of VR modules and whose classroom and teaching are represented in the segments. These stakeholders shared some overlapping goals, practices, and values. All of them are engaged and invested in (re-)shaping instructional practice and relationships in classrooms, yet they occupy different positions in relation to this practice and the way it figured in the VR observational experiences. Preservice teachers were just starting to develop understandings of and experience with instructional practice (they were largely observers of practice), the experienced ELA teacher in the segments had grown her approach over time (she, her practice, her classroom and students were the observed) and the teacher educator-researchers took up a mediating role between representations of practice, including VR, and preservice teachers' sense-making around these (they were the primary designers and facilitators of the observational activities).

THE VR SEGMENTS AND ACCOMPANYING TOOLS

The equipment used in our study were Oculus Go headsets loaded with VR segments filmed with a 360-degree camera (see figure 2.2). Oculus Go is an all-in-one VR viewing experience that comes with a portable headset and a controller that recognizes hand motion while viewing. The rechargeable headset does not need a computer or wired connection and is secured through adjustable straps. Oculus Go was chosen because it is primarily designed to bring viewing experiences to life and enhance immersion, presence, and interactivity. As our study aimed to create conditions for embodied perspective-taking, this equipment was a natural choice.

The segments we have started to use in our teacher education program (see figures 2.3 and 2.4) are drawn from three days of filming in a tenth-grade ELA classroom, in which all 25 students speak a language other than English as their home language. Reflecting the diversity that is increasingly common in K–12 schools of all types in the United States, some of the students in the focal classroom were born in the United States and had attended U.S. schools for their full academic careers, whereas others had arrived as refugees the previous school year, having never attended school at all before. In addition to diversity of languages, cultural and other

Figure 2.2 VR Headsets.

Figure 2.3 Library of VR Segments from the ELA Classroom Stored on Desktop Computer.

background experiences, and experiences with school, students in the focal classroom also had a broad range of needs and strengths, both personally

Figure 2.4   Screenshot from One of the VR Segments Filmed in a Tenth-Grade ELA Classroom.

and academically. This diverse classroom stood to provide a rich environment for novice teachers' observation through VR. The skill and experience of the ELA teacher year veteran in the building, also made this classroom an attractive choice for filming 360-degree footage destined for the VR segments. The teacher, Vaughn (pseudonym), was not only an experienced and successful ELA teacher; she was also well known for her expert integration of arts into ELA curriculum and instruction, and she had a long history of connecting with her students in meaningful ways. She lived just a few blocks from the school, organized many field trips and events that connect school life with the community and the arts especially, and she supported the school's theater and arts-oriented groups and activities. After observing Vaughn's class for a few weeks and in consultation with her, we decided to film a three-day instructional segment from a longer curricular unit on "art as resistance." The unit was connected to the grade-level Common Core State Standards (CCSS) for text-based, persuasive writing. The three-day series of lessons revolved around a poem entitled "Home" written by Warsan Shire, a British-Somali poet. Students heard, read, and annotated the poem, analyzed it for metaphor and then drafted text-based claims that could be folded into a longer essay. One researcher and two videographers from a local digital media company attended the three days in order to film. Footage was, in nearly all cases, captured from the front of the room to best approximate the teacher's authentic point of view, although alternative angles were captured when physical arrangements in the classroom space shifted. Classroom artifacts (student work, lesson plans, etc.) and still photos of the classroom setting were also captured. All of these raw materials formed the basis of the eventual segments produced for use in the teacher education program and the accompanying tools and materials that teacher educators would use with preservice teachers.

The instructional materials produced to date and used with teacher candidates include an exploration of the empty classroom as well as several segments of instruction. The empty classroom is used to highlight the notion of creating a multilingual ecology, giving novices' opportunity to notice and draw their attention to inclusion of students' home languages in the classroom displays, the classroom library, and student-created posters. The instructional segments range in length from approximately 3 to 11 minutes and provide opportunity for teacher candidates to observe and experience ELA-focused practices (such as teaching the concept of metaphor and the practice of text annotation) as well as other strategies (such as SIOP and translanguaging strategies for supporting multilingual learners and culturally sustaining pedagogies). A brief sample of these VR segments can be viewed at the following link: https://youtu.be/XPgBhNIjD6E. VR immersion is paired with readings on multilingual ecology and post-viewing teacher educator-facilitated discussions that focus teacher candidates' attention on the affordances of a classroom environment that functions as a multilingual ecology, both in terms of creating a sense of belonging in the classroom and in terms of supporting ELA learning. In most cases, teacher candidates view the segments multiple times and are prompted to respond either in group discussion led by a teacher educator or in writing to various prompts about elements of the practice. After engaging with the segments in this way, moving through a process of describing and analyzing, the participants are then often asked to answer reflection questions and to apply what they have learned through activity or lesson planning exercises. The segments were piloted during a summer institute that is part of our institution's teacher residency program and then continued to be used more extensively with a cohort of preservice teachers enrolled in a field experience class in the fall semester preceding their student teaching placements. These teacher candidates were not preparing only to become ELA teachers; in fact, our participants are preparing to become primary and secondary teachers in a wide range of subject areas in addition to ELA. Nonetheless, we have found that the use of the segments from an ELA classroom is very valuable to all teacher candidates.

DATA COLLECTION AND ANALYSIS

Preservice teachers were immersed in the VR segments across three possible visits to the university lab space where the VR equipment is housed and professional learning events for teacher education programs are held. In our first cycle of design and analysis, we offered three visits to the lab. The first was attended by all preservice teachers, and then they were given the option to return to do more VR immersion; these visits could be applied to observation hours they needed to complete to meet a state-mandated amount of observations of instruction of multilingual learners. The visits, their main focus and the types and amounts of data collected at each are provided in table 2.1.

To summarize, our data sources include recordings of the preservice teachers' pre-viewing, viewing, and post-viewing engagements with the VR tools, written responses to reflection questions and application exercises, and a brief survey sent to preservice teachers following their visits to the lab. We analyzed these data with the purpose of illuminating how immersive segments that feature teaching in a diverse tenth-grade ELA classroom can be used in an initial teacher preparation program to "observe" instructional practice. Specifically, three researchers independently coded interactional and written data, generating descriptive codes (Saldaña, 2009) related to our theoretical framework and research questions and then the group reconciled codes to solidify a common coding scheme. Codes fell into three main categories: (1) preservice teachers' sense-making about practice; (2) perspectives and stances taken up in relation to practice, and (3) design-related comments (i.e., remarks about using VR or about the lab visits in general). Codes falling into these categories are represented in table 2.2.

Our codes ultimately yielded themes around what preservice teachers noticed about instructional practice and how they took up a range of perspectives in relation to the events they observed and experienced in VR.

Findings

We present findings of these analyses by first providing data and analysis that pertain to the way the entire group of preservice teachers we studied engaged with VR as a means of observing instructional practice in the tenth-grade ELA classroom featured in the footage and their perceptions of using VR as a tool and medium for observation. With this broad picture in place, we share findings about the two preservice ELA teachers in our group, Megan and Anne, who attended more than just the first required VR session. This closer look at just two preservice ELA teachers' experiences with VR observation provides deeper insight into the value of the experience for shaping instructional practice in ELA classrooms and the potential for VR in educating future ELA teachers.

Making Sense of Culturally and Linguistically Sustaining Teaching Practices

The ways that VR "observation" shaped preservice teachers' understandings of instructional practice were first visible to us in analyzing transcripts from

Table 2.1 Overview of Data Collection Sessions

Visit	Data Collected	Session description
1	# of preserve teachers: 55 (split into four groups, required for their field experience course) Session duration: 20 minutes Type of data: Audio recordings of whole group discussions (one per group)	1. Each group arrived to lab 2. Engaged in a brief word association task—individual responses to the term *culturally sustaining pedagogy* followed by whole-group discussion 3. Immersion in 9-minute VR segment depicting a community circle arrangement as teachers and students share why they left home 4. Individual responses to a handout with guiding questions related to the footage, recording general reactions to the "observation" and some initial reflections and analysis followed by whole group discussion focused on what in the segment might relate to culturally responsive-sustaining pedagogy 5. Preserve teachers provided with state's framework and set of strategies for enacting culturally responsive-sustaining pedagogy
2	# of preserve teachers: 22 (working individually and in pairs, optional attendance but could count toward state-required observation hours) Session duration: 2 hours Type of data: Written responses to online prompts	1. Preserve teachers arrived at lab and sat at individual computer workstations that also had a VR headset at it 2. Worked individually or in pairs (if they were preparing for certification in the same discipline—math, ELA, etc.) 3. Viewed two segments multiple times, responding to a set of questions on Google Forms in between viewings. The first segment features the classroom teacher reviewing key academic vocabulary and the second depicts Vaughn and her co-teacher preparing students to analyze metaphor in the poem by explaining the task and modeling how to approach and complete it. A short handout outlining SIOP strategies was also provided and the google form questions drew preserve teachers' attention to SIOP strategies as they considered the VR footage. 4. Completed an application exercise, documenting the ways in which SIOP strategies explored in the observation task could be applied to the discipline-specific sample curricular documents they were provided. The ELA pair received a unit overview and one text from a Grade 10 curricular module entitled "Making Evidence-Based Claims" and that took up Nobel Prize speeches of Martin Luther King, Jr. and Barack Obama as focal texts. Preserve teachers only received the Obama speech for the exercise.
3	# of preserve teachers: 10 (working individually and in pairs, optional	1. Similar to procedures from visit 2, preserve teachers arrived at lab and sat at individual computer workstations that also had a VR headset at it. 2. Worked individually or in pairs (if they were preparing for certification in the same discipline—math, ELA, etc.).

(Continued)

Table 2.1 *(Continued)*

Visit	Data Collected	Session description
	attendance but could count toward state-required observation hours)	3. Viewed two short segments, the first of which featured Vaughn reviewing the concept of protest and the second the concept of metaphor. In this session, excerpts from the *Translanguaging Guide* (Celic & Seltzer, 2011) were given to students as well as curricular documents related to study of *The Great Gatsby*.
	Session duration: 2 hours Type of data: Written responses to online prompts	4. Completed questions eliciting reflection on the role of students' home languages in the classroom, what they had seen in field observations in schools, what practices they observed in the VR clips, understandings of translanguaging concepts and strategies they were developing from the guide excerpts and what translanguaging practices they would employ in re-imagining instruction viewed in the clips as well as in a *Gatsby* unit.

Table 2.2 **Analytic Codes**

Category	Codes
sense-making about practice	naming practice specifying practice through identification of constituent parts connecting practice to pedagogical purpose connecting practice to specific pedagogical actions connecting practice to impact on students reimagining practice/offering alternatives
perspectives	teacher student self as observer self as future teacher
design-related comments	Equipment experience hopes for future designs

visits that four groups of teachers initially made to the lab in connection with their field experience course. All preservice teachers in our cohort attended Visit 1. At this session, they were briefly introduced to the term *culturally sustaining pedagogy* (CSP), which in our program draws heavily on Paris and Alim's (2017) definition:

CSP seeks to perpetuate and foster—to sustain—linguistic, literate, and cultural pluralism as part of schooling for positive social transformation. CSP positions dynamic cultural dexterity as a necessary good, and sees the outcome of learning as additive rather than subtractive, as remaining whole rather than framed as broken, as critically enriching strengths rather than replacing deficits. Culturally sustaining pedagogy exists wherever education sustains the lifeways of communities who have been and continue to be damaged and erased through schooling. (p. 1)

After reviewing this term, preservice teachers were then immersed in VR, asked to complete individual written reflection through a set of guiding questions on a handout (see appendix) and then participated in whole-group discussion during which further noticing and sense-making took place in dialogic and collaborative form. Some answers to our first research question about what preservice teachers noticed about practice and how they made sense of what they viewed and experienced in VR emerged from analysis of these group sessions. Although we focus on the novice teachers' developing understandings of practice and how this was shaped through VR immersion and ensuing sense-making activities, the intentional design of the segments and the interactive sessions as well as the in-the-moment scaffolding and guidance from a teacher educator-researcher were also important elements in what preservice teachers ultimately attended to and noticed and how they made sense of these observations.

Naming Practice

While the teacher educator-researcher supplied a broad name (i.e., culturally sustaining pedagogies) for framing observation of instructional that would be the focus of the immersion and subsequent discussion, through their VR observation and ensuing individual note-taking and group conversations, the preservice teachers articulated many ways that CSP can be manifested in instructional practice, and they named several micro-practices (Grossman & McDonald, 2008), which are the possible constituent practices that make up the larger practice.

Across the four groups who attended Visit 1 sessions, the novice teachers named micro-practices that make up the broader practice of CSP represented in table 2.3.

As they named and defined practices related to CSP, the novice teachers specified micro-practices along the lines of language- and discourse-related dimensions as well as more relational dimensions.

Connecting Named Practice

As group discussion continued, the preservice teachers went beyond these general characterizations to connect practice to specific teaching goals, concrete pedagogical actions (i.e., teacher moves) and particular impacts on students that they observed in the VR segment. In this way, the novice teachers went from elaborating a vocabulary for describing CSP-related practices—what

Table 2.3   Micro-practices Preservice Teachers Specified

Language- and discourse-focused micro-practices	Translating
	repeating
	being deliberate in classroom discourse—direct, evenly paced delivery
	providing sentence frames and sample responses
	phrasing questions in inclusive ways
	making space for home languages
	encouraging students to confer in language groups
	support from bilingual assistant/translator
Relationship-focused micro-practices	asking about background
	making connection to students' personal experiences
	recognizing students' histories and linking to their present and future
	making space for students' stories
	invitation to share
	not forcing students to respond if they choose not to or to share specific details—room to not disclose
	making no assumption about what student backgrounds/experiences might be/where they are from
	letting students say who they are, not assuming or assigning identities
	teachers' self-disclosure and sharing
	connecting personal experiences to curriculum
	relationship and trust building
	exercising patience
	tough love relationship
	humor as opposed to authority
	showing care

Grossman (2011) refers to as a "grammar of practice" (p. 2839)—to orienting to the context-bound and situational enactment of the practice viewed in the VR immersion. That is, they used the vocabulary they were building to describe and analyze the focal practice to draw attention to and discuss the unique details of a particular moment, particular content and learning goals, and particular student-teacher relationships in the classroom. Excerpts from one of the group discussions in figure 2.5 illustrate what was typical across all groups.

In this excerpt, when the teacher educator-researcher (TE) asks novice teachers to identify CSP-related practices from the segment they viewed, focusing in on what the teacher and student were doing in the footage, they (S) reference particular teacher actions such as "translation and L1" (line 6) and connect this to specific pedagogical purposes such as "help[ing] the students understand the question" (lines 6–7). Across teacher educator and novice teacher contributions, many specific teacher actions are enumerated (asking for specific information, not forcing students to respond, inviting students to share, making no assumptions about students' backgrounds, teachers

1	TE:	Okay so you were immersed in six minutes of classroom experience. I
2		wonder if you could identify in what ways for you this might represent culturally and
3		linguistically responsive or sustaining teaching? What is the teacher doing or what do you
4		see in how the students are interacting that connects to this? What are the specific
5		practices?
6	S:	I saw some use of translation and L1 to help the students understand
7		the question.
8	TE:	There's space for the home languages, right? So there's translation. There's the students
9		conferring in language groups. You have the support of the Spanish bilingual assistant
10		who's a teacher in the room and a Swahili translator for some of the the students who
11		speak Swahili.
12	S:	They were asking specific information regarding the students' background and and also
13		they're not forcing students to respond if they chose not to.
14	TE:	Fantastic. So this is a connection to students' personal experience. There's an invitation to
15		share about background. There's no assumption about what those backgrounds might be
16		and there's no forcing students to share specific details. There's room to not disclose.
17		There's also the teachers disclosing to some extent as well, right? In the outro, I don't
18		know if you caught it, but it's also connected to the curriculum, so they're going to
19		analyze a poem in their very next set of activities and for several weeks actually, called
20		Home, and you heard her say, it's about, it's written by an author explaining to people
21		who don't understand why people would leave their home. And it's actually a very
22		powerful kind of poem. It fits in the curricular unit that they're doing…When do you
23		think this happened in the school year? This event.
24	S:	Maybe the beginning. It seems like an introductory thing.
25	TE:	It seems like it could be right because they're learning about each other. Any other ideas
26		on this? It happened in March. Okay? So the reason that I pose the question wasn't meant
27		to trick you. The question, I pose it that way because I'm giving you a six-minute slice of
28		the classroom experience, but there was all sorts of relationship building and trust
29		building that happened before this, so when we ask our students to share personal sorts of
30		things like this, we have to be very cognizant of the fact that we're asking them to do
31		something that is really really vulnerable.
32	S:	right

Figure 2.5   Connecting Practice to Pedagogical Purpose and Specific Teacher Actions.

disclosing their own experience) and several pedagogical purposes (helping students understand, making space for home languages to encourage a sense of belonging, making space for students' experience to encourage classroom community and trust, connecting student experiences to curricular content and learning goals). Clearly, the teacher educator talked more than the novice teachers in this excerpt and elaborates on both teacher actions and potential pedagogical purposes at greater length as they discuss what is represented in the VR footage. This highlights the important scaffolding role of the teacher educator in such analytic post-viewing discussions, as the questions posed and details offered will be central in how novice teachers develop their understanding of the focal practice.

Reimagining Practice

Preservice teachers' ways of defining CSP in instructional practice were not only expressed through descriptions of what was seen in the VR segment but also at times through referencing of what was not seen or by drawing

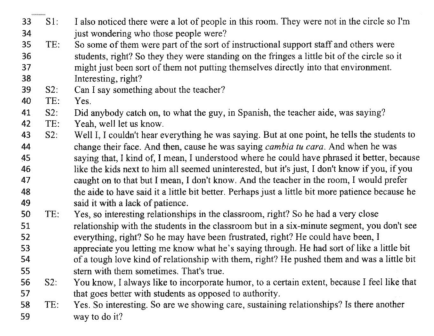

33	S1:	I also noticed there were a lot of people in this room. They were not in the circle so I'm
34		just wondering who those people were?
35	TE:	So some of them were part of the sort of instructional support staff and others were
36		students, right? So they they were standing on the fringes a little bit of the circle so it
37		might just been sort of them not putting themselves directly into that environment.
38		Interesting, right?
39	S2:	Can I say something about the teacher?
40	TE:	Yes.
41	S2:	Did anybody catch on, to what the guy, in Spanish, the teacher aide, was saying?
42	TE:	Yeah, well let us know.
43	S2:	Well I, I couldn't hear everything he was saying. But at one point, he tells the students to
44		change their face. And then, cause he was saying *cambia tu cara*. And when he was
45		saying that, I kind of, I mean, I understood where he could have phrased it better, because
46		like the kids next to him all seemed uninterested, but it's just, I don't know if you, if you
47		caught on to that but I mean, I don't know. And the teacher in the room, I would prefer
48		the aide to have said it a little bit better. Perhaps just a little bit more patience because he
49		said it with a lack of patience.
50	TE:	Yes, so interesting relationships in the classroom, right? So he had a very close
51		relationship with the students in the classroom but in a six-minute segment, you don't see
52		everything, right? So he may have been frustrated, right? He could have been, I
53		appreciate you letting me know what he's saying through. He had sort of like a little bit
54		of a tough love kind of relationship with them, right? He pushed them and was a little bit
55		stern with them sometimes. That's true.
56	S2:	You know, I always like to incorporate humor, to a certain extent, because I feel like that
57		that goes better with students as opposed to authority.
58	TE:	Yes. So interesting. So are we showing care, sustaining relationships? Is there another
59		way to do it?

Figure 2.6   Reimagining Practice and Suggesting Alternative Teacher Actions.

attention to pieces of the footage that were perceived as non-examples of CSP. In these cases, the novice teachers would also offer reimaginings of the classroom moment or general approach or articulate specific alternatives to what they had viewed. For example, in figure 2.6, which is the immediate continuation of the conversation represented in figure 2.5, we see how the ongoing descriptive, analytic, and reflective dialogue takes a new direction in which the novice teachers play a more active role in the conversation and in constructing their understandings of the focal practice.

In this excerpt, a novice teacher offers a new observation (line 33), with no prompting from the teacher educator, attempting to discern whom the various classroom participants were that she had viewed during the VR immersion. After the teacher educator clarifies that the community circle they viewed included students as well as a handful of co-teachers and instructional support staff, another novice teacher requests permission to make further commentary (line 39) and draws the group's attention to the Spanish-speaking bilingual aide in particular. Over the course of the following stretch of interaction (lines 41–59), he and the teacher educator engage in sense-making around what was observed (the aide telling the students to "change their face"), what it meant in terms of the teacher-student relationship (a "close relationship," frustration, "a tough love kind of relationship") and how it could have unfolded differently (the aide "could have phrased it better," with "a little bit more patience," or with "humor . . . as opposed to authority"). Notably, the teacher educator makes moves in lines 50–55) to situate this moment of the VR observation in a broader frame, as she had observed the class for several months; at the same time, this seeming mitigation of the aide's behavior in the shorter clip was nonetheless confronted by the novice teacher in lines 56–57, maintaining the stance of preferring an alternative course of action from the aid-based.

On several occasions across the group discussions, novice teachers offered reimaginings of the classroom events they observed in VR, stretching their understanding of the focal practice beyond what was in the clips to what could have been in that classroom or what could be in their own future teaching. At the end of this excerpt, the teacher educator summarizes by asking the question: "Is there another way to do it?" (lines 57–58), referring to what the preservice teachers had viewed and, in a sense, encouraging them to imagine alternative pedagogical actions and approaches as they process and interpret what they observe. This was a recurring theme in the conversations, to use the observed events to begin moving from description of the focal practice and definition by non-example to transforming these non-examples into other imagined courses of action. This way of expanding and deepening understandings of CSP in instructional practice was even further developed in subsequent visits to the lab and the application exercises these visits entailed.

Taking Different Perspectives

Over the course of their discussions, analysis also showed that novice teachers and the teacher educator facilitating the conversation took up multiple perspectives as they discussed the VR segment. They sometimes focused their attention and comments on teacher behavior and decision-making, sometimes on students' behaviors and contributions to the classroom interaction they had viewed, and at other times, they adopted the perspective of detached observer or of fellow future teacher. For example, in figure 2.7, drawn from a different group of novice teachers' conversation about the VR segment, a range of perspective-taking phenomena are illustrative of what we found in the broader data set.

In this excerpt, the teacher educator similarly poses a question to elicit the preservice teachers' observations about what they viewed in the instructional practice that might relate to CSP. In the novice teachers' initial responses (lines 96–107), there was a shift in pronouns that marked concomitant shifts in perspective. That is, the novice teachers spoke at times through the voice of the teacher they had observed and at other times through the voice of students

94	TE:	What did you think? What did you think in terms of what the teacher was doing in this
95		domain about culturally and linguistically response or sustaining practices?
96	S:	I like the way that she phrased the questions like instead of why did they leave home it
97		was more like why did you come to CITY and not like just saying like oh you're not like,
98		I don't know, it just seemed more like I don't know
99	S2:	It was more open
100	S3:	It wasn't targeted
101	S:	You're not from here. Yeah it was also it included them as well.
102	S4:	They shared their experiences.
103	TE:	So there was room to share their experience. The way the question was posed matters
104		right, so I left home because. What else
105	S2:	How they started, it wasn't just like oh war it was I was abused or it was opportunity, like
106		and I think two the girls were like, well they don't have the education opportunities where
107		I'm from. They don't let us have that. So I left because of that.
108	TE:	Yeah. You learn a lot about these kids in this circle, right? And some of it is
109		heartbreaking kind of stuff. But you learn a lot about the the students in the class. What
110		else?
111	S:	She offered sentence structures to them you know, she gave them sample answers I left
112		because, what was it, I was in danger or something
113	TE:	Yeah.
114	S5:	Also the gentleman who was translating obviously for the Spanish-speaking students. I
115		could understand a bit, so he was he was he kept on saying like okay well how do you say
116		or say it in you know say it in English too, you know, and the kids were asking him, of
117		how do I say this in English and *como se dice* and I'm like yeah yeah okay I got a little bit
118		but it was it was good that he was not only reinforcing their language obviously but also
119		he said okay share it so the whole of the class can understand you, you know, and some
120		of them were more quiet. They didn't want to share and then others are a little bit more
121		comfortable. So it was nice to see.
122	TE:	So translation support. Some of the students were conferring with each other before there
123		was some space made to confer as a group. You talk about it and then you can share out.
124		And there was also the option not to share, right? I think you're right. The sentence
125		structures for their
126	S3:	There were a lot of adults in the room. I think I counted seven adults.

Figure 2.7   Perspective-Taking in Responses to VR Segments.

in the classroom. Across the excerpt, it was apparent that the preservice teachers attend not only to the ELA teacher they observed and the students in the classroom but also the Spanish-speaking bilingual aide and other adults in the classroom. As in figures 2.5 and 2.6, as well as our other interactional data, we see the preservice teachers describing and interpreting elements of the focal practice, but we see them doing so by taking into account multiple vantage points on the interaction and by stepping into some of these perspectives on occasion by speaking through the voices of the classroom actors represented in the VR segment.

From the analysis of discussions our groups of novice teachers engaged in following their initial immersion in a VR segment, what they notice about CSP-related practices becomes quite clear. They identify many elements of relationship-building among teachers and students, accord significance to designing a language-resourced environment, and on occasion, reference specific ways CSP supports ELA curriculum, in this case analysis of a poem. Indeed, they show evidence of developing robust understandings of CSP-related practice following the VR observation. Moreover, we gain insight into the process through which novice teachers develop understandings of complex and situated instructional practice. They do so by naming, describing, reimagining and by exploring a range of perspectives. VR appears to encourage attention to a range of points of view and to facilitate embodied perspective-taking that is key to development of professional vision.

Novice Teachers' Perceptions

Based on analysis of survey responses and the design-related comments preservice teachers made during sessions at the lab, several insights with regard to novice teachers' perceptions of VR as a tool for observation and learning about instructional practice emerged. These perceptions ranged widely, both in terms of preservice teachers' experiences in the lab and the use of VR in teacher education more broadly. All of these perceptions were and continue to be instructive in our ongoing design process.

When asked about the overall VR experience, we found that few preservice teachers had previous experience with VR; those that did had used it primarily for gaming or other entertainment purposes. None had experienced VR in a professional learning context before. They demonstrated a wide range of responses to and comfort levels with the VR experience in the lab. A question eliciting comparison with in-person observation, which all the novice teachers had engaged in as well, similarly showed mixed responses.

On the whole, preservice teachers' perceptions were mostly positive toward using VR as a medium for teacher education, and they used a range of adjectives and verbs to describe this experience. As shown in a word

Figure 2.8 Word Cloud with Responses.

cloud generated from responses to a question asking them to describe the VR experience in a few words or phrases (figure 2.8), novice teachers most often characterized VR immersion as new, interesting, engaging, and informative. Words that appear larger in the word cloud were used more frequently in the novice teachers' responses.

One teacher indicated that "I was thoroughly impressed by the VR process and videos seen. It was easy to follow and gave us a new perspective on ESL classes we may have not yet seen." Another said, "At times it was disorienting, however, I think that it was interesting to be able to view the classroom from multiple perspectives within one video." Similarly, other preservice teachers identified positives while also expressing some of the surprises or challenges of observing through VR. Another described the experience as "fascinating, interesting and confounding, confusing sometimes, literally a roller-coaster feeling kind of experience." Despite largely positive responses, one novice teacher described the VR experience as "less than ideal." Among the few novice teachers who noted negative elements of the experience, some felt that 2D videos would be preferable and that these would more directly focus the viewers' gaze on a focus of observation. In essence, they expressed preference for a fixed perspective and clear focus of observation, defined by a 2D framing. Taken together, novice teachers' responses show that they saw value in the affordances of VR, namely its qualities of being immersive and engaging, offering multiple points of view and flexible perspective-taking, rendering a sense of being there and the possibility for less obtrusive observation that doesn't affect teacher or students in the classroom, offering the ability to view the same segment multiple times, and facilitating observation in ways that transcend boundaries of time and place, opening the possibility to observe at home or at school and to observe many more teachers' classrooms.

In the survey, teacher candidates expressed a wide range of responses to particular qualities of the VR experience. When asked how real it was to be immersed in the VR segments they viewed, twelve out of fourteen novice teachers rated the experience 2 or 3 on a 4-point Likert scale (with the remaining two rating the experience a 4 or "very real"). Responding to the question of how fluid the VR immersion experience was—in other words, how comfortable, smooth, and sustained in terms of an immersive sensation—the novice teachers' responses similarly spanned a wide range from "a little" to "a lot"; none responded that the immersion was not fluid, except for one out of fourteen novice teachers who, on the question of the sense of sustained immersion, reported that the immersion was "not at all" sustained. When asked how interactive it was to be immersed in the VR segments, three reported the immersion was "not at all interactive," seven rated the interactivity at a 2 on the 4-point scale and the remaining four rated it a 3. None rated the interactive dimension of the immersion at a 4 or "very interactive." Finally, responding to the question of how immersive the segments were, with 1 on the scale representing "felt detached, like I was not really there" and 4 representing "felt like I was there physically and mentally," the novice teachers again displayed a wide range of perceptions. Two rated the immersion at 1, seven rated it at 2, three rated it at 3, and two rated it at 4. Perceptions of how real, fluid, and immersive the VR experience were overall quite varied; when paired with other survey responses, we might understand some of this variation in light of what some participants said they were missing: the ability to interact, however minimally, with teacher and students during in-person classroom observations. These responses raised important design questions about how a stronger sense of "being there" can be cultivated through VR and how the overall immersion experience can be orchestrated to enhance fluidity, reality, and sustained immersion. Especially in terms of interaction, we can certainly imagine novice teachers taking a more active and embodied role while experiencing VR segments, taking a tour of the classroom, for example, and moving to adopt different physical positions in the classroom while observing.

When comparing their VR experience to in-person observation, preservice teachers offered mixed responses. Achieving some level of immersion and engagement did not equate for them to the human interactions and connections that are possible during in-person, real-time observation visits to classrooms. Although VR provides novices with a means to observe core instructional practices without interrupting the actual learning environment and to access forms of instruction they are not guaranteed to observe when making visits to real classrooms, they indicated VR could not provide the opportunities to interact with teachers and to build professional relationships, nor could they take notes as in their face-to-face observation of classrooms. Furthermore, over half of the teacher candidates reported that the perspective they adopted while observing was that of "an outside observer" (see figure 2.9). This is likely due to the design itself and its lack of any significant interactive features (instead functioning as a more passive type of observational

While immersed in the 10th grade ELA classroom, what perspectives did you adopt? (14 responses)

Outside observer perspective (57.1%)
Co-teacher perspective (21.4%)
Student perspective (7.1%)
Camera perspective (7.1%
"Floating ghost" (not part of the classroom) perspective (7.1%)
Teacher perspective (0%)

Figure 2.9   Pie Chart of Perspectives.

event). At the same time, we are keen to experiment with filming from different vantage points in the classroom to see if this also influences the perspective viewers take up and the professional perspectives (i.e., professional vision) they ultimately develop through these experiences.

Even though the perspective-taking facilitated by the design of the segment used during Visit 1 was limited and not as embodied an experience as VR can make possible, when asked what they attended visually as they were immersed, the novice teachers listed the teachers and the classroom environment itself but most frequently noted the students. One teacher wrote: "I found myself watching the students more than the teacher. In a typical video, the students are either not really visible or it is the back of their heads, so I took the opportunity to watch for student reactions." What this suggests is that the VR segment may have promoted focus on students especially, more than on the teacher, which is more often the case when observing in-person as observers are very often positioned at the back of a classroom. Especially when a teacher educator hopes to draw novice teachers' attention to student learning and experience, VR may prove a well-suited tool.

Design Changes to Preservice Teachers' Engagement

The survey responses and comments recorded during Visit 1 indicated several design adjustments to make as we planned for a second visit to the lab and as we considered what a revised design might look like in running this particular session again in the future. As Visit 1 was short and intended to introduce preservice teachers to VR observation, a clearly needed modification for Visit 2 was to deepen and enhance the framing of the observational activity for novices so that they clearly understood the purpose of observing practice in this new way. As a result, we staggered arrivals and took time with novice teachers as they arrived at the lab to explain that this was one form of observation intended to complement in-person observational experiences. We also opted for overall longer and self-paced interactions with the VR, through written responses as opposed to group discussion. This format allowed the novice teachers to engage in repeated viewings according to their own needs and ensured that they all responded in descriptive, analytic, and reflective fashion whereas in group discussion not all novice teachers shared their thoughts and interpretations. Repeated viewings were written into the online questions and prompts to encourage depth of engagement and sense-making (if not sustained immersion), and we were able to draft these in a way that emphasized particular language-related elements of instructional practice—SIOP and translanguaging strategies specifically. We could through the content and sequencing of questions also direct preservice teachers' attention in specific ways. From

Visit 1 to Visits 2 and 3, we made the significant change to add more reflec-tive questions and to include application exercises, so that participants could deepen their experiences around VR viewing and the focal practices.

Beyond these round-to-round design adjustments, from the survey and participant comments we gained broader insights relevant to our next phase of collecting footage from new classrooms and designing for more extensive integration of VR into our teacher education program. Some of our partici-pants expressed desire to do more in VR than simply watch video and wished to have more interactive elements to participate in the VR experience. One preservice teacher said, for example, "I think it would be more interesting if I could walk around the room and stand next to someone in the experience and pretend as if I am part of the group. Then at one point have the whole group go silent for a minute to pretend that I am responding to the question as well." This type of design represents a VR-based interaction more on the rehearsal and enactment end of the core practice cycle, and is indeed, the direction some of our future designs are planned to take. We cautiously pursue these options as VR is currently still much more effective in providing immersive experi-ences than it is in facilitating interactive simulations that rely extensively on bodily interaction. Remaining in the realm of VR observation, though, greater mobility for the preservice teachers while observing is also possible, and we have additionally entertained the possibility of enhancing in-screen cues and overlays to more immediately direct novices' gaze and attention, rather than wait until they have removed the VR headset. One of our participants provides an example of the form this might take, suggesting that we could mark who is talking and their role in the classroom to better clarify classroom actors while novice teachers observe. Finally, an overarching design insight we gained from our experiences in cycle 1 and through surveys of participating novice teachers was that further work is needed in training teacher educators in how to use VR segments and in developing the prompting questions and scaffolding comments they make when discussing these segments with novices. We plan to involve classroom teachers even further as we film and shape guiding dis-cussion and reflection questions, as well as application exercises. In this way, we intend to expand and deepen the participatory nature of our design process.

TWO ELA TEACHERS' EXPERIENCES WITH VR OBSERVATION SESSIONS

Visit 2—Preservice ELA Teachers Observing Classroom Practice

In terms of observational practice, the guiding questions in the Google Form the ELA teachers were completing oriented their gaze, attention, and responses in particular and intentional ways, so they necessarily focus on identifying academic vocabulary and SIOP strategies as well as what teachers and students are doing in the clips. As a result, much of what the two preservice ELA teachers note relates to concrete teacher and student behaviors, especially with regards to these elements of instruction and classroom interaction.

This allowed for the preservice teachers to articulate connections between Vaughn's strategies, her specific classroom moves, and pedagogical intentions. Especially because preservice teachers viewed the same clips more than once, these connections were deepened and the breadth of their noticing was expanded. Putting SIOP names to observe teacher behaviors gave the novice ELA teachers a vocabulary for describing instructional practice in an ELA classroom that attends to multilingual learners' assets and needs. One of the novice ELA teachers noted with no direction from the prompt, "I will be honest I am not familiar with most of the SIOP strategies/activities listed on this sheet (at least not by name)."

While analysis indicated that preservice ELA teachers were indeed able to start fashioning their professional vision, coming to see teacher strategies and behaviors that promote learning for multilingual learners, and to develop their professional vocabulary for discussing this facet of ELA classroom practice, there was nonetheless one evaluative comment about one of Vaughn's teaching choices (an example she gave to try to clarify the concept of metaphor for her students). The observation task, even when consciously focused on elements of practice and particular frames for interpreting that practice (here the SIOP model), critiques and evaluations from novice teachers are likely to arise.

Furthermore, analysis of data from this phase of Visit 2 showed that the way the ELA teachers were construing language learning and language teaching was based in somewhat prescriptive notion of language and privileged form-focused over meaning-focused approaches to language teaching in most cases. Notably, as the pair of novice ELA teachers progressed through the observation and answering of guided questions, their responses showed more evidence of meaning-focused strategies for supporting multilingual learners' engagement with the ELA lesson. These findings are particularly instructive as we look to developing future iterations of this design since it appears we could provide more support for the novice teachers in a pre-viewing reading or discussion such that they are introduced to the idea that meaning-focused language instruction is essential to supporting multilingual learners, which would enhance the design beyond simply providing the list of SIOP strategies. Additionally, revision of some of the guiding questions might serve to emphasize a focus on meaning as well.

Visit 2—Preservice ELA Teachers' Approach to an Application Exercise

Through the application exercise, we see evidence that the preservice ELA teachers were able to identify key academic vocabulary and match challenges in teaching these terms with particular SIOP strategies. Once they decided on six key terms central to the curricular unit provided to them (voice, justice, equality, ability, honor, genocide), they were able to identify a range of challenges multilingual learners might face in understanding or working with these terms; they wrote "could potentially bring up past traumas; Nuances from some of the terms; Different meanings, academically and personally (ex. voice)," attending to the personal responses students might have while also focusing on how the meanings of these terms could be tricky for learners. They also showed ability to list four different SIOP strategies that could be planned to address these challenges—"clustering (similarities, differences); word wall; illustrate the text (draw a picture); vocabulary bingo." These are strategies that, taken together, balance concern for learners developing meaning around the terms with the undeniable need to also focus on recognizing form and developing automaticity with academic vocabulary. With regard to academic vocabulary especially, then, we see these novice ELA teachers were beginning to enact planning processes in a way that demonstrates facility with the instructional practices they noticed and named during the immediately preceding VR observation phase. It is notable that they focused on meaning as they selected SIOP strategies, yet as found for the observation phase of Visit 2, there is also evidence that certain form-focused, more prescriptive and traditional views of language and language learning were at play in the application exercise.

When they moved on to the part of the exercise that asked them to identify "academic processes (forms of writing, analysis, discussion)" associated with the content of the unit that may be challenging to multilingual learners, the novice ELA teachers listed the four traditional skills "reading, writing, listening, speaking" rather than identifying any written genres or forms of verbally interacting. This led to the novice teachers remaining focused on vocabulary development in subsequent responses to questions asking how SIOP strategies might be applied to support these key academic processes. This was an indication to us that the design could benefit from revision, clarifying in the prompt what "academic processes" might refer to even more concretely. Interestingly, despite the identification of language skills as academic processes, the preservice teachers did go on to deepen their articulations of what challenges multilingual learners might face and to identify further SIOP strategies that could address these, even though they remained focused narrowly on vocabulary.

A question asking the novice ELA teachers to imagine themselves and an ESL co-teacher working together to draft language and content objectives for a lesson embedded in the curricular unit they were working with also showed them staying in the realm of vocabulary learning. The pair suggested the following two learning objectives:

SWBAT orally define words through a think-aloud activity.
SWBAT craft personal definitions through a four-corner vocabulary activity.

This response, as well as an objective-writing task included in the observation portion of the visit which asked the novice teachers to imagine what learning objectives Vaughn and her co-teacher had at the top of their lesson plan for the footage in the VR segment, suggests that it was difficult for these novice teachers to move beyond word learning strategies when thinking about the supports multilingual learners need to engage in academic tasks common to ELA classrooms. In essence, the preservice ELA teachers showed some ability to articulate a particular language learning goal (i.e., vocabulary learning) but not others (related to syntax, discourse conventions in the relevant genre of persuasive speeches, etc.), and they offered no learning objective that falls more into the category of content learning. For example, they could have drawn on the ELA objectives outlined in the curriculum overview of the materials they were provided to identify objectives around making evidence-based claims in both persuasive speaking and writing. What these data and analyses suggest to us in terms of our VR design and accompanying exercises is that rather than simply providing a curricular unit and asking preservice teachers to read it before answering questions, it may be beneficial to have them identify the three standards in these materials that could undergird content learning objectives. Additionally, some brief introduction to the difference between, yet interrelatedness of, content and language learning objectives could also support novice teachers better as they progress through the exercise, generating their own ideas about how they might enact lessons in the unit, drawing on notions of practice developed in the VR observation but also necessarily leaning on other instructional planning tools such as objective-writing and aligning these with curricular content and standards.

The final questions in the application exercise phase of Visit 2 prompted preservice teachers to reflect on the roles and relationships of ELA and ESL teachers as they work as co-teachers in the classroom. While the novice ELA teachers said they valued collaboration and co-teaching in general, their responses also at times reflect ideologies that position the ESOL teacher as more marginal and merely supportive, as shown in table 2.4.

These responses suggest to us that although the preservice teachers expressed positivity about collaboration, co-teaching and working with an ESL co-teacher, there was nonetheless a surfacing of entrenched views that classroom teachers are central and ESL teachers play a supportive role to the "main" instruction. It is worth noting that this was sometimes apparent in data from other preservice teachers' discussions and application exercise responses, but other novice teachers described the classroom teacher and ESL teacher on more equal footing.

Table 2.4   Novice ELA Teachers' Views on Co-teaching with an ESL Teacher

Question	Novice ELA teachers' response
How do you think you and your ESL colleague could each take up collaborative and productive roles during classroom instruction to achieve better learning for your multilingual students during this lesson?	One lead teacher could guide the class but another would be a support and add information/details/etc. as needed. Both would engage with students during activity, circulating around classroom.
Is working alongside an ESL teacher something you have thought about before today? If so, in what ways?	No, we have not thought about ESL co-teaching specifically, but have considered co-teaching as it is a leading topic in one of our classes, and we both recognize how close collaboration with other teachers can benefit all instructors. We believe that ESL teachers are great supports and should be utilized throughout all of curriculum and not merely during the "hard lessons."

During Visit 2 to the lab, the pair of ELA teachers engaged in observation and then application and reflection exercises that related to and extended the focus on instructional practices featured in the VR segments. These follow-up activities were anchored in some particular curricular documents and specific and guided planning tasks that required them to hew very closely to the focal instructional practices (SIOP in the ELA classroom in this case). Analytically, our codes for the observation portion of the visit included naming practice, appraising/evaluating practice, connecting named practices to pedagogical purposes and to specific pedagogical actions, relating practice to personal experiences, relating practice to projected future teaching, and reimagining focal practices by offering alternative options. Data from the application-reflection phase centered more on naming practice, connecting named practices to specific pedagogical purposes and to concrete pedagogical actions, and relating practice to projected future teaching.

Visit 3

Only one preservice ELA teacher, Megan (pseudonym), attended Visit 3. In response to the prompts for this session, which focused on translanguaging pedagogies and practices, she expressed a valuing of learners' home languages and noted that she had only rarely observed these languages being used by students during her visits to classrooms for observations and had never seen them being integrated by teachers into lessons or classroom dialogue. She shared:

In the ESL classes I've observed, students referred to and used their home languages to speak, but not often. Usually this was at times when clarification was needed or they didn't know how to say a term in English (other students who shared native language helped in these moments). In that sense, native languages were encouraged and welcomed but there was a clear tone in the air that learning and practicing English was a center focus in the schools. In my observations, I didn't really see that much integration of languages (except in some readings).

Given that observation of home language integration and drawing on learners' full linguistic repertoires in instructional practice was not part of Megan's previous observational experiences, the excerpts from the *Translanguaging Guide* and VR clips provided resources for naming and beginning to identify and imagine these practices in teaching practice. Although Megan's responses to questions revealed a few lingering misunderstandings about what translanguaging refers to, she demonstrated a much clearer grasp of specific translanguaging practices. In the first VR clip, the teacher, Vaughn, reviews the words *protest* and *injustice* by clearly enunciating the words, repeating them, providing clarifying contrasts that are linguistically achieved with prefixes (approval/*dis*approval and justice/*in*justice) and also by projecting translations of these two key terms in students' home languages, which she attempts to pronounce. The ELA preservice teacher, Megan, in describing how Vaughn could have further applied translanguaging strategies is able to cite word wall, cognate charts, and four-box graphic organizers as potential options:

> In this video, the teacher points out important words for students to remember (through gesture and repetition; call and response). To make this activity more inclusive of translanguaging strategies, the teacher could take this word and have students create a visual organizer that depicts the usage of this word in their native language and an expression for this word in English (index cards? poster board? giant stickie notes?). These different organizers (think: illustration/sentence—word—illustration/sentence) could be shared as a group poster to show how the class understands these shared terms as they all work through the activity. Participating in this activity helps students understand how the class is coming to understand vocabulary and why these terms are important between diverse cultures.

While Megan doesn't refer to the translanguaging practices by name, she does connect the practices with pedagogical purposes and specific pedagogical actions.

Further along in the session, Megan observed a second VR segment, in which Vaughn reviews the concept of metaphor with her students. There are no home languages used in this clip and preservice teachers were asked to imagine which translanguaging practices could be applied to create more space for learners' home languages and to promote deeper meaning-making and understanding around this particular literary device. Here Megan came up with the idea of having groups of students generate word clouds, using home languages and English, and documenting any associations they made with the term. These word clouds would then be the basis for class discussion and building a shared understanding of metaphor. In this instance, Megan was again making connections between translanguaging practices (use of multi-lingual graphic organizers to generate meaning around words and concepts) and concrete (albeit imagined) pedagogical actions while not naming these practices explicitly.

In a final portion of the session, preservice teachers were asked again to delve further into the *Translanguaging Guide* while also considering a par-ticular piece of curriculum. In the preservice ELA teacher's case, an excerpt of a unit on *The Great Gatsby* was provided. As Megan moved back and forth between reading about specific translanguaging practices and the short curriculum document she received, she wrote about using two specific trans-languaging practices and referred to them by name. In imagining a translan-guaging-infused approach to the *Gatsby* unit, Megan demonstrated not only the ability to anticipate in a broad sense what strategies and practice might apply but also to articulate what a specific lesson could look like using the "Building Background with Preview-View-Review" (Celic & Seltzer, 2011, p. 100) strategy (see table 2.5):

This final application exercise provides clear evidence that Megan was gaining facility with naming and applying translanguaging practices, mak-ing ever finer connections between the practices, their purposes and specific pedagogical actions. Across the session, she moved from observing these or recognizing potential for using these in the teaching observed through VR and made a fuller transition at the end of the session to enacting planning practices that drew on the knowledge of practice she was building. In this session especially, given the design of the VR segments where the focal prac-tices were not actually present in the featured teaching, preservice teachers were not asked to identify and name practices based on descriptions of those practices (as they were in Visit 2 when SIOP was in focus and present in the VR footage), but rather to envision the practices using the VR instruction as a point of departure and context and then to enact planning processes that would incorporate these practices. In this regard, Visit 3 to the lab involved preservice teachers moving from identification of practice to a more agentive reimagining and enactment of practice (if only in the planning as opposed to

Table 2.5 Novice ELA Teacher's Application of Translanguaging Strategies

Prompt	Megan's response
What key academic language or concepts would you target in using translanguaging strategies in this unit?	Themes: The American dream, masculinity and feminism, love and heartbreak, socialism. Literary Devices: foreshadowing, metaphor, figurative language, poetry.
Describe what a lesson including this translanguaging strategy might include.	Preview of F. Scott Fitzgerald's *The Great Gatsby* before reading the book. Students will be given a copy of the text and asked to review the front cover and summary. Preview: Students will be given different colored card stock paper with central themes/ideas/literary elements and devices that are seen/will be understood when reading the book that they are unaware of. In pairs or small group, students will come up with words and phrases or illustrations in their native language or in English that they feel are connected to the novel. View: Students will be read a short blurb about The Great Gatsby and its significance during the time (1920s New York; Great Depression era, etc.) Review: Students will then have the opportunity to share with the class the ways they felt connected to the topics that will be seen in the text (explained to students after reading) and why they matter to them in their own languages. This is the time where students can clarify unknown or foreign ideas and discuss what matters to them in terms of this text.
Finally, take a look at the Table of Contents of the *Translanguaging Guide*. Choose one more strategy to read about. Take a few minutes to read through the information on this strategy and then cite three key points you have learned about this translanguaging strategy.	Sentence Building (p. 170): Sentence building is an important skill to know in ELA at various levels of education. However, if it isn't learned well in middle school, students will struggle academically and professionally in the future. This strategy highlights that increasingly complex sentences requires a particular lens to make meaning through. This skill is especially important for ESL students as it helps construct meaning in a routine order that can be followed and transformed in different environments/contexts. 1. Sentence building can be displayed side-by-side/above and below for ESL or general education/proficient students so that they can compare meaning and order of sentences. This also provides a visual that will stick differently than just repetition or words. 2. Modeling is an important aspect of sentence building, as students probably won't understand how to do the task themselves as is. Practicing this process through direct instruction or guided instruction is important. Just as well, this can be made more challenging when you break apart the sentence (character, event, action, etc.) and have students reconstruct it to review if they understand its complexity. 3. Using color is an important part of sentence building for bilingual and ESL learners as it is another means of visual understanding to showcase how and where subjects/parts of sentences should go in comparison between English and native languages.

instructional execution phase). Consequently, we can see the various phases of the core practices cycle that different designs of VR footage and guiding conversations and questions can engage preservice teachers in.

DISCUSSION AND CONCLUSION

The specific case we have presented illuminates some of the potential of VR for preservice teacher education, some achieved in our first cycle of design and implementation and much still to be realized in our own and others' teacher education work. Thus far, we have seen evidence that VR does indeed facilitate embodied perspective-taking and that it can serve as a potent tool in teacher education programs that adopt a core practices approach. This potential needs to be weighed against the intense time and effort needed to engage in design iterations and the complexity of that process. Caution against seeing VR as a replacement for in-person observation is also required. Rather, VR is a powerful complementary tool, one that is particularly well-suited to focusing on fine details of practice, discussions, and analysis that benefit from multiple viewings, stop and start capabilities, and the ability to engage in group discussions in the moments immediately following an observation.

Having completed a first iteration of our VR-based, core practices-infused design, we can offer insights along the dimensions Bell (2004) identifies as pertinent to much Design-based Research (DBR). On the first of Bell's criteria for useful DBR projects—their ability to promote adoption of a design in a local context—we can ask "What have we learned about local appropriation of the design?" To date, we have learned that alongside challenges in creating the VR tools, the socialization of teacher educators into a new VR-mediated teacher education process is also challenging. Adoption of VR elements into preservice teacher education requires collaborative and centralized effort. We have found that the more participatory our design, the more credibility the tools and approach tend to have with our colleagues in teacher education. Among preservice teachers, we have also found that adoption will not be automatic or wholesale; they expressed reservations and criticisms as well as their appreciation for VR tools in teacher education. Mindfully framing the role of VR in their overall teacher education experience will likely be key to greater adoption among novice teachers of VR elements of their observation experiences. Additionally, greater interactivity in VR observation experiences will also likely increase willingness to adopt these tools and experiences.

Bell's second criteria of high-quality DBR projects is that they lead to new knowledge about activities that are central to teaching and learning. Through our analysis, we can now ask, what have we learned about the teacher education activity of novices observing instructional practice? What do we now know about how observation experiences can be better structured and carried out? Our analyses to date confirm that observation experiences in VR can be comparable to in-person observations while potentially offering benefits that being in a classroom does not permit. We have also confirmed that intentionally designed VR observation experiences that balance deconstruction of instructional practice with a focus on unique situational enactments and attention to classroom relationships can prompt novice teachers to reflect on connections between practice, teacher-student relationships and their own future approaches. Our analyses point to the utility of VR observation for preservice teachers across grade-level and disciplinary preparations; for novice ELA teachers, we see how VR observation assisted them to connect CSP and language-related elements of instructional practice especially to the teaching of ELA content and skills. Future VR segments can go even farther in focusing novice teachers' attention and reflection on ELA-specific instructional practices.

Finally, Bell asserts that DBR research can serve to advance theoretical understanding. In our case, we ask, "What have we learned about theories of how novice teachers observe and shape understandings of teaching practice and broader professional vision? What are the limitations of those theories are exposed as a result of the research?" On the whole, our findings support a core practices theory of teacher education and the theory of professional vision that underpins that approach. At the same time, VR as a medium blurs the lines between inquiry and enactment in the core practices cycle and makes interactivity and embodied perspective-taking (arguably, enactment to some degree) possible in the observation phase. Importantly, VR seems to offer a bridge across these two phases, serving as a stepping stone to fuller enactment of practice while still "observing" and providing a new venue for rehearsals of instructional practice in the enactment phase.

REFERENCES

Bell, P. (2004). On the theoretical breadth of design-based research in education. *Educational Psychologist, 39*(4), 243–253. https://doi.org/10.1207/s15326985ep 3904_6

Brown, A. H. (1999). Simulated classrooms and artificial students: The potential effects of new technologies on teacher education. *Journal of Research on Computing in Education, 32*(2), 307–318. https://doi.org/10.1080/08886504.199 9.10782281

Celic, K., & Seltzer, K. (2013). *Translanguaging: A CUNY-NYSIEB guide for educators.* CUNY-NYSIEB.

Cobb, P., Confrey, J., Disessa, A., Lehrer, R., & Schauble, L. (2003). Design experiments in educational research. *Educational Researcher, 32*(1), 9–13. https://doi.org /10.3102/0013189X032001009

Crawford, J., & Reyes, S. A. (2015). *The trouble with SIOP®: How a behaviorist framework, flawed research and clever marketing have come to define—and diminish—sheltered instruction for English language learners.* Institute for Language & Education Policy.

Daniels, J., & Varghese, M. (2019). Troubling practice: Exploring the relationship between whiteness and practice-based teacher education in considering a raciolinguicized teacher subjectivity. *Educational Researcher, 49*(1), 56–63.

Dede, C., Jacobson, J., & Richards, J. (2017). Introduction: Virtual, augmented and mixed realities in education. In D. Liu, C. Dede, J. Jacobson, and J. Richards (Eds.), *Virtual, augmented, and mixed realities in education* (pp. 1–18). Springer. https://doi.org/10.1007/978-981-10-5490-7

Deiker, L., Rodriguez, J., Lignugaris-Kraft, B., Hynes, M., & Hughes, C. (2014). The potential of simulated environments in teacher education: Current and future possibilities. *Teacher Education and Special Education, 37*(1), 21–33. https://doi.org /10.1177/0888406413512683

The Design-Based Research Collective. (2003). Design-based research: An emerging paradigm for educational inquiry. *Educational Researcher, 32*(1), 5–8. https://doi .org/10.3102/0013189X032001005

Fredricks, D., & Peercy, M. M. (2020). Youth perspectives on humanizing core practices. In L. Cardozo-Gaibisso & M. V. Dominguez (Eds.), *Handbook of research on advancing language equity practices within immigrant communities.* IGI Global.

Goodwin, C. (1994). Professional vision. *American Anthropologist, 96*(3), 606–633. https://doi.org/10.1525/aa.1994.96.3.02a00100

Grossman, P. (2011). Framework for teaching practice: A brief history of an idea. *Teachers College Record, 113*(12), 2836–2843.

Grossman. P., & McDonald, R. (2008). Back to the future: Directions for research in teaching and teacher education. *American Educational Research Journal, 45*(1), 184–205. https://doi.org/10.3102/0002831207312906

Lampert, M., Franke, M. L., Kazemi, E., Ghousseini, H., Turrou, A. C., Beasley, H., Cunard, A., & Crowe, K. (2013). Keeping it complex: Using rehearsals to support novice teacher learning of ambitious teaching. *Journal of Teacher Education, 64*(3), 226–243. https://doi.org/10.1177/0022487112473837

Lave, J., & Wenger, E. (1991). *Learning in doing: Social, cognitive, and computational perspectives. Situated learning: Legitimate peripheral participation.* Cambridge University Press. https://doi.org/10.1017/CBO9780511815355

Lindgren, R. (2012). Generating a learning stance through perspective-taking in a virtual environment. *Computers in Human Behavior, 28*(4), 1130–1139. https://do i.org/10.1016/j.chb.2012.01.021

Paris, D., & Alim, S. (2017). *Culturally sustaining pedagogies: Teaching and learning for justice in a changing world.* Teachers College Press.

Peercy, M. M., Varghese, M., & Dubetz, N. (2019). Critically examining practice-based teacher education for teachers of language minoritized youth. *TESOL Quarterly, 53*(4),1174–1185. https://doi.org/10.1002/tesq.533

Philip, T., Souto-Manning, M., Anderson, L., Horn, I., Carter Andrews, D., Stillman, J. & Varghese, M. (2019). Making justice peripheral by constructing practice as "core": How the increasing prominence of core practices challenges teacher education. *Journal of Teacher Education, 70*(3), 251–264. https://doi.org/10.1177/0022487118798324

Saldaña, J. (2009). *The coding manual for qualitative researchers* (2nd ed.). Sage.

Sandoval, W. (2004). Developing learning theory by refining conjectures embodied in educational designs. *Educational Psychologist, 39*(4), 213–223. https://doi.org/10.1207/s15326985ep3904_3

Skulmowski, A., & Rey, G. D. (2018). Embodied learning: Introducing a taxonomy based on bodily engagement and task integration. *Cognitive research: Principles and implications, 3*(1), 6. https://doi.org/10.1186/s41235-018-0092-9.

Tomasello, M., Kruger, A. C., & Ratner, H. H. (1993). Cultural learning. *Behavioral and Brain Sciences, 16*, 495–552.

Chapter 3

"So Similar, But So Different From My Real-Life Classroom"

Using Augmented Reality in Teacher Learning to Facilitate Discussion in Diverse ELA Classes

Jennifer M. Higgs, Megan E. Welsh,
and Steven Z. Athanases

In the context of a preservice teacher education course, Jung just completed a 15-minute augmented reality (AR) simulation where she led a discussion of literature with five middle school-aged avatars. The course was focused on guiding English language arts (ELA) preservice teachers to explore resources and classroom-based inquiry tools to develop knowledge and practice for leading discussions in culturally and linguistically diverse classes. Jung prepared for the event by reading the chapter "My Name" from *The House on Mango Street* (Cisneros, 1983), in which the protagonist, 12-year-old Esperanza Cordero, reflects on personal, familial, and cultural themes related to her name. Jung had further prepared for her AR experience by reading through a manual provided by a university-based research team with guidelines for how to prepare for the "My Name" lesson, broad objectives for the discussion, and brief biographies of the students she would meet in her AR classroom.

Jung now sat before a laptop, viewing video footage of herself facilitating the discussion that replayed her engagement with the augmented students (i.e., the student avatars). She paused the video at moments that warrant her reflection, including this one:

> I felt like we had really good discussions about the topic where we could explore
> different things, like looking at the text but also talking about our backgrounds

and their own thoughts about things . . . I wish I could've explored more and to ask more people, "What did you think about that?" "Do you think that's an acceptable thing?"

This moment captured several affordances of the AR activity and some of the research and practice themes we explore in this chapter. For example, the simulation provided Jung the opportunity to practice using recently learned discussion facilitation tools in a low-risk space. In addition, she had the opportunity to review and reflect on her responses almost immediately after her practice AR session, allowing her to exercise ownership and control of moments she chose to explore. Third, because of the interactive nature of the AR activity, Jung was able to immerse herself in leading a discussion in a way that may not have felt as authentic if she had role-played with fellow teacher candidates.

Despite such affordances, this kind of AR activity also poses numerous challenges. We explored these opportunities and challenges as part of a study in two teacher learning contexts: a teacher inquiry course and a monthly workshop for in-service teachers we refer to as Teacher Partners. The inquiry course occurred near the end of a post-Baccalaureate teacher credential program that included extended school-based practice teaching. Like the course, the workshop also focuses on class discussion, and the Teacher Partners are all alumni of the discussion-focused inquiry course. We examined the AR explorations of eight culturally and linguistically diverse teachers—five preservice, three in-service. Due to the exploratory nature of the work and the small number of teachers involved, we do not offer comparisons across these groups; instead we identify themes across the eight teachers to illuminate the potential and challenges of a particular AR platform. At times, we identify the point-in-career of individuals, but overall we refer to the group as "teachers."

We reviewed video, audio, and written reflective data of these teachers as they engaged with an AR environment called *Mursion*. The Mursion environment enables users (e.g., teachers, healthcare workers) to interact with human-controlled avatars that are engaged in real-time interactions. The avatars, controlled by a human actor or what we refer to as an AR actor, respond to the interactive environment that the user establishes and guides (with open-ended questions about a text, for example). Drawing upon this exploratory study, we articulate why AR activity is particularly suited for development of interactive moves that support facilitation of ELA discussion in an improvisational manner. We describe elements of the exploratory study, briefly summarize what unfolded, and highlight insights that shed light on affordances of the AR event and challenges in meeting project goals. We organized our findings and insights into two strands: (a) insights about potential affordances and constraints of the AR environment in supporting teacher learning about discussion, drawing on teachers' retrospective reflections on their AR experiences, and (b) emergent design principles developed through iterative design of *Mursion* scenarios with diverse stakeholders (experienced ELA teachers, literacy and assessment researchers, AR actors, and technologists).

WHAT WE KNOW ABOUT EXPLORING TEXTS IN ELA THROUGH CLASS DISCUSSION

Learning to facilitate class discussions in ELA is fundamental work, as class discussions can serve as laboratories for meaning-making, engagement with text, and development of text interpretations. We highlight key ideas from the research literature on discussion and the challenges for teachers of moving toward discussions as learning opportunities.

Toward More Dialogic Talk in ELA Classrooms

Broadly defined, class discussions are collaborative episodes of talking among teachers and students for the purpose of supporting student learning, problem-solving, comprehension, and/or literary appreciation (Murphy et al., 2011). A substantial literature has identified multiple approaches to class discussions that serve diverse pedagogical purposes. Most of these approaches, which push against teacher-centered models of instruction, fall under the label of authentic or dialogic teaching (e.g., Alexander, 2008; Nystrand et al., 2003).

Dialogic talk stands in opposition to monologic talk, which focuses power on the teacher as primary transmitter of knowledge. Although classroom discourse is never truly monologic, instruction that is organized as though it gives the teacher interpretive authority and control of talk through a discourse structure commonly referred to as IRE (Initiation/Response/Evaluation) (Mehan, 1979). These participant structures, widely documented across nations, subject areas, and grade levels, are characterized by the teacher initiating a topic with a "known answer question" (Mehan, 1985), the student responding, and the teacher evaluating or giving feedback on the student's response. Countering such long-standing school-based talk structures is a tall order for teachers.

Research in ELA classrooms associates dialogic teaching with enhanced student learning. In one study of classroom talk in hundreds of eighth- and ninth-grade ELA classes across the country, Nystrand and Gamoran (1991) found strong effects on student learning for the overall dialogic quality of classroom talk, measured by proportion of authentic (i.e., open-ended) questions; proportion of uptake (e.g., follow-up questions); and time devoted to discussion (defined as an open exchange of ideas among at least three participants lasting longer than 30 seconds). Students in dialogic classrooms were found to recall and comprehend readings better and respond to aesthetic literary elements more fully than students in monologic classes. These results were replicated in a study by Applebee et al. (2003) of 974 students in 64 middle- and high school English classrooms in 19 schools in 5 states. Applebee and colleagues found that discussion-based instruction significantly enhanced literature achievement and reading comprehension.

Literacy educators have also highlighted the important role dialogic talk can play in promoting equitable learning opportunities for all students (Freedman et al., 2005; Pacheco, 2010; Paugh, 2015). For example, in a study of emergent bilinguals/ELLs participating in small groups, Pacheco (2010) found these students benefited from talk spaces where they learned to draw on cultural knowledge and resources, challenge their teacher's and peers' contributions, develop background knowledge to engage with texts, and contribute to joint meaning-making. Paugh (2015) similarly found in her study of extended discussions in an urban elementary classroom that the teacher's inclusion of students' various academic, social, and personal resources in discussion created a classroom microculture that supported students' persistence in seeking meaning with each other.

Challenges of Enacting Class Discussion

While the value of "talking to learn" stands on strong theoretical and empirical ground, implementing dialogic talk continues to pose a problem in many ELA classrooms. Despite agreement about high-quality discussion characteristics, teacher-dominated talk is often the prevalent form of classroom discourse around the world (Howe & Abedin, 2014). What is needed is more dialogic talk, but this is difficult to achieve.

English educators have argued that a reason for the continued prevalence of monologic classroom instruction is a lack of professional development that enables teachers to make informed decisions about the use of discussion practices (e.g., Juzwik et al., 2013). With the range of available approaches to classroom discussion, preservice and in-service teachers need in-depth understandings of affordances of classroom talk and approaches to talk that are suited to their purposes, their students, their disciplines, and the contexts in which they work (Murphy et al., 2009). To bring about changes in classroom discourse, teachers need time to reexamine and reflect on their own interactions with students, try out and evaluate new behaviors, discover discrepancies between their intended goals and actual practices, and continually question their understandings of effective pedagogy (Garet et al., 2001). Despite these calls for increased attention to classroom talk and teacher education, relatively little attention has been paid to initial preparation or professional learning that helps preservice or in-service ELA teachers develop dialogic stances and practices (see Juzwik et al., 2013).

AUGMENTED REALITY ACTIVITY GOALS
ALIGNED WITH ELA DISCUSSION PRACTICES

Science Technology Engineering and Mathematics (STEM) education has utilized augmented reality, virtual reality, and mixed reality to support student and teacher learning for some years (e.g., Maas & Hughes, 2020). We are working to expand AR use to ELA. For AR, we draw upon a definition by Azuma (1997) that AR is an overlay of information or virtual objects into the real world, allowing a reality where virtual objects seem to coexist in the same space with the real world. Such activity holds promise for ELA teacher learning, and particularly in relation to class discussions. While discussions play important roles in all content areas, in ELA they are foundational spaces for meaning-making from text. This meaning-making can include exploring multiple and often divergent interpretations and linking text to personal, social, community, and cultural experiences that can potentially enhance understanding of character motivations, social conflicts, and themes (e.g., Applebee et al., 2003; Lee, 2001; Nystrand et al., 1997).

AR Uses for ELA Discussion

AR can provide opportunities for change in ELA discussion practices for several reasons. First, AR offers a low-risk environment because real students are not impacted. Second, AR activities can take the form of tailored, reusable learning environments that offer teachers sustained practice with important aspects of discussion in environments in which they may have uneven exposure (e.g., facilitating discussion in linguistically diverse classrooms). Third, AR creates opportunities for teachers to explore ways of responding in the spontaneous, ephemeral space of group talk—albeit with avatars as student discussants.

Finally, AR used for professional development offers authentic interactions that teachers can return to and iterate upon, making typically ephemeral discussions durable artifacts for analysis and improvement. In comparison with interactions with algorithm-controlled agents, physiological reactions and behaviors with human-controlled avatars are similar to those experienced when reacting to real people (e.g., Okita et al., 2008). This suggests that immersive virtual environments with avatars may provide novel, contextualized classroom talk situations that are realistic. These kinds of simulated interactions can potentially augment face-to-face preparation by repeatedly drawing teachers' attention to consequential elements of classroom discussion that can go unseen or unexplored in real-world settings.

AR Design for the ELA Discussion Activity

We planned for two aspects of AR design as essential dimensions in developing knowledge and practices of ELA teachers for class discussions: design of the tool and design of the teacher learning activities. Design of the tool is concerned with providing directions to teachers and AR actors, the human actors who control the student avatars in real-time. Directions include information about the lesson that will be taught, the class of student avatars teachers will work with, and detailed expectations for working within the *Mursion*/AR system. Design of the learning activity refers to how *Mursion*/AR fits within the larger efforts of teacher education and development in furthering teacher knowledge and practice. We first discuss the affordances introduced by different design decisions. Then we address design for teacher engagement to foster learning through interaction with *Mursion*/AR.

Design of the Tool

Developing an AR scenario requires a great deal of effort, especially when focusing on complex tasks like facilitating rich, equitable classroom discussion of a text in diverse classrooms. Our development efforts centered around designing information packets that we distributed to preservice teachers and Teacher Partners to help them prepare a *Mursion*/AR lesson. Packets included an introduction to the project; a description of the basic structure a lesson should follow; a list of lesson goals, curricular materials to center the lesson; and student avatar background information (brief biographies, examples of student work, and classroom norms).

Our lesson structure and goals aligned with National Council of Teachers of English (NCTE) positions on supporting linguistically and culturally diverse learners (National Council of Teachers of English, 2005) and with principles of close reading for the twenty-first century (Catterson & Pearson, 2017). Teachers were provided discretion to make whatever pedagogical decisions they chose within these guidelines and within constraints of the technology. However, they were asked to attend to three broad ELA instructional goals:

a. *Interpretation of text.* Build student dispositions that there are multiple valid interpretations of a piece of literature. Foster students' abilities to connect to, disagree with, and build on each other's interpretation.

b. *Foster discussion that includes the entire class.* Engage all students in classroom discussion. Center discussion around student contributions and limit teacher-dominated discussion.

c. *Honor students' voices by using identity to enrich interaction and learning.* Help students see how their backgrounds brings multiple viewpoints that enriches everyone's understanding of a text.

These goals were reinforced by student background materials and *Mursion*/AR scripts provided in packets. Background materials included student prewrites about the meaning of their names in which some students expressed challenges with their identities. For example, one prewrite activity included, "my name sounds weird and I stand out too much."

Scenario scripts were provided to AR actors only. These scripts, which our university-based research team designed with input from an in-service teacher and the AR actor, specified six moments during the lesson in which avatars would say something intended to prompt a response from the teacher. Avatar reactions were also scripted and varied depending on what the teacher said. The goals of fostering interpretation of text, inclusive discussion, and valuing of student identities were layered into these moments. For example, a student interprets Cisneros's text as asserting that women are weak. Later, a different student asserts that women are weaker than men. The student avatars' reactions to these statements depend on the extent to which the teacher shuts down this discussion, laughs it off, or invites students to critically explore these comments (e.g., "Student B is a girl and she plays taekwondo. She's the toughest one in the class").

Design of Teacher Learning Activity

AR systems like *Mursion* are useful because they provide teachers the opportunity to practice navigating challenging situations in a low-stakes environment—situations that they may not experience during actual teaching. This ability to practice in and of itself, and especially in an authentic setting, is particularly important for preservice teachers because they may have limited opportunities to lead instruction.

While opportunities to practice teaching are essential, we believe that AR simulations are most beneficial when they are combined with other educational experiences. Aligned with this principle, teachers in our project (as noted earlier) all had explored class discussion knowledge and practices for student learning in ELA. We followed a practice sequence designed to ensure that teachers had adequate opportunity to prepare for and reflect on the experience:

a. *We provided a brief overview of the tool.* During an overview, teachers participated in a brief warm-up, started a *Mursion* lesson (e.g., a lesson centered around the text "My Name"), and chatted with student avatars. We distributed packets to help teachers prepare to teach a lesson.

b. *Teachers taught lessons in Mursion.* Those lessons were taught in a separate room containing a laptop used to interact with the avatars, and were staffed with a tech support person. The teachers taught lessons that lasted about 10 minutes. The lessons were recorded and uploaded to cloud-based data storage so that they could be immediately reviewed and reflected upon.

c. *Teacher candidates immediately reflected on their experience.* They watched the video immediately after the lesson with a member of the university-based research team. The teacher paused for any moment they deemed interesting. During these pauses, the teacher commented on what they were thinking at that moment. The researcher also stopped the video and asked questions when a moment was introduced and the teacher did not comment on it. Reflections were teacher-driven; researchers did not provide feedback or their own thoughts on what they saw. Instead, they asked teachers to explain what they noticed and why they thought it was important.

We considered this process of having teachers teach, review a video of their teaching, and reflect on that experience to be a powerful educational tool, especially when student responses elicit specific instructional challenges. These experiences present an opportunity to reflect on important teaching challenges while the lesson is still fresh in the teacher's mind. The combination of designed interaction with immediate, teacher-driven reflection provides an opportunity to think about what it means to teach in ways aligned with literacy theories and practices and to consider which aspects of practice are most challenging and why. Ultimately, this reflection may help teachers reconsider challenging and potentially problematic dimensions of their instruction for future practice.

THEMES FROM AR TRYOUTS WITH MIDDLE SCHOOL AVATARS

To provide some concrete examples of how reflection on AR teaching simulations can impact teacher understanding, we selected three themes that emerged from our work with teachers exploring the AR learning space. Both the discussion practice and the think-aloud supported teachers to reflect upon, uncover, and rethink themes and practices in their discussion tryouts. The ultimate goal of the reflections is to help teachers think through different trade-offs, or tensions, that arise while facilitating discussion in diverse classrooms. The ultimate goal of these activities is to help teachers be more intentional in their practice.

1. Balancing Text and Text-to-Self: Linked Literacy Processes of Close Reading and Making Connections

Our work identified that a common challenge of facilitating literature discussions, especially for in-service teachers, is managing engagement of the two processes of (a) close reading of text and (b) making connections that link text to other knowledge sources and experiences. These are entwined literacy processes—readers draw upon prior knowledge, personal experiences, and other texts and sources as they engage with a text and make meaning from it and with it. However, this entwined nature of literacy activity often is not obvious or internalized for adolescent readers. This may be especially true when K–12 students view class discussion as an artificial schoolish activity involving pursuit of knowledge and information outside of the experiences, knowledges, and lives they bring with them to school.

The AR activity prompted teachers to navigate this pair of literacy processes. The very nature of the focus on names and identities, guided by the scenario design, prompted teachers to invite text-to-self connections. However, determining how much of the talk ought to explore sharing of such connections posed a challenge. The avatar youth spoke of liking and disliking the length, sound, and associations with their names, and wanting to invent new names for themselves as the character Esperanza wanted to do. They were ready to share such connections, and the teachers made choices about how to navigate this. Noreen, for example, felt it was important to allow sharing of such connections to flourish, reporting that "a lot of times students don't see the connection between the text and themselves." For her, these connections might develop into other forms of connecting and understandings.

For Ying, the avatars prompted her to reflect on how she *sequences* this pair of literacy processes in her discussion pedagogy:

> My thought process was we're going to talk about the text first, and then bridge it out to them. But I think what caught me off guard was the students kind of jumped to step two rather than step one, so I was trying to get them back to talk about the text first, and then we can connect the text to their names.

Ying reported that after two of the avatars reflected on their own names and identities, she had to rethink her expectation regarding sequencing: "I kind of realized, oh, so we're kind of going to try to do it simultaneously, versus doing it one at a time." Several other teachers reflected on this notion of sequencing. One teacher, for example, reflected afterward that she might have liked to start with the theme "and then maybe dive into identity," which might have helped her prompt closer attention to affordances of the text.

While not all of the teachers wrestled with assumptions about *sequencing* this pair of literacy processes, nearly all wrestled with how to balance them. As Norah reflected, "I was not exactly sure how to respond 'cause I feel like I wanted them to talk about what mattered to them, but I also had specific ideas that I wanted to cover, so sort of trying to balance that." Teachers tell us repeatedly that fostering multiparty talk, and creating space for talk to flourish in a risk-free environment is an essential step in creating discussion that feels authentic. Nonetheless, the teachers were working to comply with the scenario that asked them to do some close work with the Cisneros text and with larger ELA goals as exemplified in standards and policy statements of the discipline.

In their AR interactions with the avatar students, the language of the teachers clearly marks their attempts to ensure that adequate attention was being paid to the vignette from Cisneros's novella. David, for example, makes clear to the students that he values their sharing but wants to link this sharing to the text:

> I want you all to chime in here. We really get to pick what our names mean to us, but also we have to make that decision if we want the name that we're born with. And just to connect this back with the text, does Esperanza use the name she was born with? Does she want that name?

Here David injects text-based questions in order to expand the discussion.

Demi, a white woman who was launching her second year of teaching seventh grade in a culturally and linguistically diverse school of predominantly Latinx students, repeatedly reported a desire for personal connections while maintaining a commitment to support students' meaning-making. Her experience with the avatars prompted her to articulate her value on both literacy processes:

> So it seems like you all can relate in some way to what Esperanza is feeling in terms of her name and there's a lot of you have mentioned things that you can relate to and similar situations in your own lives, which I love you connecting that to yourself. But, I want us to look in paragraph one. It says . . . "my name means hope in Spanish."

At another point, Demi urges the focus on text even more explicitly: "Let's go back to Esperanza. I can see that you guys have your text in front of you. Can everyone go and look into paragraph number two?" Demi's repeated efforts of this kind mark a challenge that teachers in our work report: they can get discussion flowing on personal connections and linkages to popular culture, but the discussion dies when talk moves back to close attention to text.

2. Text and Language: Academic Language in Facilitating Discussion

A second theme that emerged from teachers' tryouts and reflections was a focus on language in discussion. Several teachers made explicit use of academic language in their AR tryouts, using terms such as *claims* and *evidence* in interactions with avatars. One noteworthy observation is that two middle school teachers working in culturally and linguistically diverse classrooms found the scenario prompted their reflection on academic language and its role in opportunities to learn. Carmina paused the video to reflect on equitable access:

> And then here, I was thinking, after I said "inherit," I was wondering, should I have made that one of my ALD [Academic Language Development] words, inherit? What does inherit mean, kind of thing? Because some or maybe they all know it but taking it for granted that they already know what it meant. . . . And I was like, I probably should explain what that meant or asked someone to tell me what it means.

Here she highlights a distinction between familiarity with and understanding of language.

Carmina's rumination on the role of academic language was also prompted by a moment when avatar students reflected on Esperanza's reporting of strength and weakness of women from her grandmother's generation and especially within Mexican and Chinese cultures. One of the avatar students brought up an image of Esperanza's grandmother being thrown over a man's shoulder and forced into marriage. Carmina paused the video and wondered aloud about what preparation the avatar students might have had regarding figures of speech, hyperboles, metaphors, and similes. Rethinking this moment in the discussion, Carmina proposed that she might have provided a bit of direct instruction:

> Sometimes authors use exaggerations in text to kind of give us a picture of something and make it more interesting. And Cisneros writes really figuratively, so I don't know if her grandfather really literally picked her up and made her get married.

In this way, Carmina found the avatars' remarks pointed her to needed support for meaning-making. She chose to clarify explicitly in her AR tryout:

"They don't mean it literally. They're just using it to create a picture in our head. Does that make everyone feel a little bit better about it being sexist or not?" This approach used does not foster students' puzzling through layers of language, but it appeared to be what this preservice teacher felt she could muster in the moment. Clearly, the avatar students' literal meaning-making challenged teachers to reflect on how they might deepen students' grasp of layered and metaphorical language.

3. Text to World, Text to Self: Teachers Engaging with Emotion, Identities, and Language in Discussion

A third theme that emerged from AR tryouts and reflections were teachers' ruminations on how to lead discussions when a text prompts deep consideration of personal identities and emotions among especially diverse youth. A "moment" designed for the scenario featured a comment offered by an avatar named Davi, identified as a female emergent bilingual of Cambodian descent. Davi reported discomfort about her name, noting that it sounds very Cambodian, not normal, indicating preference for a name like Amanda. She also noted that it sounded like a boy's name, which bothered her. This moment proved to be deeply unsettling for most of the teachers, as it concerned a salient and personal theme related to sociocultural concerns and voiced in an AR space in a manner that had emotional authenticity. During the think-aloud, Danielle, for example, remarked, "That broke my heart, but I was like, 'There's so much to unfold there,' and I was just like, 'What do I say?' I was definitely taken aback by that." Danielle added:

> That was difficult for me to not be able to really connect with her and feel that she was being vulnerable. And I felt like I did not handle it well. . . . Especially because she is an ELL student, and I wanted her to feel like she's part of the class.

Here the avatar experience has elicited an emotional response from Danielle, prompting her afterward to rethink what she considers an inadequate response.

Noreen reflects afterward that her response was to ensure a safe space and to validate Davi's remarks:

> I think a lot of times when kids say self-deprecating remarks, your first instinct is like, "No, don't think that way! Everyone's name is beautiful and everyone is fine." But you have to validate their feelings and so that's what was going through my mind when I said, "Thank you for sharing. Do you want to continue to share or are you ready to move on to the next person?" Because sometimes

they don't have another safe place to share, especially if it has to do with the text.

Ying recalled that another avatar reflected on how having a unique name like Davi's makes you feel like you "quote, unquote don't fit into society." Ying probed, recalling, "I felt like if I did not, Davi would go home thinking like, you know, yeah, her name is different, therefore she won't fit into society." In this way, the avatar takes Ying to a space of care, and she is responding in the moment to ameliorate harm to Davi. For many of the teachers, the text, the scenario, the AR tryout, and the think-aloud converged to create opportunities for this intimate connection, and avatar Davi has brought it to life.

Davi was not the only avatar to share references to name and identity. Dev, who is Indian, also shared, and for Carmina this then raised a question of balance:

> I was trying to figure out a way to kind of validate her in this situation, that like, oh, it's okay that it sounds Cambodian, that's actually really cool, and kind of, I don't know how to say this, and kind of making it more positive that no one else does have that name kind-of-thing. But I was also trying to make sure to include everyone.

Here Carmina reflects on the desire to validate and support the individual during a discussion, all the while considering the group as well.

LESSONS LEARNED ABOUT AR DESIGN
FOR TEACHER LEARNING

Our initial foray into designing learning activities with AR has helped us to reflect on issues that may assist others in teaching and guiding development of ELA teachers. We focused on three issues: (a) enacting authentic and respectful scenarios that address issues of equity, (b) designing AR scenarios, and (c) creating spaces for teachers to reflect on and revise instructional strategies. While AR platforms may vary in terms of degree of human presence in simulation management, we offer lessons learned from a particular model we explored, in which human actors play a key role in the in-the-moment activities.

Some AR platforms remain expensive tools that may seem beyond the budgets of most school districts and teacher education programs. *Mursion*, for example, requires a significant investment in terms of fees to the vendor and in terms of staff time to develop and enact scenarios. However, as these tools evolve, we believe they will become increasingly available and affordable within various educational contexts. Even with increased accessibility, numerous considerations and principles are salient as researchers, practitioners, and technology companies forge alliances around AR use and design for implementation that is meaningful and attentive to local needs. In what follows, we highlight some design principles and considerations that we believe help to keep classes in highly diverse schools and communities central to the work. This means striving for authentic scenarios that feature real discussion challenges in real classrooms and that invite the voices of teachers and students into the design work around text choice and languages used to make meaning of those texts.

Enacting Authentic and Respectful Scenarios about Equity

AR systems can be configured in many ways—the number of students per class, the demographic composition of students, content area, and instructional challenge can vary. One particularly promising innovation involves the extent to which students with special needs are included in the AR classroom. For teacher education, in particular, a diverse student body provides teacher candidates experiences they may not have in their student teaching placements. For example, not all classrooms will serve students on the autism spectrum. AR provides teacher candidates with experiences working with students like these who have unique needs. We therefore see AR as an opportunity to help teacher candidates experience issues of equity in the classroom that they might not otherwise be exposed to during their preparation.

While the promise seems clear, other challenges exist in designing scenarios in a respectful and authentic way. In the *Mursion* platform featured in our study, one AR actor puppeteers the entire simulation and enacts every student. They enact students who differ from them in terms of gender, race, ethnicity, and specialized educational need. Care must be taken in the design of scenarios and in the training of AR actors to ensure that the puppeteering does not essentialize any group. It must be respectful while also presenting the challenges associated with teaching students with specific characteristics (e.g., encouraging an emergent bilingual to participate in class while also not putting them on the spot during classroom discussions).

We want to be very sensitive to these issues and have thus far arrived at the following conclusions. First, it is crucial that representatives of minoritized and nondominant groups, including teachers who work almost exclusively with Black and Brown students, participate in scenario design to ensure that the scripts and challenges are authentic and respectful. Second, every effort should be made to hire AR actors who reflect the avatar population. Third, AR actors must be extensively trained to ensure that they understand how to enact diverse avatars. For example, based on a teacher recommendation, we used the term *out of pocket* (youthspeak for crazy or ridiculous) in a scenario. Teacher candidates noted that scenario felt particularly authentic in that the language used by the student avatars reflected language that they heard their own students use. Finally, there may be some issues or situations that are simply not appropriate for *Mursion*. As described earlier, our scenarios currently involve a Cambodian emergent bilingual learner expressing dissatisfaction with their "non-American" name and a middle school boy stating that girls are weak. Classroom scenarios that engage racism have not yet been enacted in our scenarios because we could not find a way to do so that we were comfortable with, but in our ongoing AR work, we aim to design in ways that provide teachers with opportunities to struggle with these challenging issues.

RECOMMENDATIONS FOR DESIGNING AR SCENARIOS

The most important thing we have learned thus far is that AR simulations are very flexible and can vary tremendously in how they are structured—the characteristics and number of student avatars involved, number and nature of challenging moments introduced in the session, and the time spent in the scenario can all vary. Careful design is needed to make the most of the opportunities presented. At the same time, the number of design choices can be overwhelming. AR developers should therefore use the goals and planned use of the scenario to drive all decisions by asking, "What elements of the simulation are most important to achieve our goals in the most efficient way possible?"

The length of each simulation is one key design consideration. Much can be accomplished in a short time span. For example, Julie Cohen and colleagues at the University of Virginia (2020) have had great success with five-minute scenarios around issues of classroom management. The benefit of this approach is that it allows many teachers to experience AR in a relatively short time span. However, our classroom-discussion based work to explore interpretation of text and issues of equity requires longer lessons because the issues are too complex for teachers to work through in 5 or 10 minutes, as a number of our teachers noted in their post-AR reflections. For example, Norah noted during her reflection that she "was starting to lecture" because she was aware that she was "running short on time," even though she would have preferred to have the students "build toward the conclusions themselves."

Related to this is the challenge of sufficiently training AR actors to implement scenarios with fidelity. The shorter and simpler the scenario, the greater the chance that different AR actors will bring the simulation to life as designed. The more complex, in terms of interpretation required and in terms of the theories driving an AR actor's work, the more training is needed. The issue of implementation with fidelity to the design is important to ensure that teachers experience the right kind of and right level of challenge. In the least desirable situations, some teachers could have highly instructive experiences and others could find the experience to be a waste of time.

CREATING SPACES FOR TEACHERS TO REFLECT ON AND REVISE INSTRUCTIONAL STRATEGIES

Ultimately, AR simulations are only useful if teachers use them to reflect on and reconsider their practice. The workload of developing and administering AR simulations is substantial, and it is easy to focus on delivery of the simulation and to underemphasize helping teachers to reflect on their experience and use it to decide in what ways they may wish to revise their practice. We have found, however, that debriefing about the AR experience is far more satisfying and instructive than anything that happens during the simulation. Ying illustrates this when she reflects that it was "putting me on the spot as a teacher":

> It really helped me to think fast to formulate my questions. And I think that's always helpful for me to . . . improve my practices. How do I construct these, like level two, level three questions quickly to get my students to think about those and then respond?

The ability to make low-stakes mistakes, review a lesson immediately after it is implemented, and reflect how to do better next time accelerates teacher learning in a way that is simply not possible when teachers have to focus on the next lesson immediately after concluding the current one. AR makes this elusive luxury in the world of day-to-day teaching possible, and we encourage teacher educators to take advantage of it. As Danielle explained, "I mean, I think right now in this moment, I'm finally realizing why this is a great tool for teachers . . . to be able to look at it in hindsight, my ordering, all those things, I really wouldn't have noticed in the middle of it."

We have found that teachers volunteer which missteps they found most troubling and what they would do differently in the future without much prompting. For example, all of the teachers who used *Mursion* were quick to offer commentary during their post-AR reflections when they viewed what they believed to be an instructional misstep during their AR discussion facilitation. Ying pointed out during her reflection, for example, that she "just kind of ended [her] convo with [a female student avatar] and [called] on someone else," but that "if given the opportunity, [she] would have probed and talked to her more about kind of the significance of having like a unique name, one that isn't common." Based on teachers' reports and our observations of the AR interactions, a meaningful next step would involve allowing teachers to reteach the lesson to experiment with new approaches in a risk-free space. While we are still working on how many iterations might be helpful, it seems that multiple iterations would be useful. A related question has to do with how to proceed with reflection and feedback. We have been using the most resource-intensive approach (one-on-one reviews with teacher education faculty), but exploring other options—such as pairs of teachers jointly reviewing each other's videos—also seems worthy of exploration.

CONCLUSION

Class discussion persists as a key challenging area of ELA teaching, for teachers across the continuum of teacher learning and practice. AR experiences create opportunities for engaging, risk-free, semi-authentic practice events to explore and expand one's practices and to engage in reflective, metacognitive inquiry into what unfolds in discussion moments and interactions. We hypothesize that our efforts could be improved upon by providing teachers the opportunity to reteach a lesson, having reflected on it and redesigned it to address the challenges they identified. An iterative cycle of teach, reflect, reteach would provide teachers the opportunity to deepen a particular practice or to try on different pedagogical approaches and identify ones most consistent with their goals and their teacher identities. Drawing on our analyses of themes in teachers' engagements in the process and on our design features and principles, our project has illuminated possibilities for AR and has highlighted challenges for design that we hope may guide projects and practice of other groups exploring such innovative tools.

REFERENCES

Alexander, R. (2008). *Towards dialogic teaching: Rethinking classroom talk* (4th ed.). Dialogos.

Applebee, A. N., Langer, J. A., Nystrand, M., & Gamoran, A. (2003). Discussion-based approaches to developing understanding: Classroom instruction and student performance in middle and high school English. *American Educational Research Journal, 40*(3), 685–730.

Azuma, R. T. (1997). A survey of augmented reality. *Presence: Teleoperators & Virtual Environments, 6*(4), 355–385. https://doi.org/10.1162/pres.1997.6.4.355

Catterson, A. K., & Pearson, P. D. (2017). A close reading of close reading: What does the research tell us about how to promote the thoughtful interrogation of text. In K. Hinchman & D. Appleman (Eds.), *Adolescent literacies: A handbook of practice-based research* (pp. 457–476). The Guilford Press.

Caughlan, S., Juzwik, M., Borsheim-Black, C., Kelly, S., & Fine, J. G. (2013). English teacher candidates developing dialogically organized instructional practices. *Research in the Teaching of English, 47*(3), 212–246.

Cisneros, S. (1983). *The house on Mango Street.* Knopf Doubleday.

Cohen, J., Wong, V., Krishnamachari, A., & Berlin, R. (2020). Teacher coaching in a simulated environment. *Educational Evaluation and Policy Analysis, 42*(2), 208–231. https://doi.org/10.3102/0162373720906217

Freedman, S. W., Delp, V., & Crawford, S. M. (2005). Teaching English in untracked classrooms. *Research in the Teaching of English, 40*(1), 62–126.

Garet, M. S., Porter, A. C., Desimone, L., Birman, B. F., & Yoon, K. S. (2001). What makes professional development effective? Results from a national sample of teachers. *American Educational Research Journal, 38*(4), 915–945.

Howe, C., & Abedin, M. (2013). Classroom dialogue: A systematic review across four decades of research. *Cambridge Journal of Education, 43*(3), 325–356.

Juzwik, M. M. Borsheim-Black, C., Caughlan, S., & Heintz, A. (2013). *Inspiring dialogue: Talking to learn in the English classroom.* Teachers College Press.

Lee, C. D. (2001). Is October brown Chinese? A cultural modeling activity system for underachieving students. *American Educational Research Journal, 38*(1), 97–141.

Maas, M., & Hughes, J. (2020). Virtual, augmented and mixed reality in K-12 education: A review of the literature. *Technology, Pedagogy and Education, 29*(2), 231–249.

Mehan, H. (1979). *Learning lessons.* Harvard University Press.

Mehan, H. (1985). The structure of classroom discourse. In T. van Dijk (Ed.), *Handbook of discourse analysis* (Vol. 3, pp. 119–131). Academic Press.

Murphy, P. K., Wilkinson, I. A., & Soter, A. O. (2011). Instruction based on discussion. In R. E. Mayer, & P. A. Alexander (Eds.), *Handbook of research on learning and instruction* (pp. 382–407). Routledge.

Murphy, P. K., Wilkinson, I. A., Soter, A. O., Hennessy, M. N., & Alexander, J. F. (2009). Examining the effects of classroom discussion on students' comprehension of text: A meta-analysis. *Journal of Educational Psychology, 101*(3), 740–764.

National Council of Teachers of English. (2005, July 31). *Supporting linguistically and culturally diverse learners in English Education.* National Council of Teachers of English. https://ncte.org/statement/diverselearnersinee/

Nystrand, M., & Gamoran, A. (1991). Instructional discourse, student engagement, and literature achievement. *Research in the Teaching of English, 25*(3), 261–290.

Nystrand, M., Gamoran, A., Kachur, R., & Prendergast, C. (1997). *Opening dialogue: Understanding the dynamics of language and learning in the English classroom.* Teachers College Press.

Nystrand, M., Wu, L. L., Gamoran, A., Zeiser, A., & Long, D. (2003). Questions in time: Investigating the structure and dynamics of unfolding classroom discourse. *Discourse Processes, 35*(2), 135–198. doi: 10.1207/S15326950DP3502_3

Okita, S. Y., Bailenson, J., & Schwartz, D. L. (2008). Mere belief of social action improves complex learning. In S. Barab, K. Hay, & D. Hickey (Eds.), *Proceedings of the 8th International Conference for the Learning Sciences* (pp. 132–139). Erlbaum.

Pacheco, M. (2010). English-language learners' reading achievement: Dialectical relationships between policy and practices in meaning-making opportunities. *Reading Research Quarterly, 45*, 292–317.

Paugh, P. (2015). Discourses as resources: Active literacy practices and a microculture of rich meaning making in an urban elementary classroom. *Literacy Research: Theory, Method, and Practice, 64*(1), 132–148.

Stewart, T. T., Coombs, D., Fecho, B., & Hawley, T. (2019). Embracing wobble: Exploring novice teachers' efforts to enact dialogic literacy instruction. *Journal of Adolescent & Adult Literacy, 63*(3), 289–297.

Wilkinson, I. A. G., Reznitskaya, A., Bourdage, K., Oyler, J., Glina, M., Drewry, R., … Nelson, K. (2017). Toward a more dialogic pedagogy: Changing teachers' beliefs and practices through professional development in language arts classrooms. *Language and Education, 31*, 65–82.

Part 2

PRACTICAL APPLICATIONS

HOW CAN VIRTUAL AND AUGMENTED REALITIES SUPPORT STUDENT LEARNING?

Chapter 4

How Am I Supposed to Teach This?

*Using Google Cardboards to Enhance
English Language Arts Learning*

Clarice M. Moran

The year is 2045, and the world has been ravaged by war. The only escape from the horrors of famine, disease, and destruction is through a simulated world called OASIS, and the only way to get to OASIS is through a virtual reality hook-up. By donning virtual reality devices, you can live in this other world, fall in love with someone's avatar, and even rule society. Such is the premise of Ernest Cline's (2011) young adult novel, *Ready Player One*. In the book, the characters must save humanity from falling into the wrong hands while fighting, racing, and living in a realm made of nothing but 1s and 0s.

Scary stuff, but also exhilarating for young people who feel powerless right now. In this futuristic virtual environment, it doesn't matter what you look like—fat, thin, old, young—or if you have physical imperfections. What matters is your mind and your ability to think quickly and problem-solve. The virtual world levels the playing field for everyone, and each person can choose their own race, gender, size, age, and capabilities.

Virtual reality (VR) in this context is nothing short of miraculous. It is a place to socialize, to work, to grow, and to be who we really are—who we wish we were—outside the confines of physical reality. In Steven Spielberg's 2018 adaptation of Cline's (2011) novel, the camera cuts continually between the virtual world (animated) and the real world (live action) to demonstrate the deeply complex change between what we experience in "real" life and what we experience in our heads. In the OASIS virtual world, players are able to show themselves as cuter or sexier, as larger or older, as muscled or slim. These are the manifestations of the mind and the spirit, and they are juxtaposed repeatedly against the reality of ordinary human beings desperately trying to project what they feel on the inside into the consciousness of others.

Fantasizing and dreaming are positive past-times, and the wild creativity that lives in the recesses and halls of the mind are important corridors to be explored. As the character Halliday says, "The OASIS lets you be whoever you want to be. That's why everyone is addicted to it" (p. 37).

Although we don't have an OASIS world yet, this chapter will argue that VR is more than a fantasy or video game. It is a paradigm that allows a viewer to enter a new domain and become someone else. VR is a portal into a realm in which users can "see" as if they are a character, "feel" as if they are in a new place, and "know" what it means to inhabit the skin of another. It belongs in the English language arts (ELA) classroom as a way to amplify traditional, canonical literature and act as an experiential tool for a deeper understanding of course content. This chapter will highlight the work of four secondary ELA teachers who have used VR in their classrooms with great success. Their complete lesson plans and reflections on the lessons are included in an effort to demonstrate that VR is practical and easily applicable to ELA content.

A SHORT HISTORY

What began as a quirky, New Wave gadget in 1984 has now emerged as a sophisticated tool poised to alter the way we see the world. Developed initially by Jaron Lanier, who founded the company VPL Research in his house in the technology-rich ether of Palo Alto, California, VR was designed as an innovative approach to viewing 3D pictures. The first VR devices featured DataGloves and AudioSpheres that allowed the user to "feel" a simulated environment and hear 360-degree, surround sounds while viewing 3D images. Lanier called the experience "virtual reality," but could not get the traction he needed to make inroads into the technical world. VPL Research went bankrupt in the 1990s, and all of its patents were acquired by Sun Microsystems. Shortly thereafter, in 2010, Oracle Corporation bought out Sun Microsystems and has since released its own VR headset and a cloud computing platform that can support VR experiences. In 2016 and 2017, a few other companies, including HTC and Sony, released their own versions of VR headsets, games, and applications.

Facebook developed Oculus, a division solely devoted to all things VR. Oculus released its own VR headset called the Oculus Rift in 2016 and is now putting new iterations on the market, including the new Oculus Quest, which promises a "room-scale experience without the need for a gaming computer or PlayStation" (Heaney, 2020). Other companies, including Google, Sony, Samsung, and Lenovo, are jumping in with their versions of headsets. A recent article in *PC Magazine* (Greenwald, 2020) rated "The Best

VR Headsets for 2020" as if they were as mundane and necessary as cars or washing machines.

There are VR-themed movies (like 2010's *Inception* and 2009's *Avatar*), games (including a Minecraft VR game for Oculus Rift), and computer applications that promise to elicit excitement, fear, and intense drama. The Franklin Institute in Philadelphia, the *New York Times*, Discovery, Google, and other respected intellectual institutions all have launched VR apps for mobile phones. And in Atlanta, there is even a VR Bar called Revery that features themed rooms with VR experiences with your favorite cocktail.

VR appears ready to take its place alongside smartphones and laptops as a must-have tool for navigating twenty-first-century life. About seventy-five years ago, television burst onto the scene and forever changed our view of communication. Virtual reality is no less ground-breaking.

DOES IT BELONG IN THE CLASSROOM?

VR may seem like just another shiny technology tool, but its place in the ELA classroom is supported by research. Kirby and Crovitz (2013) wrote that "students benefit from explorations with multimedia and multimodal forms of communication" (p. 9), and VR likely can be part of this exploratory journey. VR also may encourage students to engage in self-directed learning and to explore ideas in more depth. Dail and Vasquez (2018) wrote, "it is our responsibility as teachers to help students engage in the world critically and respond to it authentically and meaningfully" (p. 91), and it seems that critically assessing the role of VR in multimedia is becoming increasingly important.

Benefits of VR in Education

VR Promotes Student Engagement

Research on VR in the classroom is still emerging, but initial results show that it has great promise for hooking students into topics they initially rejected. A virtual trip to the Globe Theatre in London or a simulated exploration into the human body may provide the impetus and encouragement students need to pursue information further. In one recent study, students explored Roman ruins through VR and were far more interested in the material than if they had simply read about it. In the study, 13-year-old students learned about the features of architecture as they were asked to build block by block—and with the aid of a computer equipped with virtual reality software—various buildings. The exercise proved to be fun, practical, and balanced collaborative and independent work (Frontera, 2009).

In another study, preservice teachers surveyed in Australia collectively agreed that VR had the potential to engage learners and offer students experiences they might otherwise not have with other learning tools (Cooper et al., 2019). The preservice teachers reported that VR helped their students independently explore places and was a "transformative technology" for encouraging student-constructed knowledge (Cooper et al., 2019, p. 3).

VR Enhances Writing

Moran and Woodall (2019) found that VR enhanced students' writing skills by allowing them to create narratives with more vivid details. In their study, students were asked to write an essay about life in the Great Depression. They struggled, even though they had just read *The Grapes of Wrath* (Steinbeck, 1939) and seen photographs of the Dust Bowl and migrant workers. Once they were handed a VR device, though, they were able to step into the time period and tour a shanty house and walk down a dusty road in the 1930s. Moran and Woodall (2019) found that this immersive experience translated into writing filled with details. Students were more excited to put what they had seen in VR into words on a page. The result was more independent writing and student-constructed knowledge about the Great Depression. As Hanson and Shelton (2008) wrote in their analysis of VR's place in the classroom, the technology can be used to build support for students as they interact with the virtual environment and "cognitively construct knowledge for themselves" (p. 120).

VR Encourages Reading

Teachers typically provide some background information or context for students before asking them to read. Frequently this is done through a PowerPoint presentation or lecture and sometimes results in bored students who tune out. Using VR to enhance background knowledge allows students to independently explore new settings and gain an understanding *before* they read. Positioning VR as a pre-reading strategy seems to answer Gunther Kress's (2003) call for "new tools for thinking with, new frames in which to place things, in which to see the old and the new, and see them both newly" (p. 8). This is especially true when VR and novels or short stories are used in conjunction with each other. As Pilgrim and Pilgrim (2016) wrote in their advocacy for the use of VR in reading instruction, "VR can be utilized as a tool for experiential learning, as it reflects active construction of an environment" (p. 90).

VR Allows for Cross-Curricular Exploration

Sir Ken Robinson (2017) has lamented that we treat children like widgets when we box them into finite subject areas and expect them to churn out facts. Cross-pollination of subject areas is a much more natural way to learn and results in critical thinking and analysis. VR allows students to marry the worlds of science and literature, for example, when they view images of the lunar phases and then write poems or short stories about the moon. Scientific trips to the bottom of the ocean can be paired with artist's renderings of oceanic life, and historical visits to a civil war battlefield can inspire first-person narratives about life as a soldier.

The reality is that VR appears poised to become part of our lives in unimaginable ways in the very near future. In his 2018 book on VR called *Future Presence*, Peter Rubin points out that breaking the fourth wall and stepping directly into the scene of a movie will completely transform our experience of film. Rather than sitting back and passively viewing content, audiences will become part of the film. How they will view scenes, characters, and important information that supports a narrative is still to be determined. At the moment, VR films are in their infancy.

Rubin (2018) writes, "Now that VR brings you inside the frame, though, those constraints are gone. VR experiences don't have the benefit of a rectangle to bound your focus, so creators need to find ways to make you notice the things that matter in the 360-degree sphere that is the VR 'screen'" (p. 71).

Helping students navigate this new medium is absolutely the job of teachers, particularly English language arts (ELA) teachers. As the National Council for Teachers of English (2018) *Beliefs for Integrating Technology into the English Language Arts Classroom* state, teachers must be responsive to the changes that technology brings "without abandoning the kinds of practices and principles that we as English educators have come to value and know to work." VR is another tool in the growing ELA digital toolbox. Using VR in the ELA classroom is essential for helping students make sense of this new medium and developing critical literacy practices for interpreting it.

THE BEST VR DEVICES FOR THE CLASSROOM

As of this writing in 2020, the Oculus Rift VR device costs about $399—fairly cheap compared to the $250,000 nascent VR devices sold by VPL in the 1980s. However, this price tag is likely too steep for most classroom budgets. Cardboard VR devices that work with a smartphone can be found online for as low as $9 each (see appendix 3 for sources). These collapsible versions are all clones of Google Cardboards—a type of VR device that was developed by Google and presented to the public in 2014 at the annual I/O Google Conference (see figure 4.1).

It is the cardboard versions that have been used with great success with the four teachers who authored the lesson plans in this chapter. These VR devices

Figure 4.1   Google Cardboard Devices are Made of Cardboard and Use a Smartphone and Gyroscope to Interface with Virtual Reality Videos and Programs.

are available online for bulk orders suitable for a class set. They are durable and easy to use, and they can be paired with Android and iPhone devices with screens up to six inches. The Google-branded ones currently cost about $25 for a two-pack, are lightweight and pack away very easily. Plans for making a cardboard VR are available online. Most involve some type of heavy-gauge cardboard (such as a pizza box), Velcro, a ring magnet, a ceramic disk magnet, and lenses that have a 45mm focal distance, and teachers will need a high level of crafting skill to assemble their device from a plan.

A class set can be stored easily in a file drawer or other safe place and then pulled out when they are needed. In this ideal scenario, each student would get one to use in class. If money is an issue, then a pair of students can share one device. Or, five or six cardboard devices could be used in stations. In this method, five or six students would rotate to the station and use the VR

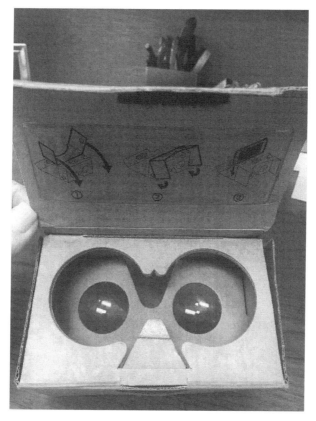

Figure 4.2   A Google Cardboard Unfolded.

devices, while the other students attended to activities in other stations. Five or six devices would run about $50.

Since the cardboard devices require a smartphone, issues of access frequently are brought up when considering whether to use VR in the ELA classroom (Moran & Woodall, 2019). Many stakeholders worry about students and their access to a smartphone or the Internet (Farjon, Smits, & Voogt, 2019). However, a 2018 Pew Research Center survey reported that 95 percent of teens aged 13–17 report owning or having access to a smartphone, and 45 percent of the teens said they are online on a near-constant basis. As one middle school teacher in a Title 1 school in Georgia said, "They might not have lunch that day, but you can be sure they have their phone" (J. McElvey, personal communication, February 4, 2020). Although issues of equity and access are beyond the scope of this chapter, mobile phones and cardboard devices may offer low-cost connections to the virtual world (see figure 4.2).

Resources for AR and VR in the ELA Classroom

It is easy to become overwhelmed by the enormous number of digital resources available for use in the classroom. VR resources are no exception. Careful consideration of apps, websites, and digital tools is essential to prevent VR from becoming simply a shiny add-on to the curriculum without added value for learning.

In our work, we have found the following apps and docs to be easily transferable to ELA content.

Google Expeditions: Google Expeditions is an app created by Google for Cardboard users to view 360-degree images of specific places. The places range from ancient Egypt (with pictures of the Sphinx and the Great Pyramid) to the American West in the 1800s (with images of covered wagons and long-horn cattle). Teachers can control the pace of the expedition and lead students intentionally to various images, or they can turn students loose and let them explore places on their own.

* *Discovery VR:* Discovery VR is an app created by the Discovery television channel. It features short VR movies (between 2 and 3 minutes) with titles such as, "Zip Down Armenia's Longest Zipline" and "Route to Everest." The immersive movies are not interactive, but they do allow users to break the fourth wall and step inside the movie, seeing everything as if they are there too.

* *NPE-AR:* This app, called the National Park Experience, allows users to visit several national parks and look around specific scenes within those parks. From Grand Teton National Park to Yellowstone, users can get a sense of the scenery and grandeur in the VR images. The app also features an AR function that offers users the ability to scan a QR code on a national park poster and transport themselves directly into the VR image from the QR code.

Classroom-Tested Lesson Plans for Cardboards

What follows are four different lesson plans for VR lessons appropriate for secondary ELA. Each of these lessons were written by in-service teachers who completed a technology-in-ELA course at a major public university in the southeastern United States. The teachers learned about VR through the course, then wrote and conducted lessons on using the technology with their own students. Many more lesson ideas can be generated by visiting the Google Expeditions spreadsheet available online at https://docs.google.com/spreadsheets/d/1M0i7JpBHAAfjPNBRSfnShfMa9OztwG7lJdN-VCpwKEg/edit#gid=1861012776.

The teachers who wrote these lesson plans said their students found VR to be an engaging and innovative way to access the curriculum. Traditional

ELA content paired with innovative VR allowed students to engage with the material in ways they may not have. After each lesson plan is a short reflective narrative from the teacher.

Lesson Plan #1

Sarah Dobson

Lesson Title: Exploring Environmental Issues with Google Cardboard
Grade Levels: 10–12

Central Focus:
Students will examine and collect information for a social movement research project by using virtual reality experiences. They will investigate a variety of Google Expeditions related to the viewing of the documentary "An Inconvenient Truth" (Guggenheim, 2006) and reading of *Silent Spring* (Carson, 1964).
This VR lesson is for AFTER READING.

Objectives:
Students will use technology to better understand environmental issues.
Students will compare digital, video, and print texts for similarities and differences.
Students will compose a thesis statement for their research project.
Common Core State Standards:
CCSS.ELA-LITERACY.CCRA.R.1
Read closely to determine what the text says explicitly and to make logical inferences from it; cite specific textual evidence when writing or speaking to support conclusions drawn from the text.
CCSS.ELA-LITERACY.CCRA.R.2
Determine central ideas or themes of a text and analyze their development; summarize the key supporting details and ideas.
Opening (10 minutes):
Think-Pair-Share
• What do Carson and Gore say about climate change? What does climate change look like? What do you think about climate change?
Instruction (30 minutes):
Explain today's agenda with the class
• Step One: Connect everyone to the school Wi-Fi network
• Step Two: Use Google Cardboards to go on an Expedition together (be sure to explain Google Cardboard for anyone unfamiliar)
• Step Three: Students will use the Cardboards to explore VR experiences related to climate change. They can choose from the following Expeditions (write these on the board so that students can refer back to them):

  ○ Polar Bears and the Arctic Ecosystem
  ○ Preserved Oceans
  ○ Recycling
  ○ The Great Barrier Reef
  ○ "Racing Extinction" videos in Discovery VR
As they explore, students will complete a short handout (appendix A) to collect information for their upcoming research project.

Closing (10 minutes):
Closing discussion
• Collect handouts and discuss the last question with the class:

   ○ What was interesting/helpful about this activity? What was challenging/distracting
     about it? Do you know more about climate change in a particular part of the
     world now? What are your next steps for your research project?

Assessments:
• Google Cardboard handout (appendix A)
• Participation in class discussion and VR activities

Sarah's Reflection

*I planned this activity for the opening week of our research unit in order to show
students how virtual reality can be informative and insightful, as well as fun and
engaging. During our opening discussion about VR, one of my students said,
"VR can be used for gaming and entertainment and educational purposes." He
emphasized the phrase "educational purposes" with dramatic air quotes. He
went on to explain how his teachers had done similar activities in middle school,
but these VR experiences turned out to be more for entertainment than for learning. This opening discussion provided me with valuable insight into my students'
existing attitudes toward VR. I was surprised to find out most of my students had
not only used VR before, but many of them had used Google Cardboard specifically. Overall, their initial enthusiasm did not quite match mine.*

*As we began our class Expedition, however, the energy in the room shifted.
As an example of how VR can inform us about American social movements,
I took my students on a tour of historical places in women's rights history.
They were impressed by how I could direct their view to specific locations in
the scene and how pictures appeared on their screens as I talked. This group
activity was the perfect opportunity for those who were unfamiliar with VR to
get comfortable with the technology before exploring on their own.*

*After our class Expedition, students were allowed to explore different VR
apps individually to find stories and activities that related to the social movement they would be researching in this unit. I had a list of suggestions on the
board. Students clearly enjoyed the freedom they were allowed. In order to
keep them on task, however, I asked them to fill out a simple handout documenting what they learned. The handout also asked them to reflect on what
worked/didn't work about the activity, as well as their opinion on the use of
VR in the classroom. These are some of the responses:*

• *"We should use VR in the classroom more often because it makes learning
  more fun."*

- *"It was helpful and way better than going on websites to look for information."*
- *"The helpful and interesting thing was that we got to see actual pictures and surroundings. The challenging thing was not being able to do virtual reality because of minor setbacks."*
- *"VR is indeed educational, but not fun when it is educational."*
- *"Finally using our phones is interesting/helpful."*
- *"I liked this activity because I can see how it is like in real life and how it feels to be there. I think VR is a good way to learn in the classroom because it was fun and easy."*
- *"It was fun, but I feel like we didn't listen because we were amused. Once we get used to it I think it would be very useful."*

Overall, this lesson went very smoothly. Students were engaged the entire time and largely stayed on task. The more VR technology becomes accessible and commonplace, the more I can see it becoming a regular tool in the classroom. The only constraints I noticed were the initial novelty of the technology and the limited number of relevant educational VR experiences.

Lesson Plan #2

Ryan Strasser
Lesson Title: Into the Virtual Wild
Grade Levels: 9–12

Central Focus: The central focus of this lesson is to help give students a look at what Chris McCandless experiences throughout the novel *Into the Wild* (Krakauer, 1996). Using a Google Cardboard Virtual Reality headset, as well as apps such as "Discovery VR" and "Expeditions," students will select different locations that match some of the locations described in the book. From this, the students will partake in place-based writing. This will put a focus on descriptive writing and imagery for the students. ***This VR lesson is for DURING READING.***

Objectives:
Students will use place-based writing with descriptive language.
Students will incorporate descriptive language into writing.
Students will use technology in the classroom to gain the knowledge needed.

Common Core State Standards:
CCSS.ELA-LITERACY.CCRA.W.3
Write narratives to develop real or imagined experiences or events using effective technique, well-chosen details and well-structured event sequences.
CCSS.ELA-LITERACY.CCRA.W.5
Develop and strengthen writing as needed by planning, revising, editing, rewriting, or trying a new approach.

Opening (10 minutes):
Think-Pair-Share
Ask students to consider the setting of *Into the Wild*. What do they think it looks like? Are there people present? How does the setting influence Chris's experiences?

Instruction (30 minutes):
• Ask students to download Google Expeditions and Discovery VR apps onto their smartphones.
• Pass around the Google Cardboard sets to the students.
• Show the students how to use the Cardboards and how to use the apps.
• Explain what descriptive language is and what it can look like in the context of place-based writing.

Structured Practice and Application (40 minutes):
• Ask students to view "Mount Everest" and "Canada's Amazing Northern National Parks" in the Google Expeditions app.
• Ask students to view "Discovery TRVLR: Antarctica" video on the Discovery VR app.
• Have students take notes on how they view their surroundings and how they would react if physically put in that location by themselves.
• Direct students to use their notes and the apps to write a narrative or poem about what they felt/how they would feel isolated in an environment similar to what is seen in *Into the Wild*.

Closing (10 minutes):
• Ask students to discuss what they saw, share what they felt, or what they wrote for their poem/narrative.
• Explain how they can use this to connect more with the main character of *Into the Wild*.

Assessments:
• Student writing can be collected as an informal assessment.

Ryan's Reflection

I was really excited to bring virtual reality into the classroom. I loved using it in my technology class, so I knew just how useful it can be when used correctly. This was something I brought up to the students at the beginning of my four to six weeks of teaching because I wanted them to look forward to it. Also, the fact that this was being used at the time we were reading Into the Wild *made me more excited because of just how perfect it fit in with the lesson. I prepared the students again two days before I actually brought in the Google Cardboard devices because I wanted them to go ahead and have the apps and specific locations ready to go.*

The two apps that needed to be downloaded were Expeditions and Discovery VR. On Expeditions, we would be looking at "Mount Everest" and "Canada's Amazing Northern National Parks." With Discovery VR, the students would follow along with the "Discovery TRVLR: Antarctica" video. Unfortunately, with Discovery VR, the video would not load correctly with the school WIFI, so we were left to use only Expeditions.

Many of the students had not followed the instructions for downloading the apps before class, so we had to wait a bit before we could get moving on the lesson. After the waiting, I passed out the Google Cardboard devices to each student and demonstrated how to put them together, how to properly insert their phones, and how the button will move from scene to scene. Most of the students were excited to use virtual reality because this is not something used in a typical classroom, and it offered a new way of learning for them. I let the students spread out around the room and even move out into the hallway to give everyone the space that would be needed to experience everything naturally. I instructed the students to please take their time with each scene and location. It is very easy to move through them quickly, but for the purpose of the lesson and the material, they needed to take their time. The point of this was to experience the environment that Chris McCandless had to deal with in Into the Wild, and to write in a similar style as the author to build their descriptive writing skills. As expected, some of the students disregarded my instruction and moved at a pace that they were comfortable with, which was rather quick. When students were finished, I allowed them to find another location on the app to explore and write about. I was lucky enough for an assistant principal and a few administrators to come visit the classroom and try on the devices.

Overall, the students really enjoyed the activity, but moved way too quickly through it. Even with going through two or three expeditions, the students completed the activity faster than I was expecting. The students who really put in the effort, which was almost all of them, even seemed to finish the expeditions faster than what I was planning. Seeing these students finish so fast is going to make me adapt this lesson for a much shorter time frame and include something else for the day rather than just the VR. I was happy to use these devices in the classroom, but I will have to change it up to make sure everyone is participating effectively and doing the best they can do.

Lesson Plan #3

Ashly Sorrells
Lesson Title: Immigration in America
Grade Levels: 7–8

Central Focus: In this lesson, students will be using Google Cardboards to build their knowledge on the significance and history of Ellis Island and the Statue of Liberty. The purpose behind the assignment is for the students to use the Google Cardboards as a way to build some foundations of prior knowledge for an upcoming text and grow their skills in supporting claims they make with textual evidence. The students will then reflect on the knowledge they have gained by discussing the information with their partner and write at least two paragraphs giving specifics on what they have learned. The graphic novel *The Arrival* by Shaun Tan (2007) is the focus text. The text is written from the perspective of someone who migrates to a new land through wordless images. In the text, the author uses the Statue of Liberty and Ellis Island, redesigned, to bring in two historical monuments that are significant.

This VR lesson Is for BEFORE READING.

Objectives:
Students will justify their answers by citing textual evidence.
Students will summarize what they have learned from multiple texts.
Common Core State Standards:
CCSS.ELA-LITERACY.CCRA.R.5
Analyze the structure of texts, including how specific sentences, paragraphs, and
     larger portions of the text (e.g., a section, chapter, scene, or stanza) relate to each
     other and the whole.
CCSS.ELA-LITERACY.CCRA.R.7
Integrate and evaluate content presented in diverse media and formats, including
     visually and quantitatively, as well as in words.
Opening (5 minutes):
Start off by putting students into pairs and passing out Google Cardboards to each
     pair. Have a volunteer pass out the handouts (appendix B).
Students should have downloaded Google Expeditions onto their smartphones prior
     to the start of class.
Instruction (15 minutes):
- Instruct students to open the "Statue of Liberty and Ellis Island" expedition in
     Google Expeditions on their smartphones. There will be a flag below the title that
     says, "National Park Service, Google Arts & Culture VR." Students should select
     "view in VR."
- Students should explore the Statue of Liberty and Ellis Island images for about 5
     minutes.
- Tell students that there are seventeen questions and a reflection in the packet
     (appendix B). Students will work together, but they both will go on their own
     expedition. As they read the content, their partner will read off the questions for
     that scene. The partner of the person who is asking the questions will write down
     their partner's answers as they are saying them. Once their partner has finished the
     last question, they should switch.
Structured Practice and Application (30 minutes):
- The teacher should do an example with the students. Select the question, "Why are
     the shackles on Lady Liberty's feet significant?"
- Teacher will ask the students, "where would I look to find the answer?"
- Wait for the students to look around.
- If no one answers, say, "to find this answer, I would look at the section that says,
     "Robe and Broken Shackles."
- The teacher should let the students know that the answer could be present under
     this section because of the key word, *shackles.*
- Teacher will read the section out loud and ask why the shackles are significant.
- Teacher will say, "the text says, 'Broken chains around her ankles show her
     forward stride. They also represent the abolition of slavery in the United States.'"
- After this example, the teacher should allow students to explore on their own,
     completing the packet and the reflection at the end (appendix B).
Closing (5 minutes):
- Ask students to discuss what they saw.
- Tell students that the Statue of Liberty expedition ties directly into their upcoming
     reading of *First Crossing: Stories about Teen Immigrants* by Don Gallo.
Assessments:
- The packet (appendix B) serves as an informal assessment. \

Ashly's Reflection

This lesson went really well! The students loved it. I made these notes as I planned so that I could address any issues:

I structured ways for my students to have discussions throughout the class. I explained all of the instructions on how to use the device and the assignment. I left space for students to ask me questions about the VR experience, the assignment, or how to find something within one of the texts. I walked around the classroom, creating opportunities for students to ask me any questions. During the structured practice, I asked the students to do the example with me. I walked them through what I saw and where we needed to look. I asked questions such as:

- *Why are the shackles on Lady Liberty's feet significant?*
- *Based off of what I just read out loud, why do you guys think that the shackles are significant?*
- *Why would we look at that section?*

I wanted to ask my students "why" questions to help them think deeper into the assignment. I wanted them to understand the answer and how we got there. I then gave students time to work with their partners after we did an example. At the end of the class, we came back to a whole group discussion on what they learned throughout the experience.

The following things did not go as planned:

1. *One partner took longer than another to complete the experience. I adjusted the assignment based on how long it took the students to complete it, giving them extra time if needed.*
2. *The students had trouble accessing the service. I changed the pairs that I created if neither of the students had a phone that would work.*
3. *A couple of students had a vision problem. A couple of students could not look into the cardboard for too long. I helped them by letting them go through the experience as a "guide." The student will not have a "class" but they were able to access the same information. The format of the "guide" is in the form of reading a text straight off of your phone.*

Lesson Plan #4

Maya Woodall

Lesson Title: The Influence of Time and Place in *To Kill a Mockingbird*
Grade Levels: 6–8

Central Focus: The focus of this lesson is on helping students understand that time and place have an effect on characters' actions in a fictional story. The setting and time period of *To Kill a Mockingbird* (Lee, 2002) are key influences on the outcome of the novel. Viewing similar settings through virtual reality devices will allow students to gain a deeper understanding of the characters' motivations.

This VR lesson is for DURING READING.

Objectives:

Students will be able to articulate the time period and setting of *To Kill a Mockingbird.*

Students will be able to describe the ways in which the time period and setting influenced the main characters in *TKAM*.

Common Core State Standards:

CCSS.ELA-LITERACY.CCRA.R.2

Determine central ideas or themes of a text and analyze their development; summarize the key supporting details and ideas.

CCSS.ELA-LITERACY.CCRA.R.3

Analyze how and why individuals, events, or ideas develop and interact over the course of a text.

Opening (5 minutes): Students should have downloaded Google Expeditions on their smartphones prior to arriving in class. Once in class, they should pair up with a friend and open the app on their phone. Students also should open a shared laptop and prepare a clean Word Doc.

(Students should have read at least the first half of the novel before beginning this lesson.)

Instruction (15 minutes):

• Ask students to imagine what the Ewell's house looked like and what the Finch's house looked like.

• Direct students to draw a quick sketch of each house with their partners. They should discuss the differences and compare what they think each would look like.

• Ask students how they think living in those types of houses would affect the characters' actions. How would the townspeople feel about the people who lived in those houses?

• Pass out the Cardboards and ask students to view, through the Expeditions app, these two Expeditions:

• Mattox Family Home at the Henry Ford Museum

• Living in a Georgian House

Structured Practice and Application (30 minutes):

• As students explore these two different houses, have them describe to their partner what they see. One person should type on the laptop while the other one describes what they see in the Cardboard. Then, switch places and add to the typed narrative.

• After students have typed descriptions about the virtual reality scenes, combine partners into small groups.

• In groups, ask them to share their descriptions and discuss which house might have belonged to Mayella Ewell and which house might have belonged to the Finch family.

• Ask students to draw conclusions about how the characters' identity and social status may have affected their actions.

Closing (5 minutes):
- Have students return to their original seat and review their drawings of the homes of the Ewell and the Finch family.
- How did the VR change or enhance their understanding of the characters?

Assessments:
- The typewritten narratives from each pair of students can be collected as an assessment.

Maya's Reflection

On the day of the VR lesson, we were amazed at the magic of the moment as we watched the pairs work together. As students virtually explored various places of the Great Depression using the Google Expeditions app, they narrated the experience for their partners to capture by typing notes. Then, the students switched roles. What we saw and heard was passion and excitement for photos of breadlines, the Dust Bowl, and Hoovervilles. Simply looking at photos would not have yielded this level of excitement—the students literally sounded like they were narrating a play-by-play commentary of a major sporting event.

To connect this experience to the novel, I thought of writing a narrative-constructed response that would mirror the one on our state writing exam in a fun way. We did that by creating a prompt with choices. These were: "1) Choose one of the settings from your VR experience, and 2) rewrite a scene from the novel changing it to the setting from your VR experience." The students continued to work with their partners and collaboratively responded to the narrative prompt.

On a standardized test in our state, the students' narrative writing involves working with texts they are given. By working with an excerpt from TKAM alongside the VR experience, the students were able to practice a necessary skill but in a more engaging and relatable way.

At the end of the VR unit, we surveyed the 105 eighth-grade students to find out their reactions to the project. Overwhelmingly, the students indicated that they enjoyed using VR in the classroom and that its immersive qualities improved their writing. They reported that seeing 360-degree scenes from the Great Depression and a Depression-era home helped clarify the setting of the novel, and they enjoyed the collaborative writing aspects of the project.

CONCLUSIONS

Although each of the above teachers' experience with using VR in their classrooms was slightly different, they all reported that students were enthusiastic and excited by the experiential qualities that the technology afforded. As Sara's student quipped, "Finally, using our phones is interesting/

helpful." With schools beginning to reopen after the COVID-19 pandemic of 2020–2021, it will become increasingly important that students who have become accustomed to using the Internet for instruction have new avenues to explore when they return. The previous novelty of asking students to access content on the Internet will have become passe. Instead, teachers may find that using VR as an accompaniment to reading/writing lessons will energize their instruction.

As these plans demonstrate, the affordances of the immersive environment offered by VR far outweigh any constraints or concerns. Introducing VR into the classroom is as simple as providing students with a device (or having them buy their own) and then pairing it with an existing writing or reading assignment. To echo the words of Christensen (1997), VR is a disruptive technology, and it is destined to alter our classrooms.

REFERENCES

Anderson, M., & Jiang, J. (2018). Teens, social media, and technology 2018. *Pew Research Center*. https://www.pewresearch.org/internet/2018/05/31/teens-social-media-technology-2018/

Cameron, J. (Director/Writer). (2009). *Avatar* [Motion Picture]. Twentieth Century Fox.

Carson, R. (1964). *Silent spring*. Crest Books.

Cervantes, M. (2003). *Don Quixote*. Penguin Classics.

Christensen, C. M. (1997). *The innovator's dilemma: When new technologies cause great firms to fail*. Harvard Business School Press.

Cline, E. (2011). *Ready, player one*. Ballantine.

Cooper, G., Park, H., Nasr, Z., Thong, L. P., & Johnson, R. (2019). Using virtual reality in the classroom: Preservice teachers' perceptions of its use as a teaching and learning tool, *Educational Media International, 56* (1), 1–13.

Crane, S. (2005). *The red badge of courage and other stories*. Penguin.

Dail, J. S., & Vásquez, A. (2018). Seeing the world differently: Remixing young adult literature through critical lenses. In. J. Dail, S. Witte, & S. T. Bickmore (Eds.), *Toward a more visual literacy: Shifting the paradigm with digital tools and young adult literature*. Rowman & Littlefield, 91–100.

Farjon, D., Smits, A., & Voogt, J. (2019). Technology integration of pre-service teachers explained by attitudes and beliefs, competency, access, and experience. *Computers & Education*. https://doi.org/10.1016/j.compedu.2018.11.010.

Frazier, C. (2017). *Cold mountain* (20th anniversary ed.). Grove Press.

Frontera, E. B. (2009). Teaching students to build historical buildings in virtual reality: A didactic strategy for learning history of art in secondary education. *Themes in Science Technology Education, 2*(1-2), 165–184.

Greenwald, W. (8 May 2020). The best VR headsets for 2020. *PC Magazine*. https://www.pcmag.com/picks/the-best-vr-headsets.

Guggenheim, D. (Director), & Gore, A. (Writer). (2006). *An inconvenient truth.* [DVD]. Paramount.

Hanson, K., & Shelton, B. E. (2008). Design and development of virtual reality: Analysis of challenges faced by educators. *Journal of Educational Technology & Society, 11*(1), 118–131.

Hawthorne, N. (2005). *The house of the seven gables.* Norton.

Heaney, D. (29 July, 2020). Oculus Quest 2? Everything we need to know about Facebook's next VR headset. *Upload.* Retrieved from https://uploadvr.com/oculus -quest-2-everything-we-know/

Kirby, D. L., & Crovitz, D. (2013). *Inside out: Strategies for teaching writing.* Heinemann.

Krakauer, J. (1996). *Into the wild.* Villard.

Krakauer, J. (1999). *Into thin air.* Anchor.

Kress, G. (2003). *Literacy in the new media age.* Routledge.

Lee, H. (2002) *To kill a mockingbird.* Harper Perennial.

Miller, A. (2003). *The crucible.* Penguin Classics.

Mitchell, M. (2011). *Gone with the wind.* Scribner.

Moran, C. M., & Woodall, M. (2019). 'It was like I was there': Inspiring engagement through virtual reality. *English Journal, 109*(1), 90–96.

National Council for the Teachers of English. (2018). *Beliefs for integrating technology into the English language arts classroom.* https://ncte.org/statement/beliefs-technology-preparation-english-teachers/

Nolan, C. (Director/Writer). (2010). *Inception* [Motion Picture]. Warner Brothers.

Pilgrim, J. M., & Pilgrim, J. (2016). The use of virtual reality tools in the reading-language arts classroom. *Texas Journal of Literacy Education, 4*(2), 90–97.

Robinson, K. (2017). *Out of our minds: The power of being creative* (3rd ed.). Wiley & Sons.

Spielberg, S. (Director), Penn, Z., & Cline. E. (Writers). (2018). *Ready player one.* [Motion picture]. Warner Brothers.

Steinbeck, J. (1993). *Of mice and men.* Penguin.

Steinbeck, J. (2006). *The grapes of wrath.* Penguin.

Stowe, H. B. (2020). *Uncle Tom's cabin.* Dover Thrift Editions.

Tan, S. (2007). *The arrival.* Arthur A. Levine Books.

Twain, M. (1994). *The adventures of Huckleberry Finn.* Dover.

APPENDIX C

FREE RESOURCES TO USE VIRTUAL REALITY DEVICES

Sources for Cardboard Virtual Reality Devices

1) Amazon: https://amzn.to/2XdqWAK
2) Google: https://bit.ly/3gk5PEp

VR Apps for Smartphones

- Google Expeditions
  - List of available Google Expeditions: https://docs.google.com/spread sheets/d/1uwWvAzAiQDueKXkxvqF6rS84oae2AU7eD8bhxzJ9SdY/edit#gid=0
- DiscoveryVR
- Google Arts and Culture
- Inception VR

Lesson Plans

Google Expedition Lesson Plans from TES:
   https://www.tes.com/resources/search/?q=%23Googleexpeditions
   Discovery Now Lesson Plans:
   http://www.discoveryeducation.com/DiscoveryNow/vr.cfm

ELA Connections and Text Pairings

Writing

In Google *Expeditions*

- "America Expands West: Life on the Range"—Narratives and first-person journals of life as a pioneer
- "Career Expeditions"—Informative or persuasive essays on the benefits of various careers; first-person journals imagining life in a specific career
- "Mattox Family House at the Henry Ford Museum"—Informative essay on life as a poor, Black farmer in Georgia
- "To the Moon with a Google Lunar XPR"—Informative essay on the moon; narratives on life as an astronaut
- "Galapagos Island"—Travel brochure; narratives; poetry

In *YouTube VR*

- "Pioneer Town VR" (https://youtu.be/JuaFUuO2Yz0)—Narratives, informative essays on life as a pioneer. Write a postcard from the town.
- "Machu Picchu in 350 (8K)" (https://youtu.be/lM8UR-aQveQ)—First-person narrative on life as an Inca or speculation on why the city was abandoned

Reading

In Google *Expeditions*

- "The Travels of Don Quixote"—*Don Quixote* (Cervantes, 2003)
- "Nathaniel Hawthorne and the Salem Witch Trials"—*The Crucible* (Miller, 2003), *House of the Seven Gables* (Hawthorne, 2005)
- "The Great Depression"—*To Kill a Mockingbird* (Lee, 2002), *The Grapes of Wrath* (Steinbeck, 2006), *Of Mice and Men* (Steinbeck, 1993)
- "The Setting of Shakespeare's Plays"—Any Shakespeare work
- "Slavery in America"—*The Adventures of Huckleberry Finn* (Twain, 1994), *Uncle Tom's Cabin* (Stowe, 2020), slave narratives
- "Roald Dahl": Phizz-whizzing collection

In *Discovery VR*

- "Route to Everest"—*Into Thin Air* (Krakauer, 1999)
- "A Letter from the Trenches"—*Cold Mountain* (Frazier, 2017), *The Red Badge of Courage* (Crane, 2005), *Gone with the Wind* (Mitchell, 2011)

Chapter 5

Designing Engaging Virtual Field Trips for Secondary English Language Art Students

Kelly Torres and Aubrey Statti

As she circulated her classroom, Mrs. Davis noticed that Jackson, a tenth-grade student, was flipping through the assigned *Murder on the Orient Express* (Christie, 2011) text. He also seemed to be investigating a specific passage of writing. Ms. Davis tried not to draw too much attention to Jackson's newfound interest in the historical detective novel. Even so, she slowly continued circulating throughout the classroom, drawing nearer to his desk. As she drew closer, Ms. Davis was pleased to see that he was "on board" the Orient Express through a virtual reality app on his Chromebook that allowed him to experience the sights and sounds of the train. Not wanting to disturb his interest in the virtual experience, she continued to walk around the classroom and answer other students' questions, but she noticed that Jackson's eyes seemed more focused than she had seen them all year. He actually seemed to be enjoying what he was reading as well as the research he was conducting in a virtual environment of this historic text. It appeared that Ms. Davis's attempts to engage her students with the *Murder on the Orient Express* mystery had been successful due to her creative use of virtual field trips in her English class' exploration of literacy.

INTRODUCTION

As educators in higher education, our curriculum development for teachers often centers around the needs of adult learners and the topics related to educational psychology and educational technology. However, we both have a passion for exploring the benefits of technology in various settings, which brought us to the investigation of virtual field trips in K–12 education.

131

Through our research, we discovered the possibilities of virtual field trips in areas of science, history, and now literacy. Interestingly, during our time writing this article, most schools across the country and many throughout the globe abruptly transitioned to remote learning due to the COVID-19 pandemic. Therefore, the possibilities of engaging students in literary work through virtual tools have become even more necessary and relevant in today's culture of remote crisis education. The following is our look into the exciting possibilities of virtual field trips in English Language Arts (ELA) classrooms both on the school campus and through virtual meeting spaces. This chapter will begin with an overview of the progression of educational technology in order to provide an understanding of its impact on student learning.

THE EVOLUTION OF TECHNOLOGY

Technology is continually evolving and is constantly influencing educators' instructional approaches and affecting how students learn. The influence of technology results in today's classrooms looking very different from prior decades and impacts how educators instruct students and how students acquire new information. Additionally, advancements in technology directly impact the instructional expectations placed on educators (O'Neal et al., 2017). Further, the inclusion of new technological tools assists in improving learning processes and students' academic experiences. Indeed, Hsu (2016) proclaimed that "higher-level technology use will enhance every aspect of students' learning experiences across curricular areas, so students will grow intellectually rather than merely develop isolated technology skills" (p. 30). Additionally, Niess (2016) proposed that "in this digital age, new and emerging technologies are more accessible and are potentially useful for teaching and learning (particularly when they are combined intelligently)" (p. 131). Chiefly, digital technologies infiltrate numerous activities engaged in by young individuals and, therefore, enable real and virtual lives to be lived together simultaneously (Cetinkaya, 2017).

Because learners are often connected to technology in various aspects of their daily lives, the pervasiveness of technology has been found to affect how students learn and communicate (Hur et al., 2016). With the expansion of educational technology, educators at all levels of education across all content areas are employing technological tools to promote student learning and enhance student motivation and engagement. For example, the addition of technology into ELA classrooms has been found to be essential in assisting students' development of reading and writing abilities (Garcia et al., 2018; Kirkpatrick et al., 2018; Wang et al., 2015), their interactions with texts

(Boche & Henning, 2015; Colwell & Hutchison, 2015) and in providing inclusion and equity (Kirkpatrick et al., 2018).

OPPORTUNITIES FOR INNOVATION
THROUGH EDUCATIONAL TECHNOLOGY

Price and Cleary (2016) argued that historically the implementation, maintenance, and management of educational technology was difficult within K–12 classrooms. However, advances in technology have resulted in classrooms moving away from single overhead projectors and shared televisions to innovative tools and platforms that provide educators the opportunity to motivate their students through novel and engaging approaches. The National Center for Education Statistics (2015) reported that approximately 65 percent of students had access to the Internet in their schools. The percentage of schools implementing high-speed Internet has continually increased to 88 percent in 2018 (National Science Foundation, 2018). School districts have enthusiastically modified their curriculum to be inclusive of technology and impact the way that instruction is delivered (NEA, 2019). Zhao (2012) shared that digital tools provide a multitude of opportunities that allow individuals to create and share through new creative ways. The inclusion of educational technology has impacted the way in which students learn and educators instruct and design their classes. In fact, Selwyn (2016) described technology as being an essential aspect of education. However, simply including technology into the curriculum does not enhance academic outcomes and needs to be carefully integrated to ensure that it supports learning.

The inclusion of new technological tools has resulted in "redefining the roles of both students and teachers throughout the learning process and are having a dramatic impact on the field of education" (Pollock & Al-Bataineh, 2018, p. 17). The inclusion of educational technology is often dependent on the perceived importance of technological tools, goal clarity, leadership support, and informal and formal exchanges among educators (Petko et al., 2018). National initiatives in the United States (e.g., Common Core Curriculum Standards) have resulted in educators depending more on educational technology for assessment, teaching, and learning processes (Pollock & Al-Bataineh, 2018). The inclusion of technological tools can be valuable in helping students engage in *deep learning* experiences (thinking more critically and sophistically about course concepts) and in their development of creativity skills (Henriksen, 2018). Further, Chew et al. (2018) shared that the advancements in technology have resulted in new applications of its use in educational environments to address the evolving academic standards placed on students. Beschorner and Woodward (2019) expressed that literacy teachers may be underprepared to integrate technology into their curriculum in meaningful ways. However, school leaders and educators can engage in professional development opportunities and provide opportunities for exploring technology to better understand the benefits associated with the inclusion of technology in classroom settings. Researchers have discovered that educators are interested in receiving more professional development opportunities related to technology integration in their classes (Mead et al., 2019; Tondeur et al., 2016). These training opportunities can be particularly vital for content areas where technology can help to bring content "to life" (e.g., exploration of literacy texts).

ENGLISH LANGUAGE ARTS
SECONDARY EDUCATION

ELA curriculum is geared toward providing learners the skill sets and expertise needed to progress and meet academic standards and develop fluency and comprehension in reading. Further, ELA is designed to enhance students' literacy skills and their comprehension of English through reading, writing, and speaking tasks. Specifically, in ELA classes, students develop reading, writing, and speaking skills that carry over to other content areas of study. Students engage in ELA curriculum through dynamic texts and meaningful digital experiences. The effectiveness of ELA curriculum is crucial to a student's overall academic success. For example, Sun (2017) postulated that "critical thinking and reading are absolutely essential skills for young people to acquire in order to equip them for today's increasingly complex world" (p. 22). Swanson et al. (2015) suggested that students may experience challenges in being able to proficiently read and understand a variety of texts and how to discern differences in vocabulary and text structures that are found in different content areas of study. However, reading comprehension is described as a key competence in information society and high demands are placed in secondary education for learners to engage with challenging and diverse literary works (Magnusson et al., 2018). Providing students meaningful learning experiences in literacy skill development is vital since Swanson et al. (2015) conveyed that within a school day, secondary students often engage in texts that include varying structures and purposes in four to five diverse subject areas.

Researchers have described digital technology as directly impacting the interactions that readers and writers have with texts (Coiro et al., 2008; Lankshear & Knobel, 2007). Colwell and Hutchison (2015) shared that digital technology in ELA curriculum provides students many benefits including increased opportunities to interact and collaborate with their peers, develop multiple perspectives, and think about content in new ways. With the advent of new technologies, educators can ensure that their students are able to apply ELA curricula and receive a wealth of experiences that guide their acquisition of multiliterate approaches. By incorporating a multiliterate approach, students are exposed to a more inclusive learning environment that encompasses linguistic, cultural, and technological diversity. Students are able to engage with a wide array of literacy methods (e.g., multimodal, linguistic, visual) in their acquisition of course content. Particularly, the inclusion of digital technology is considered to be useful for language arts instruction due to the range of digital literacies that are introduced through technological tools (Hutchinson & Colwell, 2016).

BENEFITS OF TECHNOLOGY ENHANCED CURRICULUM

Technology in classroom settings is considered to be a vital aspect of the teaching and learning process (Halim & Hashim, 2019). Essentially, the implementation of educational technology supports teachers' instructional approaches and aids in student learning. In fact, the inclusion of educational technology has been widely perceived as being one of the most effective ways to educate learners (Obiakor et al., 2018). Researchers have also found that there are numerous benefits associated with integrating technology into the classroom (Carver, 2016; Kimmons & Hall, 2018; Lowe et al., 2013; Zhuang & Xiao, 2018). For example, the inclusion of educational technology has been found to improve educational outcomes (Assefa, 2016; Luschei, 20140), enhance student engagement (Carver, 2016; Pechenkina & Aeschliman, 2017; Perrotta, 2012), and increase students' levels of motivation (Ahmadi, 2018; Calvo-Ferrer, 2015). Ahmed and Mesonovich (2019) proclaimed that "improving student performance, enhancing student learning, and getting students to be active in the learning process continue to be leading priorities in education" (p. 582). Further, Selwyn (2016) exclaimed that "digital technologies are simply part of the way that we now 'do' education, as well as how education is 'done' to us" (p. 2). Technology integration can be valuable in allowing teachers to adapt and enhance classroom activities and student learning and in providing learners higher levels of autonomy in their learning experiences (Ahmadi, 2018).

When teachers properly integrate technology into their curriculum, it can guide students' knowledge acquisition resulting in deeper understanding of course concepts. Particularly, a student's ability to gain an understanding of academic skills can increase with the use of technology (Ahmed & Mesonovich, 2019). Robb (2018) conveyed that the inclusion of educational technology is also beneficial in making learning more concrete, reducing cognitive load, promoting self-confidence, increasing growth mindset, and strengthening academic skills. Moreover, the integration of technology can assist students in their development of writing skills (e.g., brainstorming, spelling) and engagement in class lessons (Halim & Hashim, 2019). Technology in education provides teachers the opportunity to experiment with novel instructional approaches and pedagogy and make their classrooms more accessible. Additionally, technology-enhanced activities can also help prepare students for the real world in which they participate in activities that provide them experiences that allow them to explore new information, create innovative materials, and travel to exciting places.

STUDENT LEARNING THROUGH VIRTUAL FIELD TRIPS

Day (2012) shared that field trips provide a vital connection between teaching and learning. Field trips can also facilitate learning since students receive experiences in which topics and concepts taught in class can be brought to life (Friess et al., 2016). Particularly, field trips have been used to supplement lessons and enrich students' learning experiences. Kenna and Potter (2018) proclaimed that field trips help to catalyze experiential learning for students across content areas, age range, and academic abilities. Experiential learning experiences provide students the opportunity to participate in authentic learning experiences that enhance academic gains and result in lasting learning outcomes (Kenna & Potter, 2018). However, schools may be unable to coordinate field trips due to the distance of the location, lack of time, cost, or availability of other resources that are needed (Sriarunrasmee et al., 2015). Further, field trips are being limited due to increased pressures focused on standardized testing and safety and liability issues (Kenna & Potter, 2018). Nevertheless, Carver (2016) expressed that most schools have access to high-speed Internet and digital equipment (whiteboards, video projects, iPads, etc.). Although traditional field trips provide students opportunities to engage in memorable learning experiences, the advent of new technologies afford teachers the option to explore places beyond their classrooms and local communities and see and meet people they might not otherwise be able to experience (e.g., international landmarks, interactions with students across the globe). Specifically, technology has provided an alternative solution to the limitations that schools may encounter when trying to schedule physical field trips.

Virtual experiences can also be provided to students at any time in the lesson and allow for equal participation of all students. As a result, schools can offer virtual field trips in order to provide all students enriching learning activities. A virtual field trip is described as providing students' access to diverse features that they may observe during an in-person field trip, offering a sense of what it *feels* like to visit the location, and engaging learners through active learning experiences (Mead et al., 2019). Using technological tools such as multimedia, audio, videos, and video conferencing platforms, teachers are able to provide students heightened educational experiences. Virtual field trips can be created asynchronously via images, text audio, and video or through synchronous formats in which interactions occur in real time with individuals such as experts, teachers, or students located throughout the world. For example, YouTube created a channel that is dedicated to 360-degree panoramic videos that provides users enhanced experiences. These videos can be integrated into virtual field trip lessons to provide students immersive educational experiences. For instance, students are able to *ride* a rickshaw in Japan and *visit* a zoo in Australia. Other examples include providing students the opportunity to explore the ocean to visit shipwreck artifacts or travel to space to view the solar system. Asynchronous virtual field trips are typically found to be most common in educational settings (Kenna & Potter, 2018). Virtual field trips have been found to be beneficial for all areas of education due to the numerous benefits that they offer students and educators.

BENEFITS OF VIRTUAL FIELD TRIPS

By participating in engaging virtual field trip experiences, students can make vital connections to concepts, people, and places that they are studying. The use of virtual activities provides learners the opportunity to engage with environments and motivates them to learn about a particular topic (Pilgrim & Pilgrim, 2016). Students are also afforded the opportunity to explore past eras and to further discover topics of their interest. Essentially, virtual field trips provide students the opportunity to *leave the classroom* without physically leaving their schools. Additionally, students are able to explore new and unique destinations that they otherwise would be unable to visit (e.g., White House, Louvre, Egyptian Pyramids, Mount Rushmore, and Empire State Building).

Due to the extensive range of educational virtual reality applications, Han (2020) proposed that the use of virtual reality is expanding the possibility of educators being able to adopt this technology at all educational levels. The inclusion of virtual experiences can also provide students the opportunity to think critically and logically about course concepts and compare them to real-world conditions (Cox, 2012). Basically, virtual field trips provide students similar benefits as traditional field trip experiences in which they receive access to places that are able to stimulate their interests, make content more relevant, and provide opportunities for them to practice critical skills (e.g., observation, perception) (Kenna & Potter, 2016).

Further, virtual field trips do not have to be completed in the classroom. During the COVID-19 or other similar crisis or remote education, students can complete these learning experiences in their homes through their laptops and smartphones. Students can temporarily leave the four walls of their home and travel back in time or to another country to delve into the material they have been assigned. Teachers can then create dialogue and engagement regarding the students' learning experiences and reflection of curriculum through virtual discussions using Zoom or other virtual meeting place platforms.

IMPLEMENTING VIRTUAL FIELD TRIPS

The inclusion of technology into classroom settings can be perceived by educators as a challenging task (Obiakor et al., 2018). When implementing digital technologies, Hutchison (2018) cautioned that teachers' use of technological tools need to be aligned with their instructional goals to ensure that the technology enhances instruction and extends the lesson rather than simply being used as a novel approach to engage learners. Moreover, Maughan (2020) recommended establishing a learning goal as the first step in planning a virtual field trip experience. Also, for video conferencing sessions, educators should prepare their students for these virtual experiences by requiring learners to formulate possible questions that they can ask their guest presenters (Maughan, 2020). Moreover, Reinhold et al. (2020) recommended that interactive learning environments should include the following three pillars: (1) knowledge about the educational aspects of the content, (2) implications of psychological theories focused on the instructional design of multimedia elements into learning contexts, and (3) integration of technological interactive components and effective adaptive scaffolding that is needed for the acquisition of newly introduced concepts. This approach is essential in providing students realistic and effective virtual learning experiences. For instance, Han (2020) discovered that students' virtual field trips could be interesting and valuable even though they were unable to physically interact (e.g., touch zoo animals) in their virtual experiences.

When developing virtual field trips, educators could visit the targeted field site and capture videos and photos or locate multimedia resources online. Once they secure all resources that need to be included in the virtual experience, educators will need to develop a storyboard or concept map that will present the field trip. Additionally, field trips can be completed at school or in whole group activities via technology such as Smart Boards or in small groups at the classroom computer or computer labs (Cox, 2012). Students could also collaborate with peers in other classes or in different schools to develop memorable virtual activities. For example, Cox (2012) proposed that students could also work collaboratively to view different parts of a field trip site, develop questions for further discussion, and propose independent projects that they would like to pursue. Careful consideration should be used when developing these activities to ensure that they provide students the same cognitive and affective gains that they would receive if they were able to visit the actual location.

In ELA classrooms, the use of visual aids has traditionally been used to represent concepts. Thus, visualization technology can be incorporated into virtual field trips as a tool to provide experiential learning since it provides "active construction of an environment" (Pilgrim & Pilgrim, 2016, p. 90). Similar to other types of lessons, educators need to consider how to best prepare virtual field activities and determine what instructions and materials students need in order to make the lesson meaningful and compelling. Specifically, when developing virtual field trip activities, educators should ensure that the identified destinations and topics are aligned with the course learning objectives in order to make certain that the content is reflective of established educational standards (Kenna & Potter, 2016). Educators also need to consider how to connect virtual field trip experiences to previously learned content and decide how to create activities that promote student critical thinking.

During the virtual field trip lesson, educators should include prompts to have students reflect on the most salient points of the activity and determine what aspects of the experience piqued students' interest and may prompt further exploration of the topic. Following the virtual field trip, students can be provided follow-up assignments in which they develop artifacts that represent their learning and highlight the aspects of the experience that was most intriguing to them (e.g., blogs, digital stories, photo journals, reflection essays). Although post-experience activities are an important aspect of solidifying student learning (Kenna & Potter, 2016), Marcus et al. (2012) suggested that this process is rarely provided to students following a field trip activity. Essentially, virtual field trips should not be designed as stand-alone lessons and should be structured as a larger curricular experience (Kenna & Potter, 2016).

Maughan (2020) shared that educators are often able to secure support from their schools and districts on the logistics of how to integrate virtual field trips. When designing virtual field trips, educators are able to modify an existing lesson and align it with a virtual experience or they are able to use a platform and build a lesson around it (Kenna & Potter). There are a multitude of platforms that educators are able to utilize in order to create virtual field trips. Asim et al. (2020) cautioned that choice of delivery platforms for virtual contexts is vital in promoting active learning and opportunities for interpersonal skills. Examples of virtual platforms developed by other educators and industry leaders that educators can use to create their own virtual field trip or access virtual immersive learning experiences include:

- Classflow (https://classflow.com/) is a free platform that allows for the incorporation of Google Maps, 360 videos, points of interest, images, and interactive features (e.g., ability to circle images, assessments).
- Discovery Education (https://www.discoveryeducation.com/community/virtual-field-trips/) provides free live and on-demand virtual field trips that include a companion guide and hands-on learning activities.
- Tour Creator (https://arvr.google.com/tourcreator/) offers educators the opportunity to create their own virtual tours through the inclusion of 360 videos, points of interest, and image overlays.
- Skype in the Classroom (https://education.skype.com/) includes access to a global learning community that allows educators to search for topics and request access to a wide array of field virtual trips that typically range from 30 to 60 minutes in length.
- Field Trip Zoom (https://www.fieldtripzoom.com/) allows for educators to access live streaming events that are focused on a wide range of topics including holidays and international activities.
- Thinglink (https://www.thinglink.com/) provides free accounts to educators that allow for 360 and virtual reality images and videos and the inclusion of hotspots.

LITERACY ACTIVITIES

The inclusion of virtual field trips for literary activities provide students the opportunity to experience multidimensional learning encounters. Essentially, students are able to embark on virtual experiences that provide them the opportunity to visit places and landmarks mentioned in books resulting in more relevant, meaningful, and engaging learning. These types of virtual experiences provide students the opportunity to visit places of interest that they may otherwise be unable to explore. Through these experiences, students are able to *listen*, *view*, and *walk* through sites to explore literary pieces. Particularly, the evolution of digital technologies offers educators the opportunity to implement activities that extend beyond print-based reading and writing and allow students to develop skills for reading, writing, and communicating with digital tools (Hutchinson, 2018). The use of digital videos provides learners access to content that expands their ability to make interdisciplinary connections, enhance analytical skills, increase their synthesis of knowledge, develop their writing skills, and augment their levels of technological expertise (Ayotte & Collins, 2017). For example, students are able to develop literacy skills by engaging in virtual field trips that examine topics that include digital videos of content being taught. Because of these virtual explorations, students can develop valuable background knowledge about new course concepts. Cox (2012) also recommended for educators to assemble a range of texts and trade books focused on the topic of study. Prior to the field trip session, educators are able to discuss the selected books with students and engage in reader response questions and prompts to further examine the content that will be explored in the virtual field activity.

Pilgrim and Pilgrim (2016) contended students' prior knowledge impacts their understanding of a text. Essentially, students who possess prior knowledge of a topic are typically able to more effectively complete learning tasks in which they must apply this type of knowledge (e.g., writing about snow, reading about the ocean). By providing students opportunities to gain confidence in their reading skills, they are also able to improve their reading rates (Scott & Wood, 2018). To provide students background information or interactive discussions prior to engaging with literary works, educators can schedule virtual field trips in which students explore the setting of the book and have video chats with authors. For example, Skype in the classroom provides access to virtual visits with graphic novelists (Maughan, 2020).

Prior to incorporating virtual guests, educators need to prepare their students on how to appropriately communicate in the session and how to engage in call etiquette. To prepare for the virtual session, teachers need to consider their classroom design and how students' seating arrangements may impact their interactions. Designing classrooms for virtual sessions should encompass a focus on the goal of the virtual session (e.g., students may need to all be in the camera view) and parental permissions (e.g., determining if the students' photos will be taken in the session). Educators may consider having all students sit in their desks, on the floor, or moving their seats to a central classroom location. This approach will help make certain that all students are able to participate in the virtual activity. In addition to the classroom design, educators will also need to consider the student's role in the lesson. Students may be assigned roles such as greeters, interviewers, emergency responders (help provide additional feedback and information), and closers. In preparation for the virtual guest speaker, students should also be informed of appropriate call etiquette which may encompass verbal and nonverbal feedback, empathy and compassion, when to ask questions or provide feedback and comments, and how to open and close the session.

Educators are able to schedule virtual guest speakers for literary activities since these sessions provide students the opportunity to experience multidimensional learning encounters. Essentially, students are able to embark on virtual experiences that provide them the opportunity to visit places and landmarks mentioned in books resulting in more relevant, meaningful, and engaging learning. Through these experiences, students are able to explore literary novels and gain a deeper connection to the characters' lived experiences, culture and backgrounds, and geographic locations.

ENGAGING IN READING THROUGH
VIRTUAL MUSEUMS

The influence of technology on modern-day engagement with history, as well as the COVID-19 pandemic's social distancing policies necessitating that many museums close their doors to visitors, has created a plethora of virtual field trip possibilities through virtual and digital exhibits. Influential literary works, such as *Anne Frank: The Diary of a Young Girl* (Frank, 1993), *Night* (Wiesel, 2006), *Up from Slavery* (Washington, 1995), *The Ingenious Gentleman Don Quixote of La Mancha* (DeCervantes Saavedra, 2003), *The Tragedy of Julius Caesar* (Shakespeare, 2004), *Frankenstein* (Shelley, 1994), *Pride and Prejudice* (Austen, 2002), *Jane Eyre* (Bronte, 1983), and *Little Women* (Alcott, 2014) can be explored at a deeper level through the learning experiences of a virtual fieldtrip.

Anne Frank: The Diary of a Young Girl (Frank, 1993) contains the writings of a young Anne Frank during her family's two years of hiding through the Nazi occupation of the Netherlands. Through the reprinting of her diary, Anne shares her emotions and feelings during this most atrocious time in history. She often comments about her close relationship with her father and her lack of relationship with her mother as well as her observations and impressions of the others she was in hiding with. Because of the tone and openness of her writings as well as the reflections of a history, many middle school reading lists include *Anne Frank: The Diary of a Young Girl*. Hence, there are many influential sources that teachers can use to provide an immersive learning experience for their students while reading this book.

Primarily, the Anne Frank House museum provides learners with a Secret Annex virtual reality app (https://www.annefrank.org/en/about-us/what-we -do/publications/anne-frank-house-virtual-reality/) that allows viewers to "walk" through each room of the annex that Anne Frank and seven others hid in from 1942 to 1944. In the app, the secret annex is decorated with the replica furnishings of the original hiding place, allowing students the opportunity to explore Anne's hiding place in a virtual environment and to reflect on how they might have felt living in fear and confinement for two years. Teachers can also utilize other virtual sources on the Anne Frank

Museum website (https://www.annefrank.org/en/museum/web-and-digital/), including real-life artifacts, a video diary, and a 360-degree view of Anne's family home before their hiding. Other virtual sources, such as the Arts and Culture website created by Google (https://artsandculture.google.com/exhibi t/wQi4lSIy) provide learners with virtual learning through real pictures from Anne's life and a virtual timeline of her experiences, including pictures of her family's life prior to hiding.

After students have read *Anne Frank: The Diary of a Young Girl* and explored these virtual experiences, teachers can engage learners in class discussions on heavy topics such as antisemitism, prejudice and stereotypes, and discrimination and equal rights. Teachers can also assign response journal tasks in which students record their reactions to Anne's diary and other Holocaust materials that they reviewed. Additionally, students could dramatize their reflections of visiting the Anne Frank House and their emotions associated with this historical event. The Anne Frank House website (https ://www.annefrank.org/en/topics/prejudice-and-stereotypes/) provides educators with additional sources on these significant topics, including narrative videos that allow students to hear how these attitudes and beliefs continue to impact modern society and individuals of different cultural backgrounds and religious beliefs.

Night (Wiesel, 2006). Another memoir from the Holocaust, *Night* was written by a young 12-year-old Elie Wiesel. Wiesel shares his family's horrific experiences in German-occupied concentration camps. While an extremely difficult text to process for readers of all ages, high school students are often assigned this text for further understanding of the historic atrocities of this time period as well as the severe impact of German's political actions and inhumane treatment of members of the Jewish faith, during World War II. While most students will not have the opportunity to visit Germany and Poland to view these concentration camps in person and experience the haunting feelings of these locations, students can experience the enormity of this time period through virtual field trips. The State Museum of Auschwitz-Birkenau and Remember.org present a virtual tour of Auschwitz/Birkenau (http://www.remember.org/auschwitz/), allowing students to view the real locations of these heinous acts toward humanity, including the unloading ramp, the living barracks, latrines, crematoriums, saunas, and graveyards of Jewish prisoners. Additional sources such as the Yad Vashem Holocaust Museum (https://www.yadvashem.org/museum/museum-complex.html) provide learners with a plethora of virtual museum exhibits including the ability to listen to the stories of Holocaust survivors. These visuals are horrific, upsetting, and devastating. However, they allow students to see beyond the words of the *Night* text and into the lives of the concentration prisoners. In addition to creating dialogue and discussion on this significant time in history, teachers can also encourage students to reflect on their feelings while viewing these disturbing images. Written assignments such as personal reflection or the development of a digital story can allow students to process their feelings of discomfort, confusion, fear, and empathy. Students can also be tasked to make comparisons between their own identities and Elie's identity, engage in robust discussions regarding which scenes from the story were most memorable, and create digital collages that illustrate their reactions to the story and virtual tours.

Further, it is important that educators move the curriculum beyond the devastation of the concentration camps and also explore Wiesel's life after liberation from Birkenau. Wiesel lost his parents and younger sister to this concentration camp but survived with his two older sisters. He went on to live a productive, hopeful life. A strong defender of human rights, Wiesel lived until 2016 and campaigned for the victims of oppressions throughout the globe, including areas of South Africa, Nicaragua, Kosovo, and Sudan. Secondary ELA teachers can use the life of Wiesel and the *Night* text to explore a story of despair, survival, and advocating for others.

Up from Slavery (Washington, 1995). Another difficult, yet important time in history to discuss with students is detailed in Booker T. Washington's 1901 autobiography, *Up from Slavery*. Washington details his personal experiences as a slave child during the Civil War and the obstacles and challenges he faced while obtaining his education at the Hampton Institute as well as his efforts in establishing vocational schools, such as the Tuskegee Institute in Alabama, for people of color. His writing demonstrates the power of education in an individual's life, despite what may have been a bleak background. Similar to Wiesel's *Night*, Washington's writings also demonstrate the potential to overcome a valuable topic to discuss in the modern classroom. Through the discussion of these weighted topics, teachers can enhance student learning through a virtual field trip to the Smithsonian's National Museum of African American History & Culture (https://nmaahc.si.edu/explore/collection). Teachers can utilize the profusion of archives, virtual exhibits, video resources, influential biographies and collection stories to provide students with a level of "hands-on" learning that might occur in an in-person visit to the museum. Teachers may consider developing assignments that require students to utilize these sources to create their own digital work, such as through a digital timeline or presentation. Following the virtual tour, students can also be led in a discussion about the qualities that Booker T. Washington possessed that helped him become a leader and they can provide examples of times that they have persevered.

The Ingenious Gentleman Don Quixote of La Mancha (De Cervantes Saavedra, 2003). Often referred to as simply *Don Quixote*, this text written by Miguel De Cervantes Saavedra, is often referred to as the most influential literature from the Spanish Golden Age and therefore is often included on secondary student reading lists. The novel itself is very lengthy and originally published in Early Modern Spanish in two parts. Therefore, due to length, language, and tone, some students may struggle to remain engaged with the text. However, a virtual field trip may prove beneficial in engaging learners with the *Don Quixote* text. Google Arts & Culture has created a Tour of Cervantes' Spain (https://artsandculture.google.com/story/hgUBCR7bJ6h3Ig), providing learners with the opportunities to explore the real places depicted in *Don Quixote*. This virtual field trip will allow students to take a 360-degree tour of historical places in Spain, including the birthplace of Cervantes (now a UNESCO World Heritage site), the Cerro Calderico Windmills made a popular tourist site from this text, as well as various other towns, caves, and prisons discussed in *Don Quixote*. Utilizing either a computer screen or virtual reality goggles, students can "walk" through these towns and experience a country they may actually never visit. This example of a virtual field trip allows teachers the opportunity to develop dialogue around the *Don Quixote* text and to encourage students to further develop their interest and understanding of this historical text. Teachers may desire to have their students then create a virtual map of Spain, including all of the locations covered in the *Don Quixote* text, with a description of each. Students can use various forms of technology such as PowerPoint and Adobe Spark, as well as Google Images to produce and present their virtual map of Spain. Other reflection activities for the virtual field trip include students creating short comic strips or storyboards to summarize the conflicts outlined in the text or developing minds to illustrate the major story themes.

The Tragedy of Julius Caesar (Shakespeare, 2004). Another text that may be difficult for middle and high school students to fully understand is *The Tragedy of Julius Caesar*, due to the language and tone utilized by author William Shakespeare. Teachers often use the text of *The Tragedy of Julius Caesar*, as well as other works of Shakespeare, as an opportunity for students to act out various parts of the story. In addition to a traditional class play, English teachers can also use sources provided from Shakespeare's Globe to engage students with their understanding and appreciation of *The Tragedy of Julius Caesar*. A virtual tour (https://www.shakespearesglobe.com/discover /about-us/virtual-tour/#virtual-tour) of the Globe Theatre allows students to visualize how actors and audience members would have looked, behaved, and felt during the initial performances of Shakespeare's plays. In addition to a 360-degree view of the Globe Theatre, the website also includes videos, pictures, and other displays from this time period throughout the virtual theatre. Students can see where the famous line uttered by Caesar, "Et tu, Brute" ("And you, Brutus?"), was first delivered on stage. These sources can be used to further understand the importance and significance of Shakespeare's methods of writing and entertainment during the Elizabethan era. After students explore the virtual theatre, they can share how plays and performances have evolved. Further, they could be assigned to work collaboratively to create a WebQuest of the Globe Theatre.

   Frankenstein (Shelley, 1994). Written by Mary Shelley, the *Frankenstein* text is often included on many high school literacy lists. Google Arts & Culture Inspiration Station: The Places That Inspired Great Works (https ://artsandculture.google.com/story/inspiration-station-the-places-that-insp ired-great-works/AALiD0gZ5ZdpJQ) provides virtual tours of places that inspired well-known artists, musicians, and authors. One of these well-known creatives is Mary Shelley and the place depicted is Castle Frankenstein. In addition to this website as a stop on the virtual field trip, other sources can provide additional virtual experiences for students, such as Exploring Castle's The Monster Mash: Secrets of Frankenstein Castle in Germany (https://www.exploring-castles.com/europe/germany/frankenstein_castle/). According to these sources, Mary Shelley visited the castle and found her inspiration from these ruins for her gothic novel. During her visit, Shelley learned of the history beyond the castle, which included its former resident, Konrad Dippel, an eccentric scientist who was known for hair-raising and often gruesome experiments with animals and human body parts. If teachers are allotted freedom in their curriculum planning, the reading of Frankenstein and the virtual field trip through the real-life castle would provide entertaining and engaging lessons during the fall season and specifically the holiday of Halloween. In fact, Castle Frankenstein holds a rather spooky Halloween Festival every October 31 (https://frankenstein-halloween.de) that students may enjoy exploring via YouTube videos and other websites dedicated to the "monstrous" event. Once students complete this lesson, they could be tasked with recording a video that displays a place that inspired them. Additional follow-up activities may also include creating a short graphic novel or conversing about how unconventional scientific experiments could be justified in the acquisition of new knowledge.

   Pride and Prejudice (Austen, 2002), *Jane Eyre* (Bronte, 1983), and *Little Women* (Alcott, 2014). Each of these texts are commonly found on secondary reading lists and provide students with a glimpse into various themes women faced throughout history, including oppression in society, the desire for independence and influence, a love and appreciation for education, and struggles in personal relationships. While exploring these texts in ELA class, the National Women's History Museum (https://www.womenshistory.org/ womens-history/online-exhibits) provides students and educators various virtual exhibits to explore and discuss, such as biographies of influential women, archives of written documents related to the women's movement throughout history, and lesson plans on significant events impacting the feminist movement, including the path to women's suffrage. The National Women's

History Museum provides electronic field trips, various study collections, YouTube videos, and lesson plans for educators.

Additionally, Google Arts & Culture page 8 Virtual Tours of Where Powerful Women Lived (https://artsandculture.google.com/theme/_gICo M6OjTYbKQ) allows students to explore the homes of women who have fought to overcome barriers and to change the world. Jane Austen, author of six major novels including *Pride and Prejudice* and *Emma* is featured along with Maya Angelou, Amelia Earhart, and others. Students can also view *Little Women* author Louise May Alcott's home (https://artsandcultu re.google.com/theme/cgJiHqByc9S9LA) for a 360-degree view of the town in which this impressionable text was based. Utilizing these tools, teachers can move the discussion from the text themselves to the larger themes of feminism, equal rights, and the treatment and progress of women throughout history. Classroom activities may also include discussions centered on how literary texts reflect a specific period of time and culture and how these types of texts may be perceived if they were published today. Students can also share how their exploration of these texts and virtual experiences impacted their considerations of how social class impacted the characters. Additionally, students could use a T-Chart to make comparisons of the similarities and differences that they discovered among the readings and virtual tours.

ENGAGING IN WRITING DEVELOPMENT

Virtual field trips can also benefit students' development of writing skills. For example, students are able to visit locations such as Ellis Island, the Statue of Liberty, or the White House and write essays about their explorations of these places. Google Earth VR also provides students the opportunity to preview landmarks such as the Rome Colosseum and the Hoover Dam. Through this platform, students can observe 360-degree views of these places and engage in virtual tours. Virtual field trip platforms offer students the opportunity to utilize technology to travel internationally to visit places such as Machu Picchu and to explore undersea life. Upon completion of these experiences, students can be required to complete expository writing through a descriptive essay assignment. For example, Chen et al. (2019) discovered that middle school students' exploration of a virtual world expands their levels of critical thinking, enhances motivation, and promotes knowledge transition into expository writing tasks. Further, Chen et al. (2019) explained that the inclusion of virtual experiences, such as Google Earth, provide learners opportunities to develop essential schema needed for composition.

Students can also be immersed in virtual field trips in order to develop poetry writing skills. For example, after students complete a virtual field trip, they can be instructed to write a poem about their experiences. For example, students can be directed to write an observational poem regarding what they learned in which they are able to capture their impressions of the experience through their written words. Creely (2019) proposed that poetry is declining and has had less emphasis placed on it in classrooms and in curriculum. Through virtual experiences, ELA educators are able to provide students stimulating academic lessons focused on creative and personal forms of writing. Further, the inclusion of virtual environments can help students in their ability to demonstrate greater writing complexity. For instance, Lamb et al. (2019) provided students exposure to virtual marine environments and required them to respond to specified writing prompts. They discovered that students who viewed virtual immersive experiences created enhanced argumentative and summative writing products in comparison to participants who only had access to textbook content.

Educators can also provide students other types of writing tasks immediately following virtual field trip experiences. For example, students could be tasked with writing a letter to an individual who they interacted with during the field trip. Educators are able to assign each student to interact with a global electronic pal from a classroom that they visited across the globe. Asim (2020) expressed that pen pals "have long been a vital tool in the arsenal of middle school teachers" (p. 23). With the advent of technology advancements, educators are now able to move beyond students writing letters via pencil and paper to them sending electronic communications to their peers across the world. After learning more about students in an international context via a virtual context, students have the opportunity to engage in electronic communications with their e-pal to learn more about their personal interests and academic experiences. ELA educators can then have students write personal essays about their e-pal interactions and how their own cultural backgrounds are similar and/or diverse from their peers in other countries. Through these types of international activities, students develop enhanced levels of global competencies and cross-communication skills (Kirshner et al., 2016).

Further, through virtual field trips, students can also explore the writing locations of many famous authors on Google's Arts & Culture site, Famous Authors and Where They Wrote (https://artsandculture.google.com/theme/cgJiHqByc9S9LA). Students can investigate the places where iconic authors such as Sir Arthur Conan Doyle, C. S. Lewis, Harriet Beecher Stowe, Gabriel Garcia Marquez, Louise May Alcott, Sylvia Plath, and Langston Hughes penned their most famous works. After viewing these inspiring locations, ELA teachers may consider tasking students with a writing assignment where they must pen their own work from an inspired location, whether virtually or in-person. Students can then share why they selected this specific location and how they felt inspired through their completion of the writing activity. Through these assignments, students can not only enhance their creative writing skills but also deepen their understanding of the environments that influence writing, creativity, imagination, originality, and reflective thoughts.

FOLLOW-UP ACTIVITIES

Once students complete a virtual field trip, they need to receive opportunities to reflect and further process the content at a deeper level of learning. Educators should incorporate these types of activities immediately following the virtual experience since students will still have vivid memories of their interactions and the information they learned. Also, this approach will help students to make further connections to the experience and develop long-lasting memories of the learning acquired. One assignment that students can complete is to create a poster in which they make diverse connections of the text to themselves and the world. Students can also be required to interact in a social media platform to share their experience with a wider audience. Additionally, students are able to create a presentation or write a paper of their reflections and reactions to the virtual tour or develop a report from the perspective of someone else (e.g., Anne Frank).

Educators are also able to use a diverse range of technology-enhanced virtual field trip reflection activities. For example, students can create a blog that they update throughout the year to provide a reflection of the virtual sessions that they complete during the school year. Students can also use online platforms such as Flipgrid or Padlet to further highlight and share the activities and content that they found most interesting or engaging. Additionally, students can collaborate on Google Slides to present an overview of their collective reflections. Another activity that students may find engaging is creating a reflection journal that highlights an overview of the field trip, the purpose of the experience, their favorite part of the excursion, and an explanation of why it was meaningful to them.

CONCLUSION

The inclusion of educational technologies is considered to be a vital component of twenty-first-century pedagogy (Nixon & Hateley, 2013; Saudelli & Ciampa, 2016). Indeed, Hutchinson and Colwell (2016) proclaimed that "as digital tools evolve, and are increasingly capable of complex functions, user-friendly, and ubiquitous, they provide new instructional opportunities for students to learn how to read, write, and communicate digitally" (p. 1).

Technology can be a powerful tool to enhance student academic gains and provide students' learning experiences that extend beyond their classrooms. Technology implementation is already commonplace in many content areas of study. For example, ELA students are already interacting daily with technological tools that impact their reading, writing, and inquiry practices (Garcia et al., 2018). Technology is also being incorporated into curriculum to support students' development and ability to expand upon multiliterate approaches that are needed to acquire academic content (Boche & Henning, 2015). Further, information and communication skills are perceived as important in one's development of multi-literacy (Henriksen, 2018). Ayotte and Collins (2017) proclaimed that technologies are now dominated by visuals and that it would be a disadvantage if educators did not offer students the opportunity to critically examine image-driven messages that they commonly absorb each day.

One possible way to help students acquire these necessary skills is through the use of virtual field trip activities. Given that virtual field trips have been described as being robust and simple to create (Treves et al., 2015), ELA educators are able to easily provide these experiences in their classes. Additionally, virtual field trips are effective technological tools that can be utilized to provide students interactive and engaging learning experiences that expose them to a vast array of state, regional, national, and global contexts. Hutchinson and Colwell (2016) postulated that the inclusion of digital technology should be thoughtful and meaningful in order to provide students the ability to achieve academic goals and enhance their digital literacy skills. Moreover, Zhuang and Xiao (2018) proclaimed that it is vital that educators "design course materials that contain pragmatic and enjoyable technologies to encourage active learning, which in turn leads to expected learning outcomes and positive learning experience" (p. 95). As such, students need to receive engaging and meaningful learning experience that aids their acquisition of higher levels of content knowledge. Educational transformation will result from how teachers are able to effectively implement the technology that is readily available to them (Tondeur et al., 2016). One impactful educational technology experience that students can interact with in their classes is virtually visiting places in which they are able to explore new things and interact with individuals that may otherwise have been unavailable to them. Through virtual field trips, students can acquire course concepts and partake in interactive learning experiences in which they are able to visit and interact with others across the world.

Our final thoughts on the subject are that in addition to engaging students, we also envision virtual field trips reengaging ELA educators with the texts they have taught for many years and have potentially lost their initial love for due to the workload placed on teachers. We also feel that the use of virtual field trips has the potential to engage teachers with their students at a new level as they can see the initial learning and appreciation of a literary work or a time in history through the eyes of their students. Our own research for this article was influent in introducing us to the power of literary works and their historical influence on current educational movements, including a deeper appreciation for how technology can enhance the understanding of a text written centuries ago in a different language. It is exciting to see the potential for learning in education through virtual field trips and the impact that this learning will have on future literary works penned by authors in years to come who are currently developing their love for reading and writing in a secondary ELA classroom today.

REFERENCES

Ahmadi, M. R. (2018). The use of technology in English language learning: A literature review. *International Journal of Research in English Education, 3*(2), 115–125.

Ahmed, K., & Mesonovich, M. (2019). Learning management systems and student performance. *International Journal of Sustainable Energy Development, 7*(1), 582–591.

Alcott, L. M. (2014). *Little women*. Puffin.

Asim, S., Ponners, P. J., Bartlett, C., Paker, M. A., & Star, R. (2020). Differentiating instruction: For middle school students in virtual learning environments. *Delta Kappa Gamma Bulletin, 86*(3), 19–31.

Assefa, T. (2016). Educational technology implementation in Ethiopian high schools: Benefits and challenges of the instructional plasma TV. In A. Marcus-Quinn, & T. Hourigan (Eds.), *Handbook on digital learning for K-12 schools.* Springer.

Austen, J. (2002). *Pride and prejudice*. Penguin.

Ayotte, L., & Collins, C. (2017). Using short videos to enhance reading and writing in the ELA curriculum. *English Journal, 106*(3), 19–24.

Beschorner, B. & Woodward, L. (2019). Long-term planning for technology in literacy instruction. *The Reading Teacher, 73*(3), 325–337.

Boche, B., & Henning, M. (2015). Multimodal scaffolding in the secondary English classroom curriculum. *Journal of Adolescent & Adult Literacy, 58*(7), 579–590.

Bronte, C. (1983). *Jane Eyre*. Bantam.

Calvo-Ferrer, J. R. (2015). Educational games as stand-alone learning tools and their motivational effect on L2 vocabulary acquisition and perceived learning gains. *British Journal of Educational Technology, 48*(2), 264–278.

Carver, L. B. (2016). Teacher perception of barriers and benefits of K-12 technology usage. *The Turkish Online Journal of Educational Technology, 15*(1), 110–116.

Cetinkaya, A. (2017). An educational technology tool that developed in the natural flow of life among students. *International Journal of Progressive Education, 13*(2), 29–47.

Chen, Y., Smith, T. J., York, C. S., & Hayley, M. J. (2019). Google earth virtual reality and expository writing for young English learners from a funds of knowledge perspective. *Computer Assisted Language Learning, 33*(1), 1–25.

Chew, S. W., Cheng, I., Kinshuk, C. & Chen, N. S. (2018). Exploring challenges faced by different stakeholders while implementing educational technology in classrooms through expert interviews. *Journal of Computers in Education, 5,* 175–197.

Christie, A. (2011). *Murder on the Orient Express.* HarperPaperbacks.

Coiro, J., Knobel, M., Lankshear, C., & Leu, D. J. (2008). Central issues in new literacies and new literacies research. In J. Coiro, M. Knobel, C. Lankshear, & D. J. Leu (Eds.), *The handbook of research in new literacies* (pp. 1–21). Lawrence Erlbaum Associates.

Colwell, J. & Hutchison, M. (2015). Supporting teachers in integration digital technology into language arts instruction to promote literacy. *Journal of Digital Learning in Teacher Education, 31*(2), 56–63.

Day, T. (2012). Undergraduate teaching and learning in physical geography. *Progress in Physical Geography, 36,* 305–332.

De Cervantes Saavedra, M. (2003). *The ingenious gentleman Don Quixote de la Mancha.* Penguin.

Frank, A. (1993). *The diary of a young girl.* Bantam.

Friess, D. A., Oliver, G. J., Quak, M. S., & Lau, A. Y. (2016). Incorporating "virtual" and "real world" field trips into introductory geography modules. *Journal of Geography in Higher Education, 40*(4), 546–564.

Garcia, A., Stamatis, K., & Kelly, M. (2018). Invisible potential: The social contexts of technology in three ninth grade ELA classrooms. *Research in the Teaching of English, 52*(4), 404–426.

Halim, M., & Hashim, H. (2019). Integrating web 2.0 technology in ESL classrooms: A review of the benefits and barriers. *Journal of Counseling and Educational Technology, 2*(2), 1–8.

Han, I. (2020). Immersive virtual field trips in education: A mixed-methods study on elementary students' presence and perceived learning. *British Journal of Educational Technology, 51*(2), 420–435.

Henriksen, D., Henderson, M., Creely, E., Ceretkova, S., Černochová, M., Sendova, E., Sointu, & E., Tienken, C. (2018). Creativity and technology in education: An international perspective. *Technology, Knowledge, and Learning, 23*(3), 409–424.

Hur J. W., Shannon, D., & Wolf, S. (2016). An investigation of relationships between internal and external factors affecting technology integration in classrooms. *Journal of Digital Learning in Teacher Education, 32*(3), 105–114.

Hutchinson, A. (2018). Using virtual reality to explore science and literacy concepts. *The Reading Teacher, 72*(3), 343–353.

Hutchinson, A., & Colwell, J. (2016). Preservice teachers' use of the technology integration planning cycle to integrate iPads into literacy instruction. *Journal of Research on Technology in Education, 48*(1), 1–15.

Hsu, P. (2016). Examining current beliefs, practices, and barriers about technology integration: A case study. *TechTrends, 60,* 30–40.

Kenna, J. L., & Potter, S. (2018). Experiencing the world from inside the classroom: Using virtual field tips to enhance social studies instruction. *The Social Studies, 109*(5), 265–275.

Kimmons, R., & Hall, C., (2018). How useful are our models? Pre-service and practicing teacher evaluations of technology integration models. *TechTrends, 62*(1), 29–36.

Kirkpatrick, L., Brown, H. M., Searle, M., Smyth, R. E., Ready, E. A., & Kennedy, K. (2018). Impact of a one-to-one iPad initiative on grade 7 students' achievement in language arts, mathematics, and learning skills. *Computers in the Schools, 35*(3), 171–185.

Kirshner, J., Tzib, E., Zilpa, T., & Fry, S. (2016). From pen pals to global citizens. *Educational Leadership, 74*(4), 73–74.

Lamb, R. L., Etopio, E., Hand, B., Yoon, S. Y. (2019). Virtual reality simulation: Effects on academic performance within two domains of writing in science. *Journal of Science Education and Technology, 28,* 371–381.

Lankshear, C., & Knobel, M. (2007). *A new literacies sampler.* Peter Lang.

Lowe, B., D'Alessandro, S., Winzar, H., Laffey, D., & Collier, W. (2013). The use of Web 2.0 technologies in marketing classes: Key drivers of student acceptance. *Journal of Consumer Behavior, 12,* 412–422.

Luschei, T. F. (2014) Assessing the costs and benefits of educational technology. In J. Spector, M. Merrill, J. Elen, & M. Bishop (Eds) *Handbook of research on educational communications and technology.* Springer.

Magnusson, C. G., Roe, A., Blikstad-Balas, M. (2018). To what extent and how are reading comprehension strategies part of language arts instruction? A study of lower secondary classrooms. *Reading Research Quarterly, 54*(2), 187–212.

Marcus, A. S., Levine, T. H., & Grenier, R. S. (2012). How secondary history teachers use and think about museums: Current practices and untapped promise for promoting historical understanding. *Theory and Research in Social Education, 40*(1), 66–97.

Maughan, S. (2020a). In the field: We learned more about how educators are using Skype in the classroom. *Publishers Weekly, 267*(11), 32–33.

Maughan, S. (2020b). Virtual field trips and video conferencing: Accessible technology brings the world into the classroom. *Publishers Weekly, 267*(11), 29–30.

Mead, C., Buxner, S., Bruce, G., Talyor, W., Semken, S., & Anbar, A. (2019). Immersive, interactive virtual field trips promote science teaching. *Journal of Geoscience, 67*(2), 131–142.

Mishra, P., & Koehler, M. (2006). Technological pedagogical content knowledge: A new framework for teacher knowledge. *Teachers College Record, 108*(6), 1017–1054.

National Center for Education Statistics. (2015). *Computer and internet use.* https://nces.ed.gov/fastfacts/display.asp?id=46

National Science Foundation. (2018). *Instructional technology and digital learning.* https://nsf.gov/statistics/2018/nsb20181/report/sections/elementary-and-secondary-mathematics-and-science-education/instructional-technology-and-digital-learning

NEA (2019). Technology in schools: The ongoing challenge of access, adequacy, and equity. *NEA Policy Brief.* http://citeseerx.ist.psu.edu/viewdoc/download?doi=10.1.1.204.7430&rep=rep1&type=pdf

Niess, M. L. (2005). Preparing teachers to teach science and mathematics with technology: Developing a technology pedagogical content knowledge. *Teaching and Teacher Education, 21,* 509–523.

Niess, M. L. (2016). Transforming teachers' knowledge for teaching with technologies: An online learning trajectory instructional approach. In M. C. Herring, M. J. Koehler, & P. Mishra (Eds.), *Handbook of technological pedagogical content knowledge (TPACK) for educators* (pp. 131–142). Routledge.

Nixon, H., & Hateley, E. (2013). Books, toys and tablets: Playing and learning in the age of digital media. In K. Hall, T. Cremin, B. Comber, & L. Moll (Eds.), *The Wiley Blackwell international handbook of research on children's literacy, learning and culture* (pp. 28–41). Wiley-Blackwell.

Obiakor, L., Obi, S., & Gibson, L. (2018). Benefits of using computer-based technology for special education and multicultural education. In L. Gibson & F. Obiakor (Eds.), *Computer-based technology for special and multicultural education. Enhancing 21st century learning* (21–57). Plural Publishing.

O'Neal, L., Gibson, P., & Cotton, S. (2017). Elementary school teachers' beliefs about the role of technology in 21st century teaching and learning. *Computers in Schools, 34*(3), 192–206.

Pechenkina, E., & Aeschliman, C. (2017). What do students want? Making sense of student preferences in technology-enhanced learning. *Contemporary Educational Technology, 8*(1), 26–39.

Perrotta, C. (2012). Do school-level factors influence the educational benefits of digital technology? A critical analysis of teachers' perceptions. *British Journal of Educational Technology, 44*(2), 314–327.

Petko, D., Prasse, D., & Cantieni, A. (2018). The interplay of school readiness and teacher readiness for educational technology integration: A structural equation model. *Computers in the Schools, 35*(1), 1–18.

Pilgrim, J. M., & Pilgrim, J. (2016). The use of virtual reality tools in the reading-language arts classroom. *Texas Journal of Literacy Education, 4*(2), 90–97.

Pollock, B., & Al-Bataineh, A. (2018). Benefits of current educational technology: A comparison of student and teacher preparations in a rural Illinois school district. *The Online Journal of Distance Education and e-Learning, 6*(1), 17–32.

Price, G. L., & Cleary, P. F. (2016). The K-12 educational technology value chain: Apps for kids, tools for teachers and levers for reform. *Education and Information Technologies, 21,* 863–880.

Reinhold, F., Hoch, S., Werner, B., Richter-Gebert, J., & Reiss, K. (2020). Learning fractions with and without educational technology: What matters for high-achieving and low-achieving students? *Learning and Instruction, 65,* 1–19.

Robb, J. (2018). *Using instructional technology to support students with exceptionalities.* https://techandcurriculum.pressbooks.com/chapter/technology-and-exceptionalities/

Saudelli, M. G., & Ciampa, K. (2016). Exploring the role of TPACK and teacher self-efficacy: An ethnographic case study of three iPad language arts classes. *Technology, Pedagogy, and Education, 25*(2), 227–247.

Scott, L., & Wood, R. (2018). Not so elementary: Preservice teachers reflect on teaching urban middle school struggling readers. *Teaching literacy in urban schools* (pp. 19–32). Rowman & Littlefield.

Selwyn (2016), N. (2016). *Is technology good for education?* Polity Press.

Shakespeare, W. (2004). *Julius Caesar.* Simon & Schuster.

Shelley, M. (1994). *Frankenstein.* Dover.

Sriarunrasmee, J., Suwannatthachote, P., & Dachakupt, P. (2015) Virtual field trips with inquiry learning and critical thinking: A learning model to enhance students' science learning outcomes. *Procedia Social and Behavioral Sciences, 197,* 1721–1726.

Sun, L. (2017). Critical encounters in a middle school English language arts classroom: Using graphic novels to teach critical thinking & reading for peace education. *Multicultural Education, 25*(1), 22–28.

Swanson, E., Wanzek, J., McCulley, L. Stillman-Spisak, S., Vaughn, S., Simmons, D., Fogarty, M., & Hairrell, A. (2015). Literacy and text reading in middle and high school social studies and English language arts classrooms. *Reading & Writing Quarterly, 32*(3), 199–222.

Tondeur, J., Forkosh-Baruch, A., Prestridge, S., Albion, P. & Edirisinghe, S. (2016). Responding to challenges in teacher professional development for ICT integration in education. *Educational Technology & Society, 19*(3), 110–120.

Treves, R., Viterbo, P., & Haklay, M. (2015). Footprints in the sky: Using student track logs from a "bird's eye view" virtual field trip to enhance learning. *Journal of Geography in Higher Education, 39*(1), 97–110.

Wang, B. T., Teng, C.W., & Chen, H. T. (2015). Using an iPad to facilitate English vocabulary learning. *International Journal of Information and Education Technology, 5*(2), 100–104.

Washington, B. T. (1995). *Up from slavery.* Dover.

Zhao, Y. (2012). *World class learners: Educating creative and entrepreneurial students.* Corwin Press.

Zhuang, W. & Xiao, Q. (2018). Facilitate active learning: The role of perceived benefits of using technology. *Journal of Education for Business, 93*(3), 88–96.

Chapter 6

Experiencing Literature in Virtual Reality

Christine Oughtred, Louise Paatsch, and Anne Cloonan

There is a long and acknowledged history of the development of literature for children and young people, and a shared understanding of quality through critical debate, academic publications, and children's book awards (Hamer, Nodelman, & Reimer, 2017; Nikolajeva, 2015). The aesthetic quality of literature focuses on experience rather than artifact, as it fosters the opportunity to put ourselves in the place of another and has the potential to engender changed attitudes and values (Rosenblatt, 1976).

Appreciation for the importance of literature for young people also features prominently in curricula for English language arts (ELA) education globally. In Australia, this acknowledgement is affirmed in the national curriculum for English, which includes a literature strand described as understanding, appreciating, responding to, analyzing, and creating literary texts (ACARA, 2011). In the United States, it is noted that "the acts of responding to, interpreting and creating literary texts enable us to participate in other lives and worlds beyond our own and to reflect on who we are" (National Council for Teachers of English, 1996, p. 12). The curriculum also includes that "students should learn that virtually any type of text—essay, diary or film . . . can contain powerful literary expression" (National Council for Teachers of English, 1996, p. 13).

Interactive digital picture books, including virtual reality (VR) texts, are an emerging expression of literature which have the potential for use in an English curriculum. In relation to narratives within the Australian English curriculum specifically, "digital platforms and technologies are transforming the ways that we read, write, and experience textual contents" (Heyward, 2018, p. 3). The use of VR to enhance the experience of literature in the English curriculum offers potentially exciting opportunities for the use of this medium (Madigan, 2018; Moran & Woodall, 2019). However, there is currently no shared understanding of what constitutes quality in relation to a potential literary experience.

This chapter draws from a larger study which explores critical elements and criteria for evaluation of interactive digital picture books for children and young people aged 13 years and over. Specifically, this chapter investigates the "reading" experiences and responses to a narrative virtual reality experience. Readings of the virtual reality text *Wolves in the Walls* (Fable Studio, 2019) were undertaken by four young people aged 13 years or over. Following individual readings of the text, each participant was interviewed with a focus on the contribution of both text and reader to the literary experience through an aesthetic transaction (Rosenblatt, 1978). The discussion in this chapter will highlight the relevance of transactional theory for a narrative virtual reality experience. It also presents the influence of multimodality and the senses of seeing, hearing, touching, and moving on the participants' experience of the text, affirming the potential for an aesthetic transaction (Rosenblatt, 1986).

VIRTUAL REALITY

Virtual reality (VR) is an immersive experience in which wearable technology, typically a specially developed headset, generates sensory rich sounds and images to create a world either imaginary or seemingly real (Sobel, 2019). Immersive media such as VR, particularly for children and young people, have "the potential to affect . . . imagination, empathy or perspective taking, and experiential, embodied learning differently and more intensely than other types of media experiences" (Sobel, 2019, p. 8). Furthermore, VR has the capacity to prompt emotionally engaging experiences by creating the feeling of presence and immersion in the VR world with heightened emotional engagement linked to better cognitive outcomes (Vesisenaho et al., 2018). However, there is currently limited published research available on the learning potential and the literary experiences that young people encounter when reading VR texts.

Successful narrative VR experiences require a combination of interactivity, immersion, and narrativity as an optimal formula (Ryan, 2015). This highlights the importance of an immersive environment and engaging narrative structure that has the potential for an interpersonal relationship between the user and the character. Narrative VR experiences involve actively participating in the experience and "the perceptions of the various senses . . . fused in a global experience that enables the user to apprehend the virtual world through many facets at the same time" (Ryan, 2015, p. 208). Immersion must also be prompted by the story or rather the user's agency in the story world. The art of interactive storytelling is not simply a matter of including interactivity within a standard plot but should also offer the design and meaningfulness of a narrative.

In ELA, the use of a narrative VR experience has the potential to provide readers with opportunities to actively participate in a text and create a personal experience on which to reflect.

LOOKING AT VIRTUAL REALITY FROM A TRANSACTIONAL THEORY VIEWPOINT

Transactional theory (Rosenblatt, 1978) is based on reading from an aesthetic standpoint. It acknowledges the importance of text (and its qualities) while highlighting that reading involves a complex personal response. The elements of a literary text contribute to the aesthetic transaction but "form is something felt on the pulses first of all" (Rosenblatt, 1982, p. 20). It is the reader's lived-through personal experiences in response to the text which result in a literary work of art, and despite the differences in medium, this relationship is "paralleled in all the arts" (Rosenblatt, 1986, p. 127).

The close synergy of Rosenblatt's (1982) passionate philosophy of reading with narrative virtual reality becomes clear in the following passage which, while referring to print, could equally refer to the narrative VR experience. Rosenblatt (1982) writes:

> In aesthetic reading, we respond to the very story or poem we are evoking during the transaction with the text. In order to shape the work, we draw on our reservoir of past experience with people and the world, our past inner linkage of words and things, our past encounters with spoken or written texts. We listen to the sound of the words in the inner ear; we lend our sensations, our emotions, our sense of being alive, to the new experience which we feel corresponds to the text. We participate in the story, we identify with the characters, we share their conflicts and their feelings. (p. 270)

Rosenblatt (1998) describes aesthetic reading as a process which prompts an evocation or experience which is "burned through, lived through in the immediacy of awareness" (p. 895). It is an experience which should precede any call for reflection or response. Similarly, with multisensory immersive virtual reality, the moment the user puts on the headset they are "completely engulfed by visual and audio fields that appear to surround them" (Ross, 2020, p. 2), and the outside world falls away in a unique personal experience. Thus, aesthetic VR transactions are concerned not just with the quality of the text but with "the quality of the literary experience undergone" (Rosenblatt, 1960, p. 307).

In this chapter, we focus on the qualities that contribute to an aesthetic transaction and prompt a literary experience, in this case, through the VR text of *Wolves in the Wall*. Through the lens of transactional theory, we explore the experiences of readers 13 years and over who are engaged with literature in VR. We propose that an aesthetic transaction with a VR text is "lived through" during the reading event. It involves the bringing together of what the reader knows and feels with what the VR text offers. Something new is created from the interaction between the reader and the VR text. In addition, we build on this notion of aesthetic transaction to explore the place of sensory elements in facilitating such an experience.

SENSORY EXPERIENCES AND THE AESTHETIC TRANSACTION

According to transactional theory, text, as a series of signs, and the reader work together in a dynamic interplay to build an aesthetic transaction and craft a response. Since the advent of digital texts, a greater variety of text forms combining modes of representation other than language have been accessed by readers, requiring them to be multiliterate in linguistic, visual, audio, gestural, spatial, and multimodal meaning-making (New London Group, 2000). With the introduction of touch screens, further modalities have been required, including tactile modes as well as written language and oral language, visual, audio, gestural and spatial representations (Kalantzis, Cope, & Cloonan, 2010). Written language represents writing and reading, including on the screen; oral language represents live or recorded speech and listening; visual representation includes still and moving images; audio represents music and noises as well as hearing and listening; tactile represents touch, smell, and taste as well as bodily sensations and feelings; gestural representation includes movements, expressions of the face, and also demeanor; while spatial representation includes proximity, spacing, and interpersonal distance. Multimodal literacies have been further theorized to foreground the body and the senses in meaning-making (Mills, 2015, p. 149).

Multimodal and sensory theories have led to an expanded view of text beyond the language elements, which is particularly relevant in the context of virtual reality. "Embodied practices, including literacy, are constituted and experienced multi sensorially, including experiences of sight, sound, touch, posture, movement, smell, taste and other forms of bodily awareness" (Mills, 2015, p. 140). Motion-sensing technologies, which have long been part of the gaming industry, are now embedded in virtual reality, enhancing experience through movement and gesture. Haptics (related to touch) also offers further nuanced physical interaction, where touch pressure and manipulation of objects are part of the narrative experience, which when interwoven with high-quality visuals and audio, help to create a fully immersive experience.

VR can present a masterful and artistic storytelling experience within a new genealogy of reading using multimodal and sensory qualities to create a rich encounter with the narrative. Sensory literacies, foregrounding the body and senses in literacy research, are particularly relevant when discussing the potential for an aesthetic experience in virtual reality. Interaction through the multimodal text and the senses may enable a VR experience for students to engage and respond to "the wit, the wisdom, the beauty that imaginative literature can communicate" (Rosenblatt, 1960, p. 304). As such, it is useful, then, to consider how embodied literacy practices of seeing, hearing, touching, and moving as ways of engaging with textual elements in narrative VR experiences can prompt an aesthetic transaction. As Engberg and Bolter (2020) state, "Our physical senses as well as our imagination offer us a new representation of the world" (p. 87).

The potential of VR texts requiring sensory interactions for meaning-making through aesthetic transactions is under-researched (Mills, 2015). Given the importance of multimodal representation and sensory literacies and the potential affordances of VR in providing literary experiences for readers, this chapter sought to explore the following research question: *What qualities of a narrative virtual reality experience can prompt an aesthetic transaction?*

Case Study Research Methodology

The larger research project was designed using qualitative methods using a case study approach. The data presented in this chapter draws from the case study on VR using a subgroup of young people.

Participants

Invitations to participate in this research were distributed to all members of a voluntary writing group conducted after school hours, one day a week at a Regional Library in the western region of Victoria, Australia. Consent was sought from the organization, the guardians, and the young people to conduct interviews with the young people attending the writing group. Four young people aged 13 years and over, who attended different secondary schools in the area, agreed to participate.

The Virtual Reality Experience

The VR experience used in this study is based on the award-winning picture book *Wolves in the Walls* written by Neil Gaiman and illustrated by Dave

McKean, published in 2003. The VR experience (Fable Studio, 2019) is a single-user experience, a "story based drama" (Billington, 2019) for young people 13 years and older, which requires the use of a headset. However, the story displays on a laptop or large screen for group viewing while in use. The VR text used in the study was experienced by using an Oculus Rift headset.

The narrative introduces the reader to Lucy who hears the sounds of mysterious *Wolves in the Walls* in their home—claims that are dismissed by her parents and brother as harmless creatures who often inhabit an old house. Lucy's claims prove correct, and her resolution of the ensuing problem makes for a compelling, sophisticated, and rewarding open-ended story. The VR experience of this story is enriched by high-quality design and visual, auditory, tactile, and kinesthetic elements to create a blueprint for the senses. The construction of the physical environment, the sensitive audio of wolves scratching in the walls, the tone of Lucy's voice, and the opportunity to touch, hold, and move with meaning deeply enhance the overall experience. The multimodal nature of the experience and the sensory qualities in particular offer new avenues for an aesthetic transaction by capitalizing on the affordances of virtual reality.

The research for this study introduced the participants to chapter 1 of the story. The complete story, including chapters 1–3, is now available from the Oculus Store. In chapter 1 of the VR experience, Lucy explains the phenomena of the sounds of *Wolves in the Walls* and invites the user to collect photographic evidence so that together Lucy and the reader can convince her parents that the sounds are real.

Methods

Following submission of signed consent forms by the young people, their guardians, and the manager of the Regional Library, the four participants viewed chapter 1 of the Fable Studio VR experience *Wolves in the Walls*. After viewing chapter 1, each participant was interviewed for approximately 45 minutes. There were ten open-ended semi-structured interview questions that sought to elicit responses regarding the young people's literary experience with the VR text. For the purpose of this chapter, five of the ten questions were used in the analysis to explore the features of the VR text that led to an aesthetic transaction for these young people. Key concepts of transactional theory were identified and rephrased as questions for the young people using accessible language. Table 6.1 shows how each of these five VR-related questions aligned to aspects of the transactional theory. All responses were audio recorded and were later transcribed for further analysis.

Table 6.1 Transactional Theory Concepts and Interview Questions on the VR Experience

Theory concept for an aesthetic experience	VR-related questions for young people 13 years or over
Transactional Theory	
The transactional relationship between reader and text is parallel in all the arts	How would you describe the qualities of a good story?
The text is the author's means of directing the attention of the reader—what he/she hopes to make you "see, hear and feel" from a particular view of life.	What do you think the person who created the VR story *Wolves in the Walls* is trying to say or to show you or make you feel?
The author creates a "blueprint" for the senses through elements which contribute to the aesthetic transaction.	How did you think the art or illustrations, sounds, and interactivity affected the story in *Wolves in the Walls*?
The capacity of the work to activate past experience and emotion is critical.	Did you understand why Lucy in *Wolves in the Walls* behaved in the way she did? Did you understand how she felt? Did you want to try and get her to do anything else?
The transaction between reader and text creates a lived through personal experience	How did you feel part of the story in the VR experience *Wolves in the Walls*?

DATA ANALYSIS

Qualitative thematic analysis (Wilkinson, 2011) was used to analyze the data, which enabled exploration and interpretation of young people's aesthetic transactions through what they said in response to the five VR-related questions. The process involved generating initial codes from the responses of young people in relation to sensory elements activated throughout their experiences with the VR text that triggered aesthetic transactions in this group. Themes were then identified among these codes that were reviewed until all researchers agreed. The process of identifying codes and themes was an inductive process where the unit of meaning, whether a word, sentence, or phrase, was included (Herrington & Oliver, 2006).

Analysis of the young people's responses showed that three main themes emerged from the data: (1) presence; (2) connection to character; and (3) user agency. In each case, these themes described part of the reader/VR text synthesis prompting a new experience and as such, have been identified in this chapter as characteristics of an aesthetic transaction using narrative VR. These characteristics of an aesthetic transaction were enabled through the readers' senses. Participant data pertaining to each of these themes were organized according to sensory engagement (sight, hearing, touch, movement) with VR representations in the form of oral and written language, visual, audio, tactile, and gestural modes of meaning.

Findings and Discussion

The VR narrative experience of *Wolves in the Walls* generated enthusiastic reactions from the young people in this study. Young people's specific responses are presented below according to three characteristics of an aesthetic transaction: presence, connection to character, and user agency. The sensory and multisensory qualities of sight, sound, touch, and movement as well as written and oral language allowed the user to enter a dynamic relationship with these characteristics of the text, prompting the potential for an aesthetic transaction.

Presence

> *"Part of the interest of reading any literary work is the sense of participating in another world"* (Rosenblatt, 1969, p. 36).

Drawing on the representational elements suggested by Kalantzis, Cope, and Cloonan (2010) of written and oral language, visual, audio, tactile, and gestural modes of meaning, we discuss participants' interactions with Lucy and responses in the virtual attic in chapter 1 of *Wolves in the Walls* (See figure 6.1, Lucy's detective desk in the attic and figure 6.2, Lucy looking at photo evidence of wolves' paw prints).

The still shots represented in figures 1 and 2 are indicative representations of the three dimensional (3D) multimodal representations (Kalantzis et al., 2010) which readers experience. These are in the form of the visual mode, for example, moving animations of Lucy including her direct gaze, her handing the reader a Polaroid camera and darkening the set by turning off the light, examining the photos for wolf paw prints, and other evidence. The written mode is evident when Lucy's crayon is offered to the reader to enter their name in the story credits. The oral language mode includes Lucy reading from her Nana's journal. This overlaps with the audio mode which is exemplified by Lucy retelling stories from her Nana who said that when she was a little girl in Russia the wolves would come out on nights of the full moon. It also includes wolf scratching noises, a lyrical musical score, vocal humming, and creaking sounds from the old room. The tactile mode is engaged with through the readers' manipulation of touch controllers to hold a camera passed by Lucy, to take instant Polaroid photos, retract photos from the camera and pass to Lucy, and take a magnifying glass from her to examine the photo for evidence. The gestural mode is evident through the readers' ability to move around the attic, look under furniture and pick up fallen photos.

All four young people's responses to their readings of chapter 1 *Wolves in the Walls* showed that a strong sensory experience and emotional reaction were stimulated through engagement with the representational modes of the

Figure 6.1   Lucy's Detective Desk in the Attic. Reproduced with Permission from Fable Studio 2020.

Figure 6.2   Lucy Looking at Photo Evidence of Wolves' Paw Prints. Reproduced with Permission from Fable Studio 2020.

VR experience. One young person, when referring to the atmosphere of the experience, stated that:

> That kind of thing it's slightly spooky. If I had just read that from his picture book, yeah, I think I would have thought oh there's something going on. But to be actually in the room level, when the lights turned off and you could actually see all the marks [left by the wolves]. I was like geez . . . So, yeah, . . . (it can) enhance emotions towards the situation kind of thing. (Annie, 14)

Another young person reported that the VR experience enhanced the perception of the environment. The visual representation of the attic, capacity to move through the attic, and being surrounded by ambient sounds transitioned the reader into the narrative, with one young person noting that:

> Just that like eerie feeling was with the surroundings as well and that was awesome . . . I'm in an entire house and then the hallway extends and it's like OK. No wait. That was a bed that extends and that's just more eeriness. So, I found it really good in terms of environment. (Jodie, 15)

The four young people's responses also highlighted that the sense of touch was strongly aligned to a feeling of presence. One response that was typical of the group commented:

> Just the fact that this whole world disappears around you. You've immersed yourself into this whole other kind of fantasy or this fictional world yet where you can even pick things up and touch things. It's almost like you're actually there. (Hannah, 14)

The young people engaged with the multimodal representation as multisensory experiences. They also recognized that hearing the subtle scratching of the unseen wolves tied to the mysterious ambience of the attic environment ensured the audio mode (Kalantzis et al., 2010) was experienced through the sense of hearing and was a facilitator of immersive presence. As one young person noted:

> Sound is definitely very immersive, with wolves in the walls I could hear the noises and I was like, OK there are noises. I understand why you're worried about them. They do not sound nice. (Jodie, 15)

The final mode that was identified by the young people in relation to feeling a presence in another world was gestural (Mills, 2015), experienced through the sense of movement. Lucy skillfully leads the reader through the story, guiding movement and encouraging the sense of touch. Young people noted that they experienced moving in the environment physically through leaning, turning, moving their heads, taking steps, and passing things to and receiving things from Lucy as they interacted with the multimodal text. One young person commented:

> The fact you can move around the scene was really freaky like I was in the room and I would bump into the wall. It was great. I bent down to see underneath the table. It was more about exploring so you could actually be in there and look up and look down. She kept you engaged by giving you things. (Riley, 13)

The senses of sight, sound, touch, and movement in interplay with the modes of meaning ensured a visceral sense of presence. As Mills says, "[t]he body is central to the practical enactment of the interaction" (2015, p. 139), a view particularly relevant to this narrative VR experience.

All four young people recognized the social presence, interacting with another, enhancing the sense of their own and Lucy's existence through their experience with the VR text. Underscoring that visual representations were experienced through the sense of sight, including the compelling nature of "gaze" (Mills, 2015), appeared to draw the young people into a strong sense of presence. Hannah noted that:

> You felt like you were actually there with the girl because every time you moved like a certain place in the room with every part of the story she always made eye contact with you and you feel like you are a part of it. (Hannah, 14)

The above examples of young people sensorially experiencing "presence" through interaction in a VR experience demonstrate the "shuttling back and forth" interplay between user and the multimodal text in an affective aesthetic transaction (Rosenblatt, 2005a). In one way, this could be seen as almost inevitable the moment the reader puts on a VR headset, however, the immersive and transporting sense of presence, "physically being in another location, forgetting about the immersive technology involved and accepting the virtual environment as a true environment" (Decock, Looy, Bleumers, & Bekaert, 2014, p. 451), ensures it is a defining feature for participating in an aesthetic transaction. Interleaved with *presence* is a connection to character which is the next key theme evident in the experience of aesthetic transaction.

Connection to Character

> *We can encounter "personalities who become more alive to us than our next door neighbor"* (Rosenblatt, 1998, p. 895).

The second main theme that emerged from young people's responses related to the affordance of the VR text is the ability of the reader to connect to character. Young peoples' responses showed a connection to the main character, Lucy, through sensory engagement with representations in the form of oral language, visual, audio, tactile and gestural modes of meaning (see figure 6.3 Lucy holding a pig puppet with gaze directed at reader).

Responses by the young people that evidence connection to a visual representation of character included:

> I feel like the main way to have a good experience is to have a connection with the main character. So, I felt again, most connection with Lucy. Yeah, because you could like see her. You could understand her like we've all been in that situation kind of thing . . . Not as extreme as that but in a similarish kind of thing. (Annie, 14)

> "I think she was pretty lonely and I kind of understood where she was going." (Riley, 13)

The "resizing" of the reader during the experience that enabled the reader to look directly into Lucy's eyes also proved compelling. This finding was supported by comments such as:

> I was looking up at her face and she was looking at me with her eyes . . . I could see her expression and I could see her concentrating on things and looking around the room . . . and reacting to them like an actual person would. You can

Figure 6.3   Lucy Holding Pig Puppet with Gaze Directed at Reader. Reproduced with Permission from Fable Studio 2020.

see what she's seeing and what she's seeing is different from what everyone else is seeing and you're trying to convince her parents that it's actually happening 'cause no one believes her. (Riley, 13)

It was also evident from the young people's responses that they engaged with Lucy's oral language through listening to her words and talking with her and hearing her personal statements such as "I'm glad you're here." One response was:

> You actually got to engage with the characters in a way that you could understand them and the way they talk to you about their interests and how they were telling their story to you specifically rather than it just being something happening in the background of a normal book. Not discussing it with another character, actually talking with you and telling you everything. (Hannah, 14)

Hearing the embodied sense of sound represented through a particular tone of voice also allowed for a further connection to character:

> In a book it's so hard to imagine like if the author said that the character's voice was gravelly or childlike or something you have to try and figure something out based on your own experiences but then you could actually figure out what this little girl is like because you can hear her voice. (Hannah, 14)

Responses showed that touch also contributed to an emotional connection to character. For example, figure 6.4 shows Lucy handing the reader a Polaroid camera.

Figure 6.4   Lucy Handing Reader a Polaroid Camera. Reproduced with Permission from Fable Studio 2020.

Such an embodied experience through a combination of gestural and tactile modes forms a deep and personal connection to character. As one young person commented:

> I feel better if I touch things because if I'm just reading it then I'm not that immersed. It's just like OK they're pretty, move on. But like that one (VR) was good I got to touch things. The camera function was awesome. Suddenly Lucy is my small child and I love her already. I want more of it. (Jodie, 15)

These findings suggest that we are now meeting the challenge noted five years ago that "the greatest hurdle to overcome (of interactive narrative) is the creation of a kind of relation between the user's character and the synthetic agents that allows the user not only to interact verbally with these agents but also to influence their destiny and to feel personally concerned for both her character and for others" (Ryan, 2015, p. 250). This is further supported by the following young person's response:

> It's trying to make you see what the character is seeing and feeling and all of their senses and it helps you to understand a lot more what they're going through when you can see it right in front of you. You actually hear what they're saying. The fact that no one believes her because that's the thing with kids. Adults are more likely to believe another adult than a child's story. (Hannah, 14)

The young people's responses showing their connection to character highlight that "people who identify with their characters will get more involved in a presence situation . . . (which) will lead to a more powerful experience and emotional response" (Basil as cited in Decock et al., 2014, p. 453). Such responses showed that this connection to character through a range of representational modes including direct exchange of gaze and gestural and tactile opportunities, that were experienced through the senses, contributed to an aesthetic transaction in the narrative VR experience.

In addition to the characteristics of *presence* and *connection to character*, the final key theme in the experience of aesthetic transactions is *user agency*.

User Agency

> *"The reader is in a sense both spectator and participant"* (Rosenblatt, 2005b, p. 57).

The third main theme that was evident in the data related to the affordance of the VR text was the ability of the reader to employ user agency. Young people's responses showed that they were empowered to contribute to the

Figure 6.5 Lucy Drawing Reader's Hands. Reproduced with Permission from Fable Studio 2020.

development of the narrative through sensorial participation with representations in the form of oral language, visual, audio, tactile, and gestural modes of meaning. For example, after developing a relationship with the user, drawing a map of the house and explaining the problem on site in the attic, Lucy "draws hands" for the user (see figure. 6.5: Lucy drawing the reader's hands) and hands over a camera to take Polaroid photos of the room and collect evidence of the elusive wolves who "come out at night."

Collecting the photos and finding the evidence of wolf prints, for example, is an empowering moment of agency and connection with Lucy. Perfectly aligned with the narrative structure and meaning is the balancing of a finely crafted artistic portrayal of child agency within an interactive and immersive mystery/fantasy story, moving it forward as they go tell Mom.

Confirming "the concept of embodiment and literacy practice is one that allows for the human agency of the text user, and is active rather than passive" (Mills, 2015, p. 148). The four young people employed senses of sight, sound, touch, and movement as they walked through the experience with purpose and agency. As one young person noted:

> With Lucy it's just like OK I'm going on, I felt like a main character . . . Let's go, we've got wolves in the walls. Let's deal with them . . . that was very very immersive and entertaining to do. Just the ability to take those [photos] and hold the photo and look at them. (Jodie, 15)

The sense of a shared discussion and working with Lucy on the problem of the mystery sounds in the walls also fostered user agency. As one young person reflected after she negotiated with Lucy to find evidence of wolves through taking photos:

> She's trying to at least prove to someone . . . she's desperate for that understanding which is why she's talking to you. You could talk to her and try to help her convince her parents. (Riley, 13)

This notion of the evolution of the storyworld was reflected in the interest and expectation for user agency from the four young people. As one young person commented:

> I felt like people like me who enjoy that sort of thing like mystery and books come to life that would be definitely interesting. If there was a choose your own adventure aspect that would be really cool. I would definitely enjoy it if it were implemented. (Annie, 14)

This response from Annie also supports the view that "systems must be authored, and users should respond to affordances built into the virtual world and programmed into the system, rather than being entirely responsible for constructing the story" (Ryan, 2015, p. 183). As Ryan (2015) reports, "the immersion must come from the story, or more precisely, from the user's agency in the storyworld" (p. 257).

With the affordances and design of narrative VR experiences, participation and user agency has been reimagined. Along with presence and connection to character, user agency contributes to the aesthetic transaction as part of the whole experience allowing the reader to fully inhabit the story and build the narrative in partnership with the characters.

CLASSROOM OPPORTUNITIES FOR INCORPORATING THE VR EXPERIENCE

"Curriculums and classroom methods should be evaluated in terms of whether they foster or impede an initial aesthetic transaction, and on whether they help students to savor, deepen the lived through experience to recapture and reflect on it, to organize their sense of it" (Rosenblatt, 1986, p. 126).

Globally, ELA curriculum calls for examination and response to literary texts. In the Australian curriculum for English, students are called to "interpret, appreciate, evaluate and create literary texts such as short stories, novels, poetry, prose, plays, film and multimodal texts, in spoken, print and digital/online forms" (ACARA, 2011). Similarly, the Common Core State Standards (CCSS) in the United States recommends standards for ELA, including reading standards that call for "integration of knowledge and ideas" (CCSS, 2010). For example, in the reading standards for literature Grade 7, the "integration of knowledge or ideas" section suggests that students should "compare and contrast a written story, drama, or poem to its audio, filmed, staged, or multimedia version, analyzing the effects of techniques unique to each medium (e.g., lighting, sound, color, or camera focus and angles in a film)." Grade 8 standards require students to "analyze the extent to which a filmed or live production of a story or drama stays faithful to or departs from the text or script, evaluating the choices made by the director or actors" (CCSS, 2010, p. 37).

Using narrative VR opens up further potential for responding to curriculum prompts. Researchers note that the vivid detailed world of VR can aid the transfer of skills into student writing (Misak, 2018; Moran, 2019). In light of the young people's engaged responses and interpretation of the *Wolves in the Walls* VR experience in the current study, the following list of activities could be considered by teachers to support student responses to VR:

- Making a video or social media VR trailer of the experience;
- Conducting a media interview with Lucy or her brother or parents regarding the plot of *Wolves in the Walls*;
- Undertaking creative writing activities including a digital "Lucy's Diary" or script between Lucy and yourself as the character friend for the remainder of the story;
- Comparing the interpretation of artifacts, photos, illustrative techniques between the book and the VR experience of *Wolves in the Walls*;
- Identifying and interpreting central themes (child/adult relationships, fear, empowerment) through art, collage, photographs, and so on;
- Responding to intertextuality within the experience (fables, mysteries, first-person child protagonists) through writing or other media;
- Analyzing VR elements that helped to create a "lived through" experience—perspective, scene development, first-person narrative;
- Modeling or drawing (2D or 3D) the setting of the story, including lighting, room details, and so on;
- Considering the contribution of sight, sound, touch, and movement, as well as written and oral language to the story experience;
- Conducting a debate about the book versus the VR experience of stories;
- Discussing the multimedia opportunities of other picture books;
- Developing a short piece researching the processes of making a narrative VR experience; and
- Choosing another narrative VR experience to explore.

CONCLUSION

This research investigated the potential for learning experiences using narrative VR that would not otherwise be possible using traditional approaches (Gouveia et al., 2017). The responses by a small group of young people after engaging with *Wolves in the Walls* were insightful and articulate in the acknowledgement of the "lived through" experience, referring to known experiences and emotions, and demonstrating a synthesis between reader and text. For these young people, the qualities of the VR experience included the sensory engagement with the multimodal elements of the narrative text leading to an immersive sense of presence, connection to character, and created a vehicle for participation or user agency. Sophisticated and meaningful multimodal textual elements of the VR text *Wolves in the Walls* experienced sensorially by the young people prompted aesthetic transactions and created new ideas and perspectives from a personal literary experience.

REFERENCES

ACARA. (2011). *F-10 Australian curriculum: English: Structure.* Retrieved from https://www.australiancurriculum.edu.au/f-10-curriculum/english/structure/

Berleant, A. (1991). *Art and engagement.* Temple University Press.

Billington, P. (2019). Q & A with Pete Billington of Emmy award-winning Fable Studio. In *Future of Storytelling* (Ed.), Future of StoryTelling community spotlight series: A Medium Corporation. Retrieved from https://medium.com/future-of-storytelling/q-a-with-pete-billington-of-emmy-award-winning-fable-studio-164ff13c00df

Baobab Studios. (2020). *Baobab Studios home page.* Retrieved from https://www.baobabstudios.com/

Decock, J., Looy, J., Bleumers, L., & Bekaert, P. (2014). The pleasure of being (there?): An explorative study into the effects of presence and identification on the enjoyment of an interactive theatrical performance using omnidirectional video. *AI & Society, 29*(4), 449.

Engberg, M., & Bolter, J. D. (2020). The aesthetics of reality media. *Journal of Visual Culture, 19*(1), 81–95. doi: 10.1177/1470412920906264

Fable Studio. (2019). Wolves in the Walls. [Virtual reality experience]. Retrieved from https://www.oculus.com/experiences/rift/2272579216119318/?ranking_trace=0_2272579216119318_SKYLINEWEB_15x1IoCnnezmX0jqT

Gouveia, C., Cook, C., Snyder, A., & Payne, S. (2017). *"Nice to have" to "can't do without": aligning simulations and VR with current needs in the K-12 classroom.* Paper presented at the Making a difference: prioritizing equity and access in CSCL, 12th International Conference on Computer Supported Learning Philadelphia, PA.

Group, N. L. (2000). A Pedagogy of multiliteracies: Designing social futures. In B. Cope & M. Kalantzis (Eds.), *Multiliteracies: Literacy learning and the design of social futures* (pp. 9–36). Macmillan.

Hamer, N., Nodelman, P., & Reimer, M. (2017). *More words about pictures: Current research on picture books and visual/verbal texts for young people.* Routledge.

Herrington, J., & Oliver, R. (2006). Professional development for the online teacher: An authentic approach. In A. Herrington & J. Herrington (Eds.) *Authentic learning environments in higher education* (pp. 283–295). Information Science Publishing.

Heyward, M. (2018). Future text: glimpsing narrative futures through the history of digital writing. *Metaphor, 2,* 3–12.

Kalantzis, M., Cope, B., & Cloonan, A. (2010). A multiliteracies perspective on the New Literacies. In E. Baker (Ed.), *New Literacies: Multiple perspectives on research and practice.* The Guilford Press.

Madigan, P. (2018). A spotlight on virtual reality in the English classroom. *Metaphor, 2,* 56–58.

Mills, K. (2015). *Literacy theories for the digital age: Social, critical, multimodal, spatial, material and sensory lenses.* Multilingual Matters.

Misak, J. (2018). A (virtual) bridge not too far: Teaching narrative sense of place with virtual reality. *Computers and Composition, 50,* 39–52.

Moran, C. M., & Woodall, M. K. (2019). "It was like I was there": Inspiring engagement through virtual reality. *English Journal, 109*(1), 90–96.

National Council of Teachers of English. (1996). *NCTE/IRA standards for the English language arts.* International Reading Association and National Council of Teachers of English. Retrieved from https://ncte.org/resources/standards/ncte-ira -standards-for-the-english-language-arts/

National Governors Association Center for Best Practices, Council of Chief State School Officers. (2010). *Common Core State Standards.* National Governors Association Center for Best Practices, Council of Chief State School Officers, Washington DC.

Nikolajeva, M. a. (2015). *Children's literature comes of age: Toward a new aesthetic.* Routledge.

Penrose Studios. (2020). *Homepage.* Retrieved from https://www.penrosestudios .com/

Rosenblatt, L. M. (1960). Literature: The reader's role. *English Journal, 49*(5), 304–316. doi: 10.2307/810700

Rosenblatt, L. M. (1969). Towards a transactional theory of reading. *Journal of Reading Behaviour, 1*(1), 31–49.

Rosenblatt, L. M. (1976). *Literature as exploration* (3rd ed.). Noble and Noble.

Rosenblatt, L. M. (1978). *The reader, the text, the poem: The transactional theory of the literary work.* Southern Illinois University Press.

Rosenblatt, L. M. (1982). The literary transaction: Evocation and response. *Theory Into Practice, 21*(4), 268.

Rosenblatt, L. M. (1986). The aesthetic transaction. *Journal of Aesthetic Education, 20,* 122–128. doi: 10.2307/3332615

Rosenblatt, L. M. (1998). Readers, texts, authors. *Transactions of the Charles S. Peirce Society, 34*(4), 885–921.

Rosenblatt, L. M. (2005a). From "Literature as exploration" and "The reader, the text, the poem." *Voices from the Middle, 12*(3), 25–30.

Rosenblatt, L. M. (2005b). From "Viewpoints: Transaction versus Interaction." *Voices from the Middle, 12*(3), 56–58.

Ross, M. (2020). Virtual reality's new synesthetic possibilities. *Television and New Media, 21*(3), 297–314.

Ryan, M. (2015). Narrative as virtual reality. *Revisiting Immersion and Interactivity in Literature and Electronic Media* (2nd ed.). Johns Hopkins University Press.

Sobel, K. (2019). Immersive media and child development: synthesis of a cross-sectoral meeting on virtual reality, augmented, and mixed reality and young children. *Future of Childhood*. The Joan Ganz Cooney Centre at Sesame Workshop. Retrieved from http://joanganzcooneycenter.org/publication/immersive-media-and-child-developmen/

Vesisenaho, M., Juntunen, M., Häkkinen, P., Pöysä-Tarhonen, J., Miakush, I., Fagerlund, J., & Parviainen, T. (2018). Virtual reality in education: Focus on the role of emotions and physiological reactivity. *Journal of Virtual Worlds Research, 12*(1), 1–15.

Wilkinson, S. (2011). Focus group research. In D. Silverman (Ed.), *Qualitative Research* (pp. 168–184). Sage.

Chapter 7

Engaging ELA Teacher Candidates with the Power and Possibility of Geolocated Augmented Reality

William Wright

In many content areas, a tabletop-sized surface is all an educator needs to begin imagining how augmented reality (AR) might enhance their students' learning. Within such spaces, students can open up three-dimensional objects, zoom into microscopic plant cells, or witness a spotty simulation of the Big Bang, all through the lens of their cell phones. In English language arts (ELA), however, there is rarely, if ever, a phenomenon or object of study to examine so much as a skill to develop or a way of thinking to encounter. As such, when compared to geometry or the sciences, there remains a relative lack of AR applications for ELA teachers to explore and imagine their teaching through.

Much of today's sparse use of AR in K–12 settings takes advantage of a certain place-based novelty factor that quickly wears off—look, there's a dinosaur in my backyard!—or else ignores the reality behind the augmentation entirely to perform a function as equally suited for virtual reality (VR) (Akçayır & Akçayır, 2017). To make the distinction clear, VR is an experiential technology that simulates the user's physical presence in a virtual environment, usually by way of a strap-on headset that includes a stereoscopic head-mounted display (providing separate images for each eye), stereo sound, and head motion-tracking sensors; or, alternatively, the much cheaper "viewer-box" into which a smartphone is inserted, which is usually held up to the viewer's face by their own hands. The current most popular VR headsets on the market are the Oculus Quest, HTC Vive, and the Valve Index (all multiple hundreds of dollars each), while the most common VR viewer box is Google Cardboard (at just over 20 dollars). The relative affordances of these VR platforms are explored in other chapters throughout this volume, and deservingly so. They will not, however, be the focus of this chapter.

AR, on the other hand, is an interactive experience in a real-world environment (rather than an immersive experience in a virtual one). Here, the objects and environmental features that reside in our reality are enhanced by computer-generated sights and sounds that are superimposed onto the user's camera-eye view of the world through a handheld screen of some sort (phone, tablet, etc.), providing a composite scene that has been digitally "augmented." These overlays can take the form of virtual guides, informational plaques, or facsimiles of ancient architecture, to name only a very small few. But the real novelty of the technology stems from state-of-the-art algorithms that detect key indicators in the physical environment—relative depth, flat surfaces, and so on—that allow AR applications to render and realistically place proportionally accurate three-dimensional models with life-like qualities such as shadows or glares of sunlight. In many cases, users can also rotate, magnify, and activate certain features of these models with their fingertips.

Admittedly, however, the majority of VR platforms allow users to manipulate virtual objects in ways that are nearly identical to most phone-based AR applications, only in more immersive settings. Perhaps it is this dawning realization that is responsible for the rapid deterioration of the novelty effect that accompanies the use of most mobile AR applications: Shrek dancing in the school hallway is humorous (it happens); magnified ions bonding on a student's desk is neat; but, save for the background, these things can be done in VR as well—or simply on a computer screen, for that matter. And so from the onset it is important to recognize the ways in which AR can feel gimmicky and somewhat lackluster if witnessed through the inches-long screen of a cell phone, which, practically speaking, is what most students are likely to have on their person in the first place. What ELA educators must ultimately concern themselves with when using AR in their classrooms, then, is the value-added beyond surface-level engagement. In short, while there are certainly logistical reasons to prefer AR over VR—financial considerations being chief among them—ELA educators must ask themselves, pedagogically speaking, how the ability to augment reality is meaningfully different from being immersed in a virtual one. It is here that the ability to geolocate AR content (in our reality) holds critical import.

As a means of sharing some of the ELA-related uses of geolocated AR, I have chosen to frame this chapter around an activity I designed for my "Digital Tools and Social Media in English Education" course. I teach the course to fourth-year undergraduate and master's level teacher candidates during the fall semester of a year-long teaching practicum experience at a large Southeastern university, during which candidates apprentice themselves to middle and secondary mentors while taking courses on campus to supplement their experiences in the field. Put briefly, to critically engage teacher candidates with the power and possibility of this technology, I introduce them to a free iOS and Android app called *WallaMe* that allows users to hide and share messages in the real world using geolocated AR. I first unpack, in the next section, how geolocated AR (and *WallaMe* in particular) expands upon the potential of AR in ELA contexts. I then ground the activity in a short series of critical concepts before laying out the process of my inquiry and thematically describing my teacher candidates' engagement and post-reflections. Finally, I share ideas for how geolocated AR might be broadly accommodated for use in ELA settings and conclude with a brief discussion of a few literacy-related implications.

GEOLOCATED AR & *WALLAME*

Perhaps the two most prominent cultural examples of the widespread use of geolocation in the last decade have been the streamlined convenience of mobile navigation apps and the hit gaming craze *Pokémon Go*, which both use satellite data to identify the geographic location of the user in real time in order to administer location-based information and content. While both of these technologies primarily invite users to *consume* content, it is important, for the purposes of this chapter, to focus in on the small ways in which they each allow users to *produce* content as well. In recent years, for example, popular navigation apps such as *Waze* and *Google Maps* have added features that allow drivers to report speed traps via geolocation so that other users of the app will be able to adjust their speed accordingly, thereby inviting users into a participation-based virtual community. Similarly, but to a lesser extent, *Pokémon Go* allows users to update information and propose new key locations for other users of the app to interact with.

Affordances such as these are important to recognize and relate intimately to a particular imperative I drive home every year in the digital tools course, which is to emphasize that, when incorporating digital tools and social media in the classroom, opportunities for participation and creation are key. For the sake of simplicity, I often juxtaposed creation at one end of the spectrum with consumption at the other. Consumption is by far the most common way (or *direction*) that students—and adults, for that matter—interact with forms of media. One might rightly ask how it could not be with the daily barrage of targeted advertisements, *Netflix* suggestions, and dopamine-driven media feeds that pervade many of our daily lives. Consumption is clearly the default. Participation, differently, moves us away from spectatorship and toward interactivity. The ability to leave a review, chat in the comments section, upvote, or participate in community annotations opens up opportunities for dialogue between consumers and creators, making the boundary between the two more permeable. Finally, and most critically, the ability to create content enables one to issue declarative statements of their own, to realize, in other words, their potential to construct conversation pieces around which others gather—something, I urge, we would like all young people to be able to do.

But even in classrooms, where teachers ostensibly have more control over the environment and can curate, to some extent, the learning experiences of their students, consumption still tends to be the primary direction of engagement between students and digital technologies. Whether it be in the form of movies, *YouTube* videos, or online learning programs, digital learning in the twenty-first century nevertheless remains largely consumption-oriented. This is not to suggest, however, that consumption is innately detrimental for students; rather, it is to propose that consumption be leveraged, at least in part, as a stepping-stone toward participation and eventual creation. At their best, the three exist synergistically; critically conscious viewing hones thoughtful participation and future craft, which then hones further consumption, iteratively, ad infinitum (figure 7.1).

Even so, the current most accessible VR and AR applications tend to be primarily consumption-based, or else premised on a rudimentary "like and share" form of participation or "copy and paste" style of creation. This is unsurprising given that creation generally requires more technical skill and planning than consumption, which is not to dwell on the substantial intimidation factor many feel at the mere mention of virtual and augmented realities. But what happens when content creation goes beyond the confines of a single user and occurs within a shared, co-constructed virtual space atop the physical world? When users synthesize digitally augmented elements with the tangible details of their lived experience for others to see? It is here that *WallaMe*, with its low technical threshold and a high capacity for creative expression, provides a worthy case to explore.

In a nutshell, *WallaMe* is a mobile app that enables users to take pictures of surfaces and write, draw, add stickers, or superimpose photos onto them. When the creation tab is opened, the phone's camera feed is superimposed with an outline of either a green square or a red square: green to signify that the particular spot/angle being pointed to is suitable to leave a message (called Wall), or red if the surface is unsuitable (i.e., not flat enough or containing

Figure 7.1   Learning in the Twenty-First Century Encompasses Three, Synergistic Ideas: Consumption, Participation, and Creation.

enough visual indicators). After locking a green outline into place, the user is able to author a Wall using a range of fonts, images, and artistic effects. Once the Wall is completed, it is *geolocalized*—that is, digitally pinned to a physical location in the real world—and, if made public, will remain visible through *WallaMe*'s AR viewer by anyone passing by. A sample of the Walls created worldwide can be seen in a feed similar to those of social networks like *Facebook* and *Instagram*, and can be liked, commented on, and shared outside the app. A Wall can also be made private so that it is only visible to specific people.[1]

The thrill of seeking out matching surfaces to reveal the hidden, digitally augmented Walls left by other users is a compelling experience in and of itself and is, in many ways, not unlike a form of digital Geo-caching, the uncovering of invisible ink, or the discovery of virtual graffiti. The act of *creating* geolocalized AR Walls, however, of speaking back to and, in a sense, annotating reality itself, brings with it a powerful and innovative opportunity for critical engagement. As we shall see, it is not an exaggeration to say that students who put *WallaMe* to use are able to "read and write their world" (Freire & Macedo, 2005) in ways that would not have been possible only a few years ago.

PLACE-BASED CRITICAL REMIX

I pitch this project to my teacher candidates as an act of what I call "place-based critical remix." The place-based component stems from the ability to geolocate content, discussed previously. But what do I mean by "remix," and how exactly is it "critical?"

Remix, for starters, as both a noun and a verb, originally stems from disc jockeys spinning records at live music shows and has more recently come to signify the creation of digitally altered remakes of popular songs. And yet in the current age of the Internet, *all* media is ripe for play. Alvermann (2011) suggested as much when she wrote that in the twenty-first century especially, "sound clips, images, video games, podcasts, message boards, newsgroups, blogs, and the like" have increasingly become subject to a wide range of widely accessible editing techniques (p. 541). Knobel and Lankshear (2008) cast a similarly wide net when observing that remix generally "means to take cultural artifacts and combine and manipulate them into new kinds of creative blends" (p. 22). These definitions encompass a range of practices that entail using the capacities of digital devices to author new content from existing material—crafting book trailers (Ibarra-Rius & Ballester-Roca, 2019), race-bending popular characters (Thomas & Stornaiuolo, 2016), upending popular advertisements (Wright, 2017), and so on. What these definitions have yet to do, however, is adequately encompass one's physical location as a viable element to bring to the mix.

While existing research largely explores the purposes for digital remixing—having fun, expressing affinity, making political or social statements, composing an argument, and participating in communities (Edwards, 2016; Knobel & Lankshear, 2008)—other, more recent literature discusses digital remix as a meaning-making experience (Dail, Witte, & Bickmore, 2018; Serafini & Gee, 2017). A common theme in this body of scholarship points to the profound, agency-building experience of taking received signals in a social environment and recasting them at a frequency of one's own choosing. Creating shared digital overlays atop the environment itself through geolocated AR might thereby be said to represent a substantive new modality, as one becomes able to remix, recast, or re-story (i.e., augment) the lived details of their everyday life.

Relatedly, the critical component of this project is embedded through my introducing teacher candidates to the tradition of *culture jamming*, a term first used mock-seriously in 1984 by the band Negativland to describe billboard alteration and other forms of media sabotage. In its modern incarnation, culture jamming signifies attempts to "jam" the signals of omnipresent, mass-media corporations who have overtly and covertly woven these transmissions into our mental environment. Those, for example, like me, who cannot think of the word *love* without occasionally having to suppress the melodic follow-up phrase: "it's what makes a Subaru a Subaru" are a by-product of such a system, what critic and essayist Mark Dery coins the "Empire of Signs" (Dery, 1993). To challenge this supremacy, culture jammers engage in a practice called "subvertising," a portmanteau of subvert and advertising, which refers to the practice of satirizing corporate and political advertising campaigns, essentially using the tool against itself.[2] The ultimate aim is to slice through the ruse and, for a moment, relay a deeper truth.

I do not go so far as to suggest to my teacher candidates that all of modern life has been reduced to representation and propaganda—though indeed some have and still do. Instead, I offer up the idea that the world that we live in is always already coded with an endless array of subtle cues about how to behave, which way to walk and communicate, what is valued and deemed presentable, and what is not. Evoking such traditions sets this project squarely in the field of critical literacy, an inherently political outlook toward pedagogy asserting that readers must learn to examine the ways in which power is at work in the writing, silencing, framing, and uptake of texts broadly defined (Aukerman, 2012; Freebody & Luke, 1990). The conditions of possibility that allow texts to take on the meanings that they do must similarly be questioned. Critically trained readers investigate, for instance, whose voices may be missing by challenging the stereotypes at work (Vasquez et al., 2013) and looking for counter-narratives (Johnson & Rosario-Ramos, 2012) that challenge dominant thinking.

I invite teacher candidates to take such a perspective to heart during this project and in their future teaching as well, reading the world as a contingent, contestable, sociopolitical space. It is with an aim toward developing this critically conscious eye that I ask my teacher candidates to take *WallaMe* out beyond the walls of the classroom to interact with the world around them for the next week. My hope is that the ability to produce and geolocate digital layers of augmentation, visible only through the screen of a phones' camera (there, and yet not there), will perturb their thinking about the environment without physically, in that moment, perturbing the environment—representing, in my mind at least, a fun, novel, even radical way to promote thinking anew about their habitual settings.

METHOD

After considering the ideas of remix and culture jamming in light of the capabilities of geolocated AR, teacher candidates were asked to spend the next week roaming around town using *WallaMe* to create Walls that critically interacted with the environment in some way. The assignment was left deliberately open-ended—with no real setup or implemented privacy settings—only the understanding that we would all process and discuss what happened when we next met together.

While I have now introduced *WallaMe* to two different cohorts of teacher candidates, it was not until the second iteration (in the fall of 2019) that I chose to approach the project from a direction of formal inquiry. As a literacy researcher bent on better understanding emergent literacy practices, my intent was not to supply generalizable results derived from systematic analysis of captured data, but rather to provide a "descriptive case study . . . that could serve as part of a knowledge base" (Schwandt & Gates, 2018, p. 598) about the use of geolocated AR in the context of ELA teacher education and, by extension, K–12 ELA instruction more generally. The guiding research questions I asked (and continue to dwell upon) are:

- How do ELA teacher candidates use geolocated AR to critically remix and respond to their physical environment?
- How do they then reflect on this experience as future educators?

My data corpus included recordings of class discussion (approximately 90 minutes in total), reflective memos, brief targeted follow-up interviews with select participants, and uploaded screenshots of the roughly sixty Walls my teacher candidates left around town. Homing in on these data sources allowed me to be more present during class time and eventually enabled me to track four notable themes that developed through an iterative process of observation, examination, and reflection. I expound upon these themes in the following section in semi-narrativized form.

POST-REFLECTIONS

When I first introduced *WallaMe*, not a single teacher candidate in the course had understood my admittedly outdated reference to the hit 1988 Hollywood movie *They Live*, in which the protagonist, peering through special sunglasses (or in this case, a phone's camera), is finally able to see the way things "really are." While it is highly unlikely that a covert race of aliens is hiding subliminal messages in our environment to control and manipulate our collective behavior, most teacher candidates, after engaging with *WallaMe* for the week, seemed on board with the general gist of my allusion, meant to offer up a playful nod to the futuristic and politically fraught ways new technologies provide new ways of seeing and being in the world.

Having toyed with *WallaMe* for a week, teacher candidates arrived to class eager to talk. Two students, Kayla and Brent (all names are pseudonyms), began to share their excitement at having been able to "speak back" to their environment in ways they felt to be both subversive and unobtrusive. I elicited everyone's help unpacking the apparent contradiction here. On the one hand, teacher candidates relished the opportunity to critically interact with their daily surroundings. It felt "empowering" to "call things out" and "stamp surroundings with [their] opinion." And yet, as one candidate, Tyler, pointedly asked, was it really "speaking back" if no one heard or saw what you had done (a veritable "tree falls in the woods" scenario)? Others chimed in—it was often this very discretion that eased them into expressing their opinions in the first place. Regardless of whether anyone else saw it, it was "out there now" and the "possibility" that someone *could* see it was exciting enough.

In one cheerfully reported instance, a student, Sara, shared her experience happening upon Walls left by another student, Mina, on the central quad of campus. Sara shared how she took "a few minutes to track them down" and laughed aloud when she found them. She also, in an unanticipated move, added an augmentation of her own to accompany Mina's. Mina, writing in ornamental font, had first left an augmentation describing the freshly mown grass as "wo-manicured" (figure. 7.2). A day later and a few yards off, Sara had then drawn an arrow to the socially layered pun and written "I see you!" Learning of this, Mina expressed great delight that her augmentation had been found, appreciated, and endorsed.

Figure 7.2 Screenshots of Participants' Geolocated Augmented Reality Posts in *WallaMe.*

I then asked, and was not surprised to find that, for the second year in a row, no one had been privy to *WallaMe* before it was introduced. Some did, however, zoom-out on the map to find other Walls scattered about town, though we soon surmised that most had been left by the previous year's cohort. The app thus remains relatively obscure by all accounts, an aspect that both reinforces and detracts from its appeal for various ends. When asked, for instance, about the ways they conceived of an audience for their Walls, most reported feeling that their target viewers simply included themselves, their friends, or their in-class peers; that, or else a largely imagined, theoretical audience—a kind of "a message-in-a-bottle" form of solidarity with others who might be out there, now or in the future.

Others, however, reported imagining their audience as members of the community who might be out of touch or misinformed. Kayla, for example, called attention to how the very presence or absence of sidewalks in a neighborhood all too predictably disclosed the economic means of those who called it home by writing "Sidewalks = privleged spaces" on a doubly wide sidewalk near campus (See figure 7.2). A few also indicated that they perceived their audience in somewhat vague, adversarial terms—"the man" or "the powers that be" for instance. To these students, the geolocated digital overlays they left represented a discreet act of rebellion. One, for example, had used the app to poke fun at the name of the law school *on* the law school's front entrance. Here I took a moment to ask the obvious question, just to be sure, and was assured by everyone that the majority of their Walls had been left in good fun, and that they had refrained, in every instance, from leaving messages that were in any way cruel or vindictive.

TRANSGRESSIVE FREEDOM AND
THE BIGGER PICTURE

Inevitably, the all-too-easy potential for future students to use *WallaMe* in such a way that undermined or overstepped the critically conscious intentions laid out in this activity worried more than a few candidates. Some admitted outright how impossible it was to see themselves trusting their students enough to show them technologies like this, indicating that most of their students were frankly not mature enough to "handle that kind of power."

It was at this point when I felt the conversation became truly generative. Not only were these concerns entirely valid, they were also related intimately to questions surrounding the purposes of schooling itself. To what extent, that is, are we seeking to prepare students to thoughtfully engage with the world's dynamic challenges—those we, ourselves, have yet to fully comprehend—while at the same time passing down a body of knowledge that we deem beneficial? I never pretend to deny that, in many ways, asking students to leave geolocated AR messages in their environment transgresses the norms of today's schools. As a former English teacher, I am quite mindful of the fact that the majority of K–12 schools out there do not share the same degree of instructional latitude granted to universities. At the same time, I am also well aware and have written about (Wright, 2020) the ways in which hardline schooling environments that are beholden to test scores and good PR are often run in such a way that is restrictive to and, in many cases, outright adverse toward pedagogical explorations of the very same networked technologies (Facebook, YouTube, Tik Tok) that continue to shape the world we know in profound and momentous ways. As such, I made the case to my teacher candidates that deciding with finger-in-ear certainty to foreclose even the possibility of proactive institutional engagement with these technologies too often leaves today's youth fending for themselves in the digital environments that most affect them, not to mention ignores educational standards related to facilitating digital empathy and social responsibility through online interactions. I was quick to point out, however, that the specific forms of boundary-pushing enabled by this technology would not necessarily be appropriate everywhere, at least not automatically. Teacherly courage, after all, is always context dependent (Robinson, 2018).

Here, and over the course of the semester, I emphasized to teacher candidates the importance of having constructive conversations with students about the impacts of technology that are grounded in shared experience, and of how vital a healthy degree of trust is to this process. As a result of this turn in the conversation, I chose to assign Hobbs's (2019) article "Transgression as Creative Freedom and Creative Control in the Media Production Classroom" for reading. In the article, Hobbs recognizes creative freedom—"the means by which students experience true authorship"—and creative control—"the mechanism by which educators design learning experiences to meet specific outcomes or educational goals"—to be on a continuum requiring careful balance (p. 213). Hobbs goes on to argue that we need not fear student transgression per se, and instead positions activities that might at first seem too trusting as an empowering teaching move. Inviting students to engage in potentially transgressive activities, she winds up suggesting, "provides considerable opportunities for authentic learning and personal growth"; and that, moreover, when feared, "it inevitably reflects particular ideas about professionalization, job security and the power of social norms" (p. 214). While there are, of course, entirely understandable reasons why a beginning educator may be hesitant to engage students with participatory AR tools such as *WallaMe*—reasons that are, themselves, worthy of our attention and study—the capacity to author AR texts will only continue to grow. As such, it may well quickly become irresponsible for educators to ignore opportunities to thoughtfully and proactively engage with these technologies with their students in the near future, if indeed it is not so already.

"BEING THERE" IN RELATION TO THE PASSAGE OF TIME

Another interesting and somewhat lighter theme that emerged was the simple pleasure candidates derived from "getting out" and "being there" to create and find geolocated Walls in their surroundings. In fact, well over half of the Walls candidates created were not directly critical at all, instead expressing an abiding appreciation for nature or pointing to quaint characteristics that passersby might not have seen. Several discussed how nice it was to have an excuse to roam about in the afternoon and attend more readily to details they might not have noticed before. Others mentioned "look[ing] at the world differently" when seeking out potentially compelling or thought-provoking spots for their augmentations.

Specific ways candidates made use of the physical presence of their surroundings included one screenshot of the base of a gigantic tree, where a smiley face with eyes raised suggested that viewers "be sure to look up." The student, Susan, later reported that the upper reaches of the tree had been especially magnificent. Another student, Jessica (in the sole production of a Wall that included more than words and hand-drawn images), posted a picture she had found online of the campus landmark she was standing in front of, except in the spring, captioning it: "For those wondering what it looks like when the flowers are in bloom."

Teacher candidates were also curious about how, exactly, the app worked; many wondered, for example, what happened to Walls that were pinned to locations that changed over time. Signs get taken down, trees removed, buildings demolished, sidewalks covered in snow. Often, it seemed, a Wall's intent might be lost. I looked around and waited patiently for ideas, expecting technical explanations for those who may have experimented with the app's functional limits. Instead a few brilliant musings came forth to fill the void: perhaps future users, happening upon these messages months and perhaps even years from now, would be forced to consider "the passage of time" in profound ways; or maybe they could "turn it into a game" and try to figure out what was originally meant by the person who had left it, like archeological sport. While delighted, I eventually explained that the flat surfaces upon which the original Walls were left might themselves no longer be surfaces one day, and that the AR viewer would therefore have trouble finding where, exactly, to place the augmentation. Alas, a message might be unable to be called forth from its intended spot ever again (i.e., without the "key" of its original surface). Still, the ability to experience and experiment with presence was what teacher candidates seemed to enjoy most.

WHO OWNS DIGITAL SPACES?

As our discussion wound down, students expressed curiosity over whether companies or homeowners or universities (etc.) had a right to control or be notified about the ways their physical locations were being augmented in geolocated virtual space. As a class, we could imagine any number of entangled ethical quandaries regarding whose land, whose image, whose app, and whose intellectual property was allegedly mismanaged and how. The reality is that the jury is still out when it comes to determining formal ways of dealing with AR and many other new and emerging technologies. Regardless, we all tended to agree that for the time being, as long as we refrained from either outright lying or profiteering off of the Walls we created, small fish to fry as we were, we were probably okay.

Mires of regulation aside, it is often the case that digital environments provide much-needed sanctuaries in a world where physical locales rarely "belong" to young people in meaningfully determinative ways. Candidates implied as much when they likened the app to a "Marauder's Map" and spoke of the potential for friends to band together and leave secret messages for each other. Forms of digital back channeling, such as *WallaMe*, might thus provide a means to elevate the observer's role in the meaning-making process by creating opportunities for marginalized voices to be recognized, and to recognize each other. In this way, new lines of communication and feelings of ownership might also develop beyond, or underneath, the visible establishment. In the end, we want students to feel connected to their surroundings and experience a sense of agency over its future. Furtively threaded virtual realms overlaying the physical may provide one such medium to convene and imagine differently.

IN ELA SETTINGS

As with any learning tool, I do not feel it is my place to provide an immediate, ready-made, context-specific application for *WallaMe* or geolocated AR more generally. It is up to the reader, in other words, to think through the possibilities that apps like *WallaMe* open up, and to consider how, and in what ways, such tools might be employed for specific learning purposes. I see *WallaMe*, then, as an opening, an alluring challenge even, not an impasse or a solution to a problem. In this way, this chapter is also an invitation—an invitation to further trailblaze and inquire into how geolocated AR might enhance both the instructional latitude of teachers and the critical capacities of their students. I have nevertheless ventured to provide ten entry-level ideas that hinge upon some of the unique capacities made possible by geolocated AR (figure 7.3). These ideas, brainstormed with the assistance of my teacher candidates and colleagues, represent an effort to help jumpstart the imagination of ELA educators seeking to integrate geolocated AR into their instruction. As was the case with the exploratory project described in the body of this chapter, the ideas presented here are left deliberately open-ended. Adapt

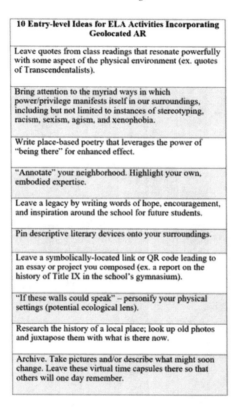

10 Entry-level Ideas for ELA Activities Incorporating Geolocated AR
Leave quotes from class readings that resonate powerfully with some aspect of the physical environment (ex. quotes of Transcendentalists).
Bring attention to the myriad ways in which power/privilege manifests itself in our surroundings, including but not limited to instances of stereotyping, racism, sexism, agism, and xenophobia.
Write place-based poetry that leverages the power of "being there" for enhanced effect.
"Annotate" your neighborhood. Highlight your own, embodied expertise.
Leave a legacy by writing words of hope, encouragement, and inspiration around the school for future students.
Pin descriptive literary devices onto your surroundings.
Leave a symbolically-located link or QR code leading to an essay or project you composed (ex. a report on the history of Title IX in the school's gymnasium).
"If these walls could speak" – personify your physical settings (potential ecological lens).
Research the history of a local place; look up old photos and juxtapose them with what is there now.
Archive. Take pictures and/or describe what might soon change. Leave these virtual time capsules there so that others will one day remember.

Figure 7.3   Ideas for Integrating Geolocation Activities into English Language Arts.

them. Take them in new and unexpected directions. Stick different cords into different sockets and see what lights up.

Certainly there are a number of instructional paths that a teacher might take. Still, it is important to bear in mind that it remains far more critical for educators to engage students in constructive conversations *about* the technology they use than it is to successfully carry out hitch-free implementations of the technology itself. It is therefore suggested that teachers approach *WallaMe* and other AR applications like it as worthy pedagogical encounters unto themselves, rather than as clever means to particular ends. We want students to have positive experiences that "turn them on to learning" (Grant & Sleeter, 2006), but it is easier than we might think to slip into superficial applications of new technologies. To counteract this, plenty of instructional time should be set aside to probe the many uncertainties such tools can bring about. Debriefs, too, should always occur afterward. What a tool does, after all, is far less important than what it does *to* us. The interactions that we have, with each other and the world, are shaped by the technologies we use on a daily basis, and it continues to be necessary for educators to help their students hone the kind of metacognitive thinking strategies required to engage and critique these technologies constructively.

While there are plenty of reasons to proceed thoughtfully, AR technologies nevertheless provide refreshing means to think and do differently in the current educational climate of the United States and elsewhere. State and federal mandates of standardization, in particular, tend to foreclose rather than expand possibilities for connected learning that is curiosity-driven (Ito & Martin, 2013), a phenomenon that Vasudevan and Campano (2009) describe as "the real risk" of schooling, namely that "the expansive sense of self that many youth are experiencing in their out-of-school lives is being constricted or homogenized in schools" (p. 326). In light of this worry especially, the ability to geolocate shared AR messages represents a welcome new dimension, one that effectively manages to take reading and writing off of the page and into the world. Finding wordplay in Shakespeare is one thing; attributing Shakespeare's wordplay to the lived details of one's own experience is something else entirely. Whether opening up means of participating in the traditions of remix and culture jamming, engaging new juxtapositional forms of rhetoric, or simply recontextualizing literary quotes in modern-day settings, geolocalized AR offers students the chance to trace connections between what they learn and how they experience their reality. Such a capability aligns with the ambition of any transformative literacy educator seeking to use the power and possibility of mobile technology to create ubiquitous learning environments that are no longer constricted by predefined places at predefined times (Peng, Chou, & Chang, 2008; Shih, Chu, Hwang, & Kinshuk, 2011)—much less in predefined ways.

IMPLICATIONS

Although this study represents an attempt to examine a small number of teacher candidates' interactions with *WallaMe*, I wish to take this opportunity to share a few final thoughts regarding the implications of geolocated AR amid several broader literacy-related conversations happening today.

Though scholars have elsewhere chronicled the practices of youth using GPS-mapping to chronicle their experiences (Wargo, 2015) and articulated the use of photovoice (documenting one's experience through photos) as a method of civic engagement (Greene, Burke, & McKenna, 2018), never before have these competencies been considered in light of one another or through the networked capabilities of mobile-based AR technology and the expressive freedom its creation tools afford. Regardless, young people coming of age near the end of the first quarter of the twenty-first century have increasingly begun to use technology to speak back to environmental hazards and a mediatized world rife with infomania and competing agendas; and yet so many also succumb to the impression that knowledge is accessible (and, for that matter, exclusively producible) by way of lofty, regulated channels and not intimate, embodied involvement in particular contexts. Scholars have thus indicated the need to better understand and account for the complexity of youth civic participation in today's connected world. In their recent article "Civic Writing on Digital Walls" in the *Journal of Literacy Research*, for example, Kalir and Garcia (2019) observed that "Civic writing has appeared on walls over centuries, across cultures, and in response to varied political concerns (p. 420)—"appear[ing] atop and . . . circulat[ing] among information environments as dissent, expression, and an invitation for dialogue" (p. 421). While the digital walls in this study examined the use of browser-based web annotations, I wish to extend, in this chapter, the notion of "civic writing on digital walls" to both encompass and account for geolocated AR overlays made possible by the likes of *WallaMe*. Such a move effectively extends the concept of digital walls beyond the confines of an Internet browser to include embodied, nomadic encounters as far and wide as the world itself.

Furthermore, I wish, briefly, to consider the significance of geolocated AR in relation to the widely framed teaching concept known as *writing in the margins*—that is, the classical reading strategy wherein students learn to interact with texts at the blank edges of the page. At the risk of sounding too forthright, I would like to suggest that geolocalized overlays in augmented reality represent a new kind of margin. This is, of course, an ontological claim in addition to a pedagogical one; however, technology (and AR technology in particular) "does not simply refer to objects that we use to extend capacities for action" (Ahmed, 2006, p. 45) but instead becomes "the process of 'bringing forth' or . . . to make something appear, within what is present" (p. 46). We cannot therefore ignore the ways in which digitally rendered Walls placed atop physical locations in the "real" world interact and inform one another in ways that would be impossible if they were separated; how they, in effect, say something together that they could not have said alone. Massey (2005) hit upon this entanglement of self, place, and technology in her book *For Space*, asserting that "What is special about place is precisely that throwntogetherness, the unavoidable challenge of negotiating a here-and-now (itself drawing on a geography of thens and theres); and a negotiation which must take place within and between both human and nonhuman" (p. 114). The AR Walls described in this chapter thus offer lively margins for these very real encounters to take place. As a reimagined pedagogical concept, then, such a medium represents new horizons for teachers encouraging students to use technology to form connections with broadly defined, location-based texts.

While these assertions are indeed big, so, too, is our responsibility toward what comes next. No one knows what the future will bring. But the rampant investment in AR start-ups and whispers of the development of wearable AR tech suggest that engagements with augmented reality have indeed become a trend, not a fad, as some have speculated. We owe it to our students to encounter these technologies proactively, particularly in a world in which online platforms have increasingly compartmentalized communities into wholly contained media ecosystems (Döveling, Harju, & Sommer, 2018). All this is to suggest that broad-based abilities to augment reality may eventually prove a means to either bridge or further isolate differing perspectives, and how such tensions play out is likely to affect lived realities both inside and outside of classrooms. In the wake of the COVID-19 global pandemic especially, with coursework going online and distance learning becoming more commonplace, it will be important to foster new forms of connection and actively engage the ongoing mediation of spaces beyond computer screens.

NOTES

1. It is also important to note that, save for a few apps catering to the tourism industry (which do not allow users to create content anyway), *WallaMe* is the only mobile-based AR application premised on geolocation that I have been able to find, and I have spent a good deal of time searching. In addition to being free, there are also no ads, paywalls, subscriptions, or upgrades available for a fee.

2. Readers who are curious to see examples of subvertising are encouraged to visit www.adbusters.org.

REFERENCES

Ahmed, S. (2006). *Queer phenomenology: Orientations, objects, others.* Duke University Press.

Akçayır, M., & Akçayır, G. (2017). Advantages and challenges associated with augmented reality for education: A systematic review of the literature. *Educational Research Review, 20,* 1–11.

Alvermann, D. E. (2011). Popular culture and literacy practices. In M. L. Kamil, P. D. Pearson, E. B. Moje, & P. P. Afflerbach (Eds.), *Handbook of reading research: Volume IV* (pp. 541–560). Routledge.

Aukerman, M. (2012). "Why do you say yes to Pedro, but no to me?" Toward a critical literacy of dialogic engagement. *Theory into Practice, 51*(1), 42–48. https://doi.org/10.1080/00405841.2012.636335

Dail, J. S., Witte, S., & Bickmore, S. T. (2018). *Young adult literature and the digital world: Textual engagement through visual literacy.* Rowman & Littlefield.

Dery, M. (1993) *Culture jamming: Hacking, slashing and sniping in the empire of signs*. Open Magazine Pamphlets. Retrieved from http://project.cyberpunk.ru/idb/culture_jamming.html

Döveling, K., Harju, A. A., & Sommer, D. (2018). From mediatized emotion to digital affect cultures: New technologies and global flows of emotion. *Social Media + Society, 4*, 1–11.

Edwards, D. W. (2016). Framing remix rhetorically: Toward a typology of transformative work. *Computers and Composition, 39*, 41–54. https://doi.org/10.1016/j.compcom.2015.11.007

Freebody, P., & Luke, A. (1990). Literacies programs: Debates and demands in cultural context. *Prospect, 5* (3), 7–16.

Freire, P., & Macedo, D. (2005). *Literacy: Reading the word and the world*. Routledge.

Grant, C. A., & Sleeter, C. E. (2011). *Doing multicultural education for achievement and equity*. Routledge.

Greene, S., Burke, K. J., & McKenna, M. K. (2018). A review of research connecting digital storytelling, photovoice, and civic engagement. *Review of Educational Research, 88*(6), 844–878.

Hobbs, R. (2019). Transgression as creative freedom and creative control in the media production classroom. *International Electronic Journal of Elementary Education, 11*(3), 207–215. https://doi.org/10.26822/iejee.2019349245

Ibarra-Rius, N., & Ballester-Roca, J. (2019). Digital storytelling in teacher training: Development of basic competences, creativity and multimodal literacy through book trailers. In M. L. Carrió-Pastor (Ed.), *Teaching language and teaching literature in virtual environments* (pp. 241–254). Springer.

Ito, M., & Martin, C. (2013). Connected learning and the future of libraries. *Young Adult Library Services, 12*(1), 29–32.

Johnson, L. R., & Rosario-Ramos, E. M. (2012). The role of educational institutions in the development of critical literacy and transformative action. *Theory into Practice, 51*(1), 49–56. https://doi.org/10.1080/00405841.2012.636337

Kalir, J. H., & Garcia, A. (2019). Civic writing on digital walls. *Journal of Literacy Research, 51*(4), 420–443. https://doi.org/10.1177/1086296x19877208

Knobel, M. & Lankshear, C. (2008). Remix: The art and craft of endless hybridization: Digital remix provides an educationally useful lens on culture and cultural production as well as on literacy and literacy education. *Journal of Adolescent & Adult Literacy, 52*(1), 22–33. https://doi.org/10.1598/jaal.52.1.3

Massey, D. (2005). *For space*. Sage.

Peng, H., Chou, C., & Chang, C.-Y. (2008). From virtual environments to physical environments: Exploring interactivity in ubiquitous-learning systems. *Educational Technology & Society, 11*(2), 54–66. https://doi.org/10.1109/icicic.2007.318

Robinson, T. B. (2018). Lights, camera, courage: Authentic assessment and multimodal composition. *English Journal, 108*(1), 25–31.

Schwandt, T. A. and Gates, E. F. (2018). Case study methodology. In N. K. Denzin & Y. S.Lincoln (Eds.), *The SAGE handbook of qualitative research* (pp. 341–358). Sage Publications.

Serafini, F., & Gee, E. (Eds.). (2017). *Remixing multiliteracies: Theory and practice from New London to new times*. Teachers College Press.

Shih, J.-L., Chu, H., Hwang, G.-J., & Kinshuk (2011). An investigation of attitudes of students and teachers about participating in a context-aware ubiquitous learning activity. *British Journal of Educational Technology, 42*(3), 373–394. https://doi .org/10.1111/j.1467-8535.2009.01020.x

Thomas, E. E., & Stornaiuolo, A. (2016). Restorying the self: Bending toward textual justice. *Harvard Educational Review, 86*(3), 313–338.

Vasquez, V. M., Tate, S. L., & Harste, J. C. (2013). *Negotiating critical literacies with teachers: Theoretical foundations and pedagogical resources for pre-service and in-service contexts.* Routledge.

Vasudevan, L., & Campano, G. (2009). The social production of adolescent risk and the promise of adolescent literacies. *Review of Research in Education, 33*(1), 310–353. https://doi.org/10.3102/0091732x08330003

Wargo, J. M. (2015). Spatial stories with nomadic narrators: Affect, snapchat, and feeling embodiment in youth mobile composing. *Journal of Language and Literacy Education, 11*(1), 47–64.

Wright, W. T. (2017). Subvertising to illustrate transcendentalist ideals. *Utah English Journal, 45,* 44–46.

Wright, W. T. (2020). Within, without, and amidst: A review of literacy educators' perceptions of participatory media technologies. *Journal of Media Literacy Education. 12*(2), 1–12. https://doi.org/10.23860/JMLE-2020-12-2-1

Part 3

INTERDISCIPLINARY WORK IN ELA CLASSROOMS

WHAT ARE THE BOUNDARIES AND FRONTIERS OF VIRTUAL AND AUGMENTED REALITIES?

Chapter 8

"It's the Actual Bomb!"

Middle School Females Using Virtual Reality to Develop Twenty-First-Century Literacies

Rick Marlatt

The class alarm clock sounded, letting everyone know that it was time to rotate to the next learning station. Eliza (all names are pseudonyms) and five female peers had completed the *Shakespeare 360* virtual reality (VR) tour and were the next group scheduled for the "Bomb Defusing" station. As our class of eighth-grade English language arts (ELA) students migrated from one station to the next, Marco, a male student whose group was departing from the bomb activity having been unsuccessful at disarming the weapon, smirked when Eliza's group approached. "Bruh, I can't wait to see the ladies try to defuse that thing. There's no way they are going to beat it. It was so hard." There seemed to be a presumption held by Marco and his male peers who laughed at this comment that Eliza's group was doomed to fail. The sense of frustrated tension his comment sparked was overmatched by a heavy dose of curiosity exhibited by Eliza and her peers as they began reading the instructions for the game, *Keep Talking and Nobody Explodes*. As practitioners, we redirected Marco by wishing him better luck next time and reminded him that all groups have the same set of tools and resources to be successful at each station. As researchers, we could not help but notice that a kind of challenge had been raised, and that Eliza's group was digging in with excitement, eager to answer the call.

In this practitioner research study, two teacher educators set out to better understand how integrating VR-based activities with reading engagement, navigation of nonfiction texts, and descriptive language could impact the way students operationalize content knowledge and skills while expressing them-selves and their personal learning experiences across the digital landscapes of the ELA classroom. The inquiry was driven by the following question: How can students leverage virtual reality (VR) to develop twenty-first-century literacies around nonfiction texts in middle school? In this chapter, we showcase our attempt to answer this question by first offering a review of the scholarly literature in the areas of VR and video games that informed our work before outlining our conceptual framework and describing the contexts, methods, and implementation of focal participants' interdisciplinary VR activities. We then present the findings of the activity, which resulted in increased cooperation, creativity, computational thinking, and more. Finally, we offer a discussion of our practitioner research including interpretations, limitations, and implications for VR in standards-based ELA education.

LITERATURE REVIEW

The International Society for Technology in Education (ISTE) outlines seven criteria for measuring how well today's students are prepared to succeed in an increasingly global, digitized society. While offering suggested instructional applications and recommendations for curricular assessment, ISTE (2019) standards posit that twenty-first-century learners (figure 8.1) are (1) empowered learners, (2) digital citizens, (3) knowledge constructors, (4) innovative designers, (5) computational thinkers, (6) creative communicators, and (7) global collaborators (ISTE, 2019). To position students for success across these standards, ELA teachers combine traditional disciplinary components such as literature study, writing instruction, and reading engagement with interdisciplinary applications of digital literacies and intersections of technology and texts that account for students' multimodal literacy practices and contemporary meaning-making (Marlatt, 2019a). The use of VR to enhance teaching and learning is one promising area being increasingly explored by ELA researchers and practitioners (Freina & Ott, 2015).

Lexico, the online dictionary, defines VR as "the computer-generated simulation of a three-dimensional (3D) image or environment that can be interacted with in a seemingly real or physical way by a person using special electronic equipment" (para. 1). Devices such as headsets and smartphones make VR accessible to students through computer-generated sensory input that can be tailored toward specific content and learning applications (Harvey, 2018). By integrating VR activities with traditional, print-based literacy exercises, secondary teachers position students for complex textual engagement that is representative of their socially situated identities (Lankshear & Knobel, 2011). Rapidly growing interest in VR is a recent example of ongoing efforts to integrate impactful technology applications into ELA curriculum in support of students' twenty-first-century learning (Rice, 2016).

Moran (2019) supported comprehensive implementation of VR in classroom settings, arguing that virtual players and assignments promote student engagement, enhance reading and writing, and allow for cross-curricular

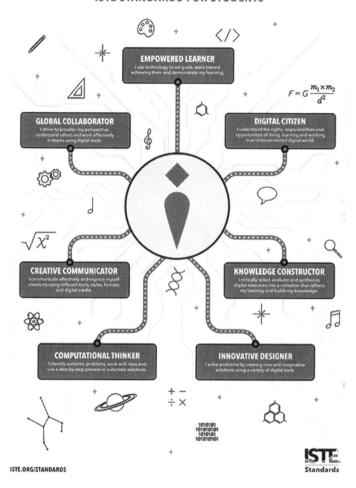

Figure 8.1   ISTE Standards.

exploration through cost-effective programs. VR presents opportunities for student-driven, station-based collaboration for learners, especially alongside ELA content that has traditionally been facilitated through lecture (Harvey et al., 2019). Interactive learning stations in which students combine multiple literacy practices and VR to solve problems and self-propel standards-based inquiry helps ELA break away from traditional lecturing which de-emphasizes student autonomy and can result in isolated, inert consumption of non-contextualized information (Calvert, 2015). VR has the potential to help practitioners design multimodal instruction that supports students' digital literacies, aligns with academic standards, and transcends content area boundaries, all the while positioning ELA education for greater equity with regard to technology integration in schools (Rybakova et al., 2019).

DISRUPTING THE STEM GENDER GAP WITH VR-BASED VIDEO GAMES

VR implementation enables interdisciplinary connections between literacy and other content areas such as science, technology, engineering, and mathematics (STEM), which carry the potential for disrupting harmful gender constructs. Recent studies investigating curriculum and instruction within STEM-based contexts involve predominantly male participants and stakeholders (Ireland et al., 2018). By using VR to democratize and enhance literacy education through STEM applications, ELA teachers can problematize gender stereotypes that inhibit students from achieving academic growth and personal development. Interest in designing ELA curriculum and instruction featuring VR continues to increase as technology becomes more affordable and potentially more accessible for schools (Moran, 2019). These current contexts present an ideal opportunity for educators to consider how VR can enhance ELA experiences for students while making connections between digital literacies and academic standards.

Although STEM concepts encourage collaborative principles in adolescents' academic and social aptitudes, a significant gender gap in STEM fields has been replicated in K–12 settings for decades (Reinking & Martin, 2018). Recently, schools across the United States have implemented numerous initiatives designed to strengthen girls' access to STEM learning, including an after-school pilot program, sponsored by Microsoft and Dell, that affords girls opportunities to engage in coding and computational thinking using Minecraft: Education Edition (Friedman, 2019), school-wide student profile systems that match girls-specific academic interests and career aspirations with desired STEM skill sets (McCarthy, 2019), and collaborative approaches to assembling outlets for girls to enact quantitative reasoning and literacy practices (McMillen et al., 2018). Increasingly, scholars have demonstrated equal interest in offering middle school girls STEM opportunities, overseeing action research projects studying river quality restoration (Burrows et al., 2016) and phenomenological case studies investigating girls' use of programmable electronics to create e-textiles (Searle et al., 2019). This combination of heightened practitioner and scholarly attention on the issue of girls and STEM has resulted in a positive trend whereby middle school curriculum and instruction is helping to combat long-held gender discrepancies (Hill et al., 2010).

Video game-oriented middle school teachers and after-school esports clubs have helped to interrupt a similar gender gap related to girls and video games, resulting in more female students becoming involved in gaming programs (McCarthy, 2020). While the benefits of esports have been touted in recent years, including increased participation with school activities and improved levels of engagement in academics, video games have mostly and incorrectly been equated with boys rather than girls (NASEF, 2020). However, according to a recent Pew Research Center study, 75 percent of girls have access to gaming consoles and even more (83 percent) regularly play video games on some device (Perrin, 2018). Pyles (2019) found that at least 48 percent of gamers now identify as female and argued that increased opportunities to play recreationally and competitively in school-based settings is helping to bring about more inclusivity and equity for girls who believe that "feeling uncomfortable while engaging in activity that you love inserts unnecessary and undesirable pressure and stress along the way" (para. 4).

Video games featuring VR components occupy an increasingly pivotal role in literacy education, especially at the secondary level, where instructors are able to leverage the adaptive, generative learning principles of gaming toward increased engagement with traditional curricular priorities such as reading comprehension, descriptive writing, literary analysis, and more (Gee, 2007; Lewis Ellison, 2017; Marlatt, 2018a). Contemporary ELA settings that blend gender-inclusive approaches to gaming, STEM applications, and standards-based literacy instruction reflect the dynamic, interdisciplinary nature of digital-age learning, a phenomenon that McCarthy (2020) described as the nexus between esports and academics, where "ISTE Standards for Students, global professional skills, and preparations for college and career opportunities are integrated into curriculum standards in knowledge, application, and higher order thinking" (p. 5).

VR GAMES IN ELA: TEXT-BASED AFFINITY SPACES

To understand how students might leverage VR to develop twenty-first-century literacies around nonfiction texts in middle school, we integrate the seven ISTE standards for the digital-age learner with Gee's (2004) paradigm of affinity spaces, digitally driven locations where "newbies and masters and everyone else" (p. 85) collaborate in informal, interactive learning. As VR video games catalyze meaning-making communities that often operate outside of traditional institutions, affinity spaces act as an "attractor" (p. 28) whereby students can utilize reading and writing competencies to compete, both individually and as part of a team, while enacting myriad socially situated literacy practices to engage with normalized, print-based academic material (Gee, 2017). Combining the technical components of instructional texts with the iterative process of using descriptive language and precise word choice to communicate those sequences with peers within the lively terrain of VR gaming presents a multi-contextual affinity space where "People can be cooperative within these spaces and communities, but they can also compete fiercely for status" (Gee & Hayes, 2012, p. 135). Today's ELA classrooms have a responsibility to be inclusive, both of the youth we serve, as well as their multiliteracies. The New London Group (1996) argued, "To be relevant, learning processes need to recruit, rather than attempt to ignore and erase, the different subjectivities, interests, intentions, commitments, and purposes that students bring to learning" (p. 18). In light of this pursuit, the following study aims to offer an example of how inclusivity can spark engagement for adolescent learners.

INFUSING VR INTO ELA CONTENT

In a large urban school district in the Southwest United States, eighth-grade ELA students participated in a sequence of VR-driven learning stations designed to promote media literacy alongside ELA domains of reading, writing, listening, and speaking. The stations were facilitated by Rick, a teacher educator interested in digital literacies, and Miles, a teacher educator and classroom teacher interested in the power of games to enhance literacy learning. Our central objective with the unit was to afford adolescents spaces to extend their textual interactions to include STEM applications and literacy operations that aligned with ISTE standards. A total of twenty-nine students participated in the VR unit (table 8.1), which spanned ten one-hour class periods and tasked six small groups with a variety of text-based activities as they alternated daily between seven different stations. In addition to station-specific materials, students also wrote in a reflective journal following the completion of each day's activities. While the VR applications and activities were downloaded for classroom use, the expectations and procedures within each station were designed and facilitated by us.

On Day 1, we introduced the unit and modeled how to operate the VR headsets. Next, students took turns acclimating themselves to the virtual space with the beginner application, *Welcome to Virtual Reality* and used the *Guided Meditation* tool to practice focusing on their breathing. On Day 2, groups began their assignments at different stations. In *BBC VR*, students explored news stories of their choice such as updates on Brexit and other parliamentary happenings. *Athens VR* offered a virtual tour and orientation of ancient Greek culture. Groups spread a safe distance apart from others and explored their artistic sides with *Sculpt VR*, where students created their own sculptures. The high-stakes activity, *Medical Training Simulator*, required

Table 8.1   VR Stations and Learning Targets with ISTE Standards

VR Station	Learning Target and ISTE Standard
Station 1 Welcome to VR Orientation	* Students will use an introduction VR app to practice active listening skills to recognize the rights, responsibilities, and opportunities that virtual reality offers while giving students the chance to listen and reflect using VR meditation. *ISTE Empowered Learner 1d. Students understand the fundamental concepts of technology operations, demonstrate the ability to choose, use and troubleshoot current technologies and are able to transfer their knowledge to explore emerging technologies.
Station 2 BBC VR	*Students will use a VR news app to broaden their perspectives and enrich their learning by collaborating with others and working effectively in teams locally and globally. *ISTE Global Communicator 7d. Students explore local and global issues and use collaborative technologies to work with others to investigate solutions.
Station 3 Athens VR	*Students use a historical VR simulation to broaden their perspectives and enrich their learning by collaborating with others and working effectively in teams locally and globally. *ISTE Global Collaborator 7a. Students use digital tools to connect with learners from a variety of backgrounds and cultures, engaging with them in ways that broaden mutual understanding and learning.
Station 4 Sculpt with VR	*Students use a VR art app to create three-dimensional ideas using various mediums to identify and solve problems by creating new, useful, or imaginative solutions. *ISTE Innovative Designer 4a. Students know and use a deliberate design process for generating ideas, testing theories, creating innovative artifacts or solving authentic problems.
Station 5 Medical Training Simulator	*Students will use VR to take on the role of a medical professional to save a patient in the emergency room about to go into surgery. Students will explore medical solutions for the patient using feedback from the game to better understand how to treat their patient. *ISTE Empowered Learner 1c. Students use technology to seek feedback that informs and improves their practice and to demonstrate their learning in a variety of ways.
Station 6 Altspace VR	*Students use VR to broaden their perspectives and enrich their learning by collaborating with others and working effectively in teams using the Altspace app. *ISTE Global Collaborator 7a. Students use digital tools to connect with learners from a variety of backgrounds and cultures, engaging with them in ways that broaden mutual understanding and learning.
Station 7 Shakespeare 360	*Students will use VR to analyze and explore Shakespeare and the times centered around his famous works in world literature. *ISTE Knowledge Constructor 3a. Students plan and employ effective research strategies to locate information and other resources for their intellectual or creative pursuits.
Station 8 Keep Talking and Nobody Explodes	*Students will use a VR bomb-defusing game to practice communicating clearly and to express themselves in small groups. Students will practice active listening and speaking skills while reading and defusing at the same time. *ISTE Creative Communicator 6c. Students communicate complex ideas clearly and effectively by creating or using a variety of digital objects such as visualizations, models, or simulations.

students to apply scientific vocabulary and perform anatomical procedures. Students were also able to socialize with other VR users around the world by playing a series of academic games in *Altspace VR*, and in *Shakespeare 360*, students learned about the Bard of Avon and the Globe Theatre. Finally, in the highly challenging and equally engaging, *Keep Talking and Nobody Explodes*, groups spent three days working together to defuse a dangerous bomb.

Although the VR activities illustrated in this study are situated within the middle school ELA setting, the ISTE standards and STEM-based competencies they position students to exhibit are interdisciplinary and can be implemented as part of a variety of standards-based instruction and curricular tasks. In addition, VR is positioned to impact classrooms across a range of socioeconomic contexts. The sixth- through eighth-grade Title 1 Program school at which this study was conducted enrolled 1,100 students, 50 percent of whom received free and reduced meals. In addition, 64.2 percent of the student body as Hispanic, and many students were served as English Language Learners. The interactions described in this chapter are positioned to disrupt any assumptions that VR and other digital technology tools are inaccessible for particular subgroups.

KEEP TALKING AND NOBODY EXPLODES

Groups completing the bomb-defusing station shared an *Oculus Go* VR headset and wand with the *Keep Talking and Nobody Explodes* game downloaded and complex manuals containing meticulously sequenced instructions on how to disarm a ticking-time explosive. Each student took her turn as the defuser while the other group members served as squad supporters. With a running clock starting at 5 minutes in the corner of the defuser's point of view (POV), she attempted to deactivate a bomb by describing the maze-like surroundings in front of her so that her teammates could help her orient the virtual scene, and most importantly, navigate the intricate web of wires and button-control series composing the deadly device. She must efficiently locate the bomb and carry out the disarming process by describing key details in her POV (figure 8.2), all the while listening intently for clues and instructions from squad supporters, who must precisely comprehend and concisely relay the steps illustrated in the manuals. The defuser must listen carefully to her team, and, as supporters are not *with* their partner in the scene and are unable to see her surroundings, communication is paramount to success. With their combined advantages and limitations, the team must work together to overcome the tension and save the day.

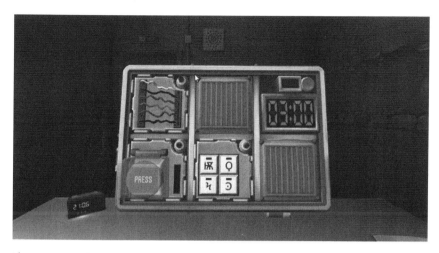

Figure 8.2   A View of the Bomb from the Defuser's VR Perspective.

The game and corresponding manual contain various modules that offer numerous defusing assignments ranging in level of difficulty. With teammates taking turns performing different roles and alternating modules chosen at random, the game's activities and its myriad required literacy practices remain fresh. Because players are accessing and generating information through different lenses, fluent speaking and listening between group members is essential to avoid catastrophe, as are textual and visual comprehension, adaptability, problem-solving, orientation via context clues, and critical thinking. Command of alpha-numeric key words and phrases is vital for success at each module's series of challenges. Supporters help diffusers decide which colored wire to cut, what buttons to press, proper directions to turn, and correct number sequences to input into the master keypad. Symbol literacy is equally important, as diffusers identify shapes and icons in their view while supporters match those descriptions with order of operations in the text (figure 8.3). As the clock ticks down, teams are afforded two mistakes per module. On the third wrongly snipped wire or incorrect code, the bomb detonates.

METHODOLOGY

A group of six eighth-grade ELA students who all identify as female—Eliza, Axilla, Tela, Carini, Magilla, and Reba—consented to serve as focal participants in our study. This group was by far the most successful bomb-defusing team, as each member was able to disarm the explosive at least once over the

Keep Talking and Nobody Explodes v. 1　　　　　　　　　　　Keypads

On the Subject of Keypads

I'm not sure what these symbols are, but I suspect they have something to do with occult.

- Only one column below has all four of the symbols from the keypad.
- Press the four buttons in the order their symbols appear from top to bottom within that column.

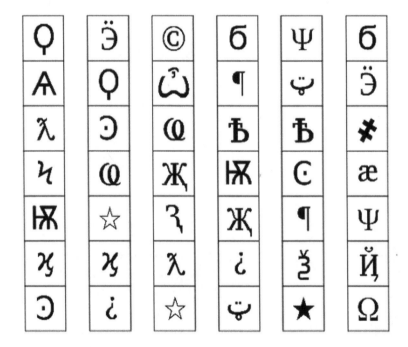

Figure 8.3　A Page from the Bomb-Defusing Manual Illustrates Symbols That Must Be Processed.

course of three class periods. Whereas other groups were less successful and often succumbed to breakdowns in communication and failures to follow correct orders of operations, this team's collaboration around multiple literacy practices integrating digital and printed materials helped them stand out among their peers. As practitioner-researchers, we were drawn to the ways in which this all-girl group's heightened STEM engagement and savvy with VR gaming appeared to problematize the persistent belief that technology-driven practices involving engineering, video games, and computational thinking are reserved for students who identify as male (Reinking & Martin, 2018).

A variety of data was collected to help answer the central question, *How can middle school students leverage VR to develop twenty-first-century literacies using nonfiction informational texts?* Data collection was made possible through our positionality as facilitators of student-driven learning stations. Once stations were up and running and groups were collaborating toward assignment completion, we offered minimal support as needed, but we operated largely as researcher-observers by taking field notes and recording the action. Group interaction was video/audio recorded with an iPad as participants cooperated against the clock by actively listening to one another's discourse, engaging with the text, making use of descriptive language, exercising problem-solving, and more. At the conclusion of each day's station work, participants responded to prompts in reflective journals, which asked them to reflect upon their experiences with VR and literacy tasks. Finally, at the conclusion of the VR unit, we conducted semi-structured interviews with Eliza and her teammates, inviting the girls to share insights on a range of topics including literacy and STEM learning, digital literacies, nonfiction reading, and more.

In the weeks following the VR unit, we began the analysis phase by transcribing audio exchanges from bomb-defusing recordings and interviews. These transcriptions, along with our field notes, participants' reflective journals, and class video recordings, were examined using thematic analysis (Braun et al., 2019). After reviewing the data several times in chronological order, we generated an initial list of codes such as "used new terms to get meaning across" and "had to find a way to get us there" which were collapsed into larger categories of ISTE (2020) digital-age learning competencies such as "creative communicator" and "innovative designer" (Braun & Clarke, 2006). We then approached the work of describing participants' literacy interactions within their affinity space (Gee, 2017) using rich description (Donmoyer, 2013). We must acknowledge the high degree of privilege that we as researchers enjoyed in this setting with regard to the school's affluency and access to equipment, as well as our participants' competency in utilizing technology schools in ways that many of their peers are not as fortunate. In the following section, we present findings from a subset of data focusing on focal participants' activities during the bomb-defusing station. Their collaborations consistently reflected ISTE standards and demonstrated STEM competencies in ways that problematized gender constructs.

FINDINGS

Results from the practitioner research investigation of middle school students leveraging VR to develop digital-age competencies using nonfiction texts in ELA are presented in this section. ISTE (2020) themes are narrated in linear fashion, offering interpretations of the focal group's activities as they progressed through the three-day bomb-defusing station from start to finish, including excerpts from participants' interactions, reflective journals, and interviews.

Day 1: Empowerment, Communication, and Computational Thinking

Day 1 began with excitement as the girls situated their desks into a pod formation and chatted about their upcoming bomb-defusing challenge. They rolled their eyes at the light teasing being thrown their way by some of their male peers whose groups had been less than successful at disarming the explosive. When Marco warned from across the room, "Watch out, we couldn't beat it. That thing is tough," Eliza responded confidently, "We'll see." She then peered at her teammates and asked, "Right?" The girls laughed and began passing out the defusing manuals, reviewing their station's objectives, and acclimating themselves with the VR headsets (figure 8.4). After a brief silence during which the girls took in the text's dense assembly of information, codes, symbols, and steps, Axilla suggested, "Here, should we just look at it all first? Then decide our plan? This is a lot." Her teammates nodded their heads and exhaled.

Figure 8.4   Group Members Acquaint Themselves with their Materials and Beginning Setting Goals.

For the first 10 minutes, the girls took turns pointing out textual features in the manual that appeared interesting or complicated. Carini then looked up and asked, "OK, should we keep going through this, or do you think we should just start and see what we come across?" The girls agreed that they would dive into the game, but they each kept their manuals open to a different page so as to collectively offer support as efficiently as possible. Eliza, who had been the only member not to don the headset, smiled and asked, "So, who's going first?" Magilla smacked her hand on her desk, snatched the headset from Eliza, slid it around her head, and proclaimed, "Let's do this. We're all going to have a turn anyway. I don't want to be the only one who explodes."

After hitting the red *start* button on the game's main menu, Magilla took a deep breath, calibrated the screen with her *Oculus* wand and said, "Here we go. Don't judge me." Although Magilla was determined, she was rendered speechless by her surroundings, taking small steps forward and backward and rotating in different directions. Her supporters eagerly anticipated clues or hints, but none were provided. Carini questioned the defuser, "What do you see? Can you see? What do we need to do?" Still silent, Magilla bit her lip and turned around once more. Suddenly, she shot her head back and shouted, "Crap! It's the actual bomb! I'm trying to turn this briefcase over on the table. I see a bunch of wires and buttons with those weird symbols." Her team cut her off with an onslaught of pressing questions about the wire colors, symbol descriptions, serial numbers, and more. Magilla seemed overwhelmed and shouted, "Just hold on a sec! I can't hear when you all bark at me. One at a time, please! I don't even know where to start." The group apologized and quickly instituted a procedure for ensuring one supporter spoke at a time. Reba reached into her pocket and pulled out an object: "Whoever has the speaking stretchy will be the speaker," she exclaimed. The girls agreed, with Carini chiming in, "All hail the magic stretchy." With their norms now established, the group was reenergized. For the next 10 minutes, Magilla's supporters took trial runs at helping her through the virtual space.

Reba began by asking Magilla, "How many wires do you see? It looks like there are different steps for different scenarios." Magilla replied, "I see four wires." Tela flipped quickly to a manual page she had bookmarked (figure 8.4), whispered for the *speaking stretchy*, and calmly replied, "Well, it says here, if there are no red wires, cut the second wire." Magilla hesitated for a moment: "But I see a red wire, so what do I do? There's only 1 minute left. Hurry!" Supporters took *stretchy-enabled* turns reading from the manual in response to Magilla's descriptions. Magilla proceeded to cut two wrong wires over the next several seconds, costing her both of her allotted mistakes. With the tension rising in the module's final seconds, Magilla was down to two wires and asked for directions. Carini responded, "Cut the blue one." Magilla

On the Subject of Wires

Wires are the lifeblood of electronics! Wait, no, electricity is the lifeblood.
Wires are more like the arteries. The veins? No matter...

- A wire module can have 3-6 wires on it.
- Only the <u>one</u> correct wire needs to be cut to disarm the module.
- Wire ordering begins with the first on the top.

---

3 wires:
If there are no red wires, cut the second wire.
Otherwise, if the last wire is white, cut the last wire.
Otherwise, if there is more than one blue wire, cut the last blue wire.
Otherwise, cut the last wire.

---

4 wires:
If there is more than one red wire and the last digit of the serial number is odd, cut the last red wire.
Otherwise, if the last wire is yellow and there are no red wires, cut the first wire.
Otherwise, if there is exactly one blue wire, cut the first wire.
Otherwise, if there is more than one yellow wire, cut the last wire.
Otherwise, cut the second wire.

---

5 wires:
If the last wire is black and the last digit of the serial number is odd, cut the fourth wire.
Otherwise, if there is exactly one red wire and there is more than one yellow wire, cut the first wire.
Otherwise, if there are no black wires, cut the second wire.
Otherwise, cut the first wire.

---

6 wires:
If there are no yellow wires and the last digit of the serial number is odd, cut the third wire.
Otherwise, if there is exactly one yellow wire and there is more than one white wire, cut the fourth wire.
Otherwise, if there are no red wires, cut the last wire.
Otherwise, cut the fourth wire.

Figure 8.5   Directions from the Bomb-Defusing Manual on Cutting Wires from the VR Bomb.

took a deep breath and then smiled, saying, "Module completed!" The girls cheered for a moment before Magilla cut their celebration short: "Great. Now we start another module."

Invigorated with confidence at having completed their first module, the team briskly moved on to the next, which presented a set of symbols stacked in columns. Magilla described the symbols to the best of her ability, stating, "They're not normal symbols, but one of them has a backwards "E" with two dots on top, and the one near it looks like a railroad track or something. Do you see that?" Eliza replied, "It says only one column below has all four of the symbols from the keypad on the bomb. You need to be more specific.

Figure 8.6 Magilla Explains the Bomb's Symbols while her Supporters Match them with Instructions.

What are the other symbols that you see?" The group searched for clues, working to match the symbols present in the module with the possible combinations detailed in the manual (figure 8.6). With under a minute remaining, having made two mistakes already, Magilla pressed the wrong button before exchanging vital information on a final step with her supporters. Magilla screamed as the bomb detonated, "I just blew up! That was so scary. I'm sorry, guys." The team congratulated her on progressing so far into the game on her first try and reassured her that they would find success.

Although these early phases continued to result in multiple failures, the girls pressed on, each member taking notes on paper regarding different module sequences or textual features. When Magilla resigned from her initial diffuser role, she held the headset out for the next contender. The girls appeared eager, except for Eliza, who was still nervous, saying, "You guys go ahead. I'm not trying to get blown up today." The other four, Tela, Reba, Carini, and Axilla, took turns as diffuser for the next 30 minutes, and although the girls got closer each time to completing successful missions by integrating their notes and discussions into the modules, each attempt ended with a detonation. Finally, with only 10 minutes remaining in the class, Eliza, to the cheers of her teammates, blurted, "OK, fine. Let's do this" and tried her hand as a diffuser. Excitedly, her supporters leaned in, listening to Eliza's descriptions of her POV, and flipped to the corresponding manual pages. Eliza calmly followed the directions of her group, asking for clarifications when needed. And only 2 minutes into the module, the team erupted into celebration, as Eliza defused the bomb. High-fives and hugs were shared all around.

The girls' initial getting-started strategies differed greatly from the other groups. Whereas previous students jumped into the virtual space and simply began playing the game without consulting teammates or formulating a plan, the girls appraised their understanding of the station's fundamental concepts and objectives, articulated a series of goals using the resources at their disposal, and developed various approaches to accomplish their aims. While numerous groups before them simply took turns from the outset of their station and even broke up into divisions with the two headsets, the girls remained cohesive and maintained their roles for an extended duration. They accepted the fact that they would likely fail multiple times on their way toward compiling a collective of experiential troubleshooting and provided that feedback to one another. From the way they positioned their desks in the class period's opening moments to the way they worked in unison toward common targets, the girls constructed their own personalized learning network and customized their environment to maximize their incremental progress.

After a hectic beginning to their activities, the girls quickly solved their communication issues with a creative solution. The *speaking stretchy* provided a simple, easily transferable tool that allowed for efficient use of time and effective speaking and listening. With one supporter speaking at a time with the defuser, and the other members actively listening, taking notes, and preparing subsequent statements, the girls created appropriate platforms for meeting their objectives. The group maneuvered their way through complex situations by remixing their materials to help one another facilitate purposeful communication between presenters and audience. These tactics helped them far outperform their peers as many groups failed to move past shouting at one another or electing to pursue their own course without team support.

In her interview, Eliza described the emotions she experienced when the group finally broke through: "It felt kind of powerful. I was relieved because we did it, but super happy for our team. We worked so hard in small ways for something bigger. There was a ton to memorize and think about in the moment." Assessing the structural design that diffusers described, squad supporters identified relevant data sets from their printed models and related problem-solving steps back to their diffusers, who used virtual tools to exec-utive-specific computations on behalf of the group. Facilitating the correct wire cuts in the correct sequence and collaborating on inputting the proper codes for disarmament was team-oriented exploration. By taking their time initially through guided practice, they broke their complex challenges down into manageable parts.

Day 2: Innovative Design and Knowledge Construction

The girls endured some adversity to begin Day 2 of their bomb-defusing activities. Because a school assembly slated for later that afternoon had triggered a shortened class-period schedule for the day, the team had only 42 minutes to complete their modules instead of the full hour. Moreover, the

Figure 8.7   The Team Breaks off into Two Smaller Groups with the VR Devices.

assembly had pushed the start of each class period up by 15 minutes, which meant that Tela would be late returning to school from her dentist appointment that had originally been scheduled during her study hall period. With less time, and down one teammate on their roster, the girls improvised their strategy. Carini suggested a plan for the day's attack: "OK, today let's split up." The girls agreed to divide forces and try to complete as many of the modules as they could, being sure to take copious notes along the way (figure 8.7). They also strategically decided to immediately start a new game if they were presented with a repeated module. While few of their peers were able to successfully complete more than a module or two, the girls' objective was to establish a collective expertise with which they could master the game. Carini and Reba relocated to one end of the pod, while Axilla, Eliza, and Magilla formed a trio.

Carini and Reba struggled at first to initiate momentum. As the defuser, Reba experienced difficulty describing the new explosive's composition to her supporters. Likewise, Carini displayed frustration with being unable to pinpoint resources needed to support the mission. As time ran out and their first attempt failed, Reba expressed, "It's a crazy big puzzle, nothing like yesterday." Carini advised that they select a different module; however, Reba responded, "No, it's OK. We got this. I think we just needed a little warm up." Reba restarted a few times until the game conferred the same puzzle configuration, and the pair began again. Following two more attempts, the girls succeeded and quickly switched roles to explore the next module. Their three teammates seemed locked in from the outset, unlocking two modules before meeting with any mishap. Both groups demonstrated patience and perseverance, and despite laboring with the manual's opaque directives and complex structures the day before, the girls now worked seamlessly through the text to locate and communicate information.

Describing her idea for splitting into two teams during her interview, Carini discussed the need for her group to be efficient with their time and efforts, offering, "By then we were really into the game and bummed out about the shorter class. We just tried to make the best of it with what we had. We wanted to beat it, so we did what we had to." Their design appeared to pay off over the next 20 minutes, as both groups were able to each complete two modules. The girls' innovation did not cease at collapsing their members; once one defuser was able to disarm the bomb, she immediately switched places with a supporter. The team then restarted the game until they found the most recent module, and the former diffuser offered immediate feedback to her successor on the module's best practices. The girls even interchanged themselves between the two groups as needed to ensure that each member had a chance to compete with the support of a teammate who had moments ago been successful herself. Even down one member, by doubling their impact, the girls had far exceeded the progress made by the other groups.

With 15 minutes remaining in the class, Tela burst into the room to the delight of her teammates. She plopped her things onto the pod's empty desk and blurted, "Where that bomb at? I'm ready to save the world!" Axilla handed her the headset and wand and wished her good luck, saying, "We got your back. We have so many tricks. The codes are actually simple once you pick them up. Help us out when we get to a problem in the manual, and we'll get you what you need." With the help of her five supporters who circulated notes, marked manual pages, and their trusted *speaking stretchy* like a finely tuned machine, Tela was able to defuse the bomb less than 5 minutes after walking through the door. The girls were progressing from newbies to masters.

Figure 8.8 Tela Writes in her Reflection Journal About her Experiences on the Second Day.

As they did throughout the unit, the girls spent the final few minutes of class scribing in their reflective journals. Characterizing her experiences from the day's station activities, Tela focused on her interactions with peers, which she felt positioned her team for success (figure 8.8):

> I think it's hard to play this game because some people aren't good with details and seeing and describing them and listening for perfect clues is even harder. I know what I'm talking about all that but it doesn't always make sense to another person. Like you can just tell the player is thinking but they aren't talking so you have to wait and let then work it all out. Plus you have to be able to read and follow hard directions that are easier if you just use your own words. This game is more about working with people than a freaking bomb. Doing the codes and wires is scary but my group got better because we really tried. We probably weren't ready for all this at first but we make a darn good team. It's kinda sad because tomorrow is the last day but I hope we do VR again.
>
> (Tela's journal entry)

By breaking into smaller teams, transposing personnel, manipulating the game's platform to their advantage, and incorporating the knowledge and skills accumulated from the day before, the girls constructed a deliberate design process that allowed them to test theories about each module and generate ideas about how to solve specific problems along the way. The girls demonstrated an ability to not only survive as a team under adverse conditions, but they were able to thrive by refining their approaches in ways that considered their unique constraints but maintained their overall objectives. Together, they planned and executed collaborative strategies that allowed them to adapt to the dynamics of game-based learning and utilize various resources within the fluid reality of school schedules. Their interaction was meaningful and effective.

Day 3: Global Collaboration and Digital Citizenship

On the third and final day of the bomb-defusing station, Axilla and a female peer from another group were the first to arrive to class. When they entered the classroom, Axilla exclaimed, "Oh my gosh, let me show you this bomb thing." After demonstrating what appeared to be the most reserved disposition on her team throughout the unit, outside of the group's interaction she now seemed much more engaged with the station. She had been soft-spoken during class; however, she was now beaming with pride and jabbering on about symbols, codes, and wire-cutting sequences as she shared her new knowledge and experiences (figure 8.9). While she had fulfilled her role

Figure 8.9 Axilla Walks her Friend Through Features in the Manual and Shares her Knowledge of a Module.

on the team in modest fashion, her demeanor in a slightly different setting was far livelier than she had previously showcased. When asked about this observable shift during her interview, Axilla admitted, "Our team is great and we get stuff done. I'm not the closest to them, most of my friends are in other classes but I can do what I need to do at that time. We all do that." Axilla went on to share that she had connected during our unit with a close friend who recently moved back to Mexico with her family via Twitter and Snapchat, to share her experiences with the game. She added, "I'm into this stuff. I might be quiet, but I love digitals and computers. I write code with my brother at home. I'd like to be an engineer like my uncle in Peru. I told him about the game, too." Axilla extended her VR interaction beyond the classroom and integrated it with her own personal aspirations, many of which complicate persistent gender stereotypes related to STEM fields such as engineering.

The girls decided they would spend Day 3 as a single group, completing as many modules as they could. Whereas their first attempts had been marred by simultaneous shouting and expressions of frustrations at the lack of communication, their interactions on the final day were precise and efficient. Each diffuser was able to complete at least one module during the class period, a feat that seemed far out of reach only days earlier. Having assumed multiple roles and incorporated numerous resources to continually redefine their affinity space in ways that afforded them opportunities for success, the girls had demonstrated a variety of digital-age competencies. With 20 minutes remaining, the class was given the chance to preview their next station. The girls were slated to begin the *Altspace VR* station on the following day, so they spent some time playing different academic games with other players around the world. Reba expressed

Figure 8.10   Reba Moves into New Realms of Educative Gaming in the Altspace VR Application.

excitement with starting a new series of challenges using VR (figure 8.10). In her interview, Reba talked about how her engagement in the bomb-defusing station informed how she would approach fresh tasks in new digital spaces. Describing her team's ability to assess and augment their available resources toward achieving their targets, Reba said, "I like using technology to find things out and do things. I know this is VR, but real life in school and jobs is just like that. You use what you have to make things happen and to help people."

As the girls prepared to connect with learners from other backgrounds and cultures, their collaboration around VR, digitized tools, and ELA domains were positioned to serve them well. In addition to the computational knowledge they had constructed, the girls also practiced respectful digital interaction throughout their bomb-defusing station work. Carini wrote in her final reflective journal about the process of treating fellow VR colleagues with dignity:

You can't see your team but you can hear them. And their voices help you decide what to do and think. This reminds me of comments and likes on Instagram where sometimes we don't see how much we can affect someone. Using VR at school was the same as sending our friends snaps and texting with them. We always hear how you should choose words carefully. My mom always tells us to be kind. This can be annoying but it's true! (Carini's journal entry)

In their team-oriented roles, the girls cultivated identities that made them aware of their own decisions and also cognizant of others who are impacted by their actions. VR provided a safe, inspiring platform through which inquiry could be facilitated in a positive manner.

DISCUSSION

This study makes contributions toward understanding the myriad ways VR can motivate secondary learners and enhance ELA curriculum by extending the kinds of academic outcomes that are acknowledged as part of instruction and assessment procedures. While the literacy operations participants enacted and the generative skills they practiced as part of their station work are also observable through normalized means such as vocabulary quizzes and comprehension tests, engagement increases when ELA pedagogies are inclusive of multiliteracies and allow for digital play and interactive knowledge construction (Marlatt, 2019b). Though situated in ELA, the significance of VR and STEM affordances extend beyond individual disciplines. Game-accelerated competencies and ISTE (2020) benchmarks related to developing learners who are collaborative, computational, and creative carries numerous cross-curricular ramifications and contributes to ongoing efforts to impact equity with justice-driven technology implementation (Rybakova et al., 2019). The girls' success with cultivating digital-age proficiencies by playing a VR-based video game alongside nonfiction texts complicates the stereotype that STEM opportunities should be exclusive to male students (Ireland et al., 2018). Axilla's description of her career aspirations, along with her STEM-driven engagement, are powerful examples of how this study's data can help disrupt harmfully untrue gender narratives. The notion of empowerment is vital to understanding the significance of this study. The girls were empowered to explore and discover through standards-driven interactions afforded by VR.

The possibility stands for qualitative research conducted by educators within their own classrooms to facilitate compelling results; however, while the present study yields a number of potential implications, its practitioner research design is not without limitations. Although genuine excitement and textual engagement were regularly observed during the focal group's interactions, a prospect persists that the girls could have consented to participate in order to maintain harmony with their instructor, and they also may have responded positively to station activities as a way to validate the researchers' instructional design efforts. We acknowledge the power differential that exists between adults and adolescents in classrooms, and all researchers should empathize with students' vulnerability and desire to please, which can result in purposefully agreeable behavior. The present study is also limited in scope due to its small sample size; thus, its results lack broad authority to generalize literacy experiences of girls who may be interested in VR or STEM on a larger scale beyond this single locale.

We also note the high level of affluence enjoyed by teachers and learners who operate at the school in which the present study took place with regard to technology implementation, materials, and resources. Clearly, not every ELA classroom is equipped with VR headsets and video game-based curricular models. And while recent data supports an overall increase in the use of technology to enhance academic achievement within standards-based learning environments (Anderson & Jiang, 2018), access to Internet-capable technology applications and availability of digital devices remains an issue of inequity in many areas of the United States. Further, nationwide transitions from physical classrooms to remote learning programs caused by the COVID-19 pandemic have the potential to exacerbate current disparities between the opportunities some students have to engage in digital literacies at home. We join other teacher educators who are committed to culturally sustaining teaching practices involving technology in advocating for justice-oriented policies that support students' academic achievement through game-based learning, multimodal engagement, and STEM applications.

CONCLUSION

As scholarly interest and practitioner implementation around the integration of VR and STEM in ELA settings intensifies, educators and teacher educators must continue to establish productive working partnerships whereby adolescents' digital literacies, and the interdisciplinary exploration they enable, are prioritized in curriculum and instruction. In conjunction with literacy objectives and academic standards for digital-age learners, VR and STEM represent future pathways through which twenty-first-century students can be inspired to engage in traditional ELA domains of reading, writing, listening, and speaking. Inquiry-based communication through and alongside multiple texts, authentic analyses of literary works, and powerful compositions in assorted genres and presentation styles, are only a few of the opportunities for literacy education afforded by VR applications. If ELA can truly embody *the bomb* for young people, we must not defuse their interest by turning them away from the platforms that define their contemporary meaning-making. Instead, we invite literacy instructors and researchers to provide a spark that can ignite students' engagement by further investigating the role of VR in our learning spaces.

REFERENCES

Anderson, M., & Jiang, J. (2018). *Teens, social media & technology 2018.* http://www.pewinternet.org/2018/05/31/teens-social-media-technology-2018/

Braun, V., & Clarke, V. (2006). Using thematic analysis in psychology. *Qualitative Research in Psychology, 3*(2), 77–101. https://doi.org/10.1191/14780 88706 qp063oa

Braun, V., Clarke, V., Hayfield, N., & Terry, G. (2019). Thematic analysis. In P. Liamputtong (Ed.), *Handbook of research methods in health social sciences* (pp. 843–860). Springer.

Burrows, A., Lockwood, M., Borowczak, M., Janak, E., & Barber, B. (2018). Integrated STEM: Focus on informal education and community collaboration through engineering. *Education Sciences, 8,* Article 8.

Calvert, H. (2015). Letting go of stand-alone technology: How to blend technology into literacy stations. *The Reading Teacher, 69*(2), 147–155. https ://doi.org/10 .1002/trtr.1373

Donmoyer, R. (2013). Generalizability and the single case study. In R. Gomm, M. Hammersly, & P. Foster (Eds.), *Case study method: Key issues, key texts* (pp. 45–68). Sage.

Freina, L., & Ott, M. (2015). A literature review on immersive virtual reality in education: State of the art and perspectives. In I. Roceanu, F. Moldoveanu, S. Trausan-Matu, D. Barbieru, D. Beligan, & A. Ionita (Eds.), T*he 11th international scientific conference "eLearning and Software for Education* (Vol. 1, pp. 133–141). "Carol I" National Defence University Publishing House.

Friedman, S. (2019). Girls who game program provides access to STEM opportunities. *The Journal.* https://thejournal.com/articles/2019/10/14/girls-who-game-program-provides-access-to-stem-opportunities.aspx

Gee, J. P. (2004). *Situated language and learning: A critique of traditional schooling.* Routledge.

Gee, J. P. (2007). *What video games have to teach us about learning and literacy.* Palgrave Macmillan.

Gee, J. P. (2017). Affinity spaces and 21st century learning. *Educational Technology, 57*(2), 27–31.

Gee, J. P., & Hayes, E. (2012). Nurturing affinity spaces and game-based learning. In C. Steinkuehler, K. Squire, & S. Barab (Eds.), *Games, learning, and society: Learning and meaning in the digital age* (pp. 129–155). Cambridge University Press.

Harvey, M. M. (2018). Video games and virtual reality as classroom literature: Thoughts, experiences, and learning with 8th grade middle school students (Doctoral dissertation). Retrieved from https://digitalrepository.unm.edu/educ_l lss_etds/90/

Harvey, M. M., Deuel, A., & Marlatt, R. (2020). To be or not to be: Modernizing Shakespeare with multimodal learning stations. *Journal of Adolescent and Adult Literacy, 63*(5), 559–568. https://doi.org/10.1002/jaal.1023

Hill, C., Corbett, C., & St. Rose, A. (2010). Why so few? Women in science, technology, engineering, and mathematics. AAUW. https://www.aauw.org/files/2013/02/Why-So-Few-Women-in-Science-Technology-Engi-neering-and-Mathematics.pdf

International Society for Technology in Education. (2019). ISTE standards for students. https://www.iste.org/standards/for-students

Ireland, D. T., Freeman, K. E., Winston-Proctor, C. E., DeLaine, K. D., McDonald Lowe, S., & Woodson, K. M. (2018). (Un)Hidden figures: A synthesis of research examining the intersectional experiences of black women and girls in STEM education. *Review of Research in Education, 42*(1), 226–254.

Lankshear, C., & Knobel, M. (2011). *New literacies: Everyday practices and social learning* (3rd ed.). McGraw-Hill.

Lewis Ellison, T. (2017). Digital participation, agency, and choice: An African American youth's digital storytelling about Minecraft. *Journal of Adolescent and Adult Literacy, 61*(1), 25–35.

Marlatt, R. (2018). Literary analysis using Minecraft: An Asian American youth crafts her literacy identity. *Journal of Adolescent and Adult Literacy, 62*(1), 55–66. https://doi.org/10.1002/jaal.747

Marlatt, R. (2019a). "I didn't say, 'Macbeth,' it was my Google Doc!": A secondary English case study of redefining learning in the 21st Century. *E-learning and Digital Media, 16*(1), 46–62. https://doi.org/10.1177/2042753018817544

Marlatt, R. (2019b). Get in the game: Promoting justice through a digitized literature study. *Multicultural Perspectives, 20*(4), 222–228.

McCarthy, J. (2019). Frameworks for fostering the skills students need for the future. *Edutopia.* https://www.edutopia.org/article/frameworks-fostering-skills-students-need-future

McCarthy, J. (2020). *Engaging students through esports in K-12 education: Understanding the value and potential impact.* Dell Technologies and Advanced Learning Partners.

McMillen C. M., Graves-Demario, A., & Kieliszek, D. (2018). Tackling literacy: A collaborative approach to developing materials, for assessing science literacy skills in content classrooms through a STEM perspective. *The Language and Literacy Spectrum, 28*(1), Article 2.

Moran, C. M. (2019, March 1). 5 reasons why virtual reality belongs in every classroom. https://corwin-connect.com/2019/03/5-reasons-why-virtual-reality-belongs-in-every-classroom/

NASEF. (2020). *Esports are for everyone.* https://www.nasef.org/resources/esports-for-everyone/

Perrin, A. (2018). *5 facts about Americans and video games.* Pew Research Center: FactTank. https://www.pewresearch.org/fact-tank/2018/09/17/5-facts-about-am ericans-and-video-games/

Pyles, B. (2019). *Women in gaming: An introduction.* North American Scholastic Esports Federation. https://www.nasef.org/news/blog/women-in-gaming/

Reinking, A., & Martin, B. (2018). The gender gap in STEM fields: Theories, movements, and ideas to engage girls in STEM. *Journal of New Approaches in Educational Research, 7*(2), 148–153.

Rice, M. (2016). A phenomenological inquiry into the technological curriculum making of secondary English Language Arts teachers in rural settings (Doctoral dissertation, University of Kansas). https://kuscholarworks.ku.edu/handle/1808/22029

Rybakova, K., Rice, M., Moran, C., Zucker, L., McGrail, W., McDermott, M., Loomis, S., Piotrowski, A., Garcia, M., Gerber, H., Marlatt, R., & Gibbons, T. (2019). A long arc bending towards equity: Tracing almost 20 years of ELA teaching trends in CITE. *Contemporary Issues in Technology and Teacher Education, 19*(4). Retrieved from https://citejournal.org/volume-19/issue-4-19/english-la nguage-arts/a-long-arc-bending-toward-equity-tracing-almost-20-years-of-ela-teac hing-with-technology/

Searle, K. A., Tofel-Grehl, C., & Breitenstein, J. (2019). Equitable engagement in STEM: Using E-Textiles to challenge the positioning of non-dominant girls in school science. *International Journal of Multicultural Education, 21*(1), 42–61.

Virtual reality. (n.d.). In *Lexico.* https ://www.lexico.com/en/definition/virtual_reality

Chapter 9

Integrating Culturally Responsive Pedagogy and Virtual Reality

Preparing Preservice Educators for Secondary Language Arts Classes

Rebecca Smith, Nichole Ralston,
and Benjamin Gallegos

In the current world of cell phones, social media, virtual and augmented reality, and the recent and rapid transition to online learning as the result of a global pandemic, the need for technologically competent teachers is not only helpful but also imperative. However, teacher preparation programs appear to be lacking in adequate preparation of tech-savvy teachers: in instruction related to online learning (Kennedy & Archambault, 2012), in how to integrate technology into lesson planning, and in teacher knowledge of technology standards (Alger & Kopcha, 2009; Chesley & Jordan, 2012; Mishra & Koehler, 2006). Research indicates that new teachers do not feel adequately prepared to effectively use technology in their classrooms (Sang et al., 2010), which is perhaps related to a reported lack of technology integration in practicum settings (Liu, 2012). Specifically, Liu (2012) advocates for embedding technology use and exposure throughout methods courses rather than teaching technology in isolation. Preservice teachers must leave teacher preparation programs ready to bring learning to life through technology in their K–12 classrooms.

The majority of students in teacher preparation programs today are part of the iGen (Twenge, 2017), which begins with students born in 1995. Many of these students had smartphones when they entered adolescence, which affects how they interact with the world compared to previous generations, including how they spend their time, their behaviors, and their attitudes toward religion, sexuality, and politics (Twenge, 2017). Yet, research on iGen suggests great disparities in digital competence, with factors such as socioeconomic status, age, and gender-impacting technology exposure and competence (Bayne & Ross, 2011; Li & Ranieri, 2010). These technological disparities call for differentiation in how teacher educators scaffold preservice teacher learning.

Our digital world necessitates technology-competent educators who can effectively teach K–12 students how to use technology as a tool for learning (Rybakova et al., 2019). Literature suggests that teachers may not be integrating technology effectively and efficiently into their practice, which can also adversely affect K–12 students' future opportunities (An & Reigeluth, 2011; Hammonds et al., 2013). Research has indicated that hands-on, experiential, and scaffolded practice with technology can improve teacher competence in teaching with technology (i.e., Anderson et al., 2017; Olofson et al., 2016). Furthermore, perceived self-efficacy of VR has been shown to impact perceived ease of use of VR (Huang & Liaw, 2018), so the constructivist nature of hands-on, scaffolded learning of the VR is one way to support teacher learning with this new technology.

In addition to the diverse forms of technology present in education today, the diversity of our K–12 student population also necessitates culturally responsive pedagogy (CRP) (Gay, 2010; Ladson-Billings, 1995) to support student learning and growth. Ladson-Billings (2014) defines CRP within three domains: (1) academic success, which includes intellectual growth experienced by students as a result of classroom learning; (2) cultural competence, which involves students gaining an appreciation for both their own culture and celebrating the cultures of others; and (3) sociopolitical consciousness, which focuses on students' abilities to identify, analyze, and solve real-world problems. Honoring students' lived experiences is perhaps more important now than ever, with the COVID-19 pandemic requiring remote learning (Kirkland, n.d.). Students and families must be collective agents of their own learning, and students, and teachers must recognize the inequities embedded in remote, technology-based learning, and challenge these disparities by supporting students' social-emotional health, affirming racial and cultural identities, and designing learning experiences that respond to the diverse social and cultural assets of our students (Kirkland, n.d.). Technology can serve as the conduit for integrating CRP into K–12 classrooms, whether it is remote or classroom-based learning environments.

INTEGRATING CULTURALLY RESPONSIVE TEACHING AND VIRTUAL REALITY

One technology platform that has the potential to bring learning to life in innovative and culturally responsive ways is virtual reality (VR). For the purposes of this study, VR was utilized in the form of a handheld headset, to which a smartphone device was attached; the phone contained a 360-degree picture of a physical space. Participants held the VR headset to their eyes and moved their head in all directions in order to see various perspectives of the virtual location. Research around VR in education is still limited, and yet there appear to be both academic and affective benefits for both students and teachers that align with Ladson-Billings's (2014) CRP framework. Research has shown that teachers who have students participate in virtual field trips are able to extend and enhance existing curriculum to improve student learning (Bashir, 2018; Klemm & Tuthill, 2003). Furthermore, VR can promote literacy engagement in high sensory, multimodal environments, such as through integrated science and literacy lessons involving data collection and interpretation (Hutchison, 2018). The potential for hands-on engagement in virtual environments, in addition to culturally rich VR content, provide a natural fit between CRP and VR.

Virtual reality can also support culturally responsive pedagogy in its capacity to connect classroom learning to the "collective lived experiences" (Kirkland, n.d., p. 2) that is needed in CRP. VR has the ability to be interdisciplinary in nature (Pellas et al., 2017) and can provide students with a platform for solving real-world problems. Additionally, VR can expose students who are economically disadvantaged with experiences they may otherwise never have, such as field trips around the globe, into the ocean, or to outer space (Klemm & Tuthill, 2003; Stainfield et al., 2010). These global cultural immersion experiences support Ladson-Billings's (2014) call to "incorporate the multiplicities of identities and cultures that help formulate today's youth culture" (p. 82). Through VR, students can be exposed to cultures and people far beyond their local, national, or even global contexts.

There are benefits to VR that go beyond academics. VR has the capacity to build student empathy (Alsever, 2017), reduce anxiety, and improve student confidence (Ferguson et al., 2014). One study (McLean, 2010) found that virtual spaces gave an immigrant adolescent student a sense of home and a connection to the life they left behind. These activities of connecting the challenges and injustices in lived experiences of students provide a culturally responsive and draw on a critical pedagogical lens (Giroux & Simon, 1989), allowing for students to "rethink how people give meaning and ethical substance to their experiences and voices" (p. 237). The abundance of benefits associated with both an integration of culturally responsive practices and the use of VR calls for an integration of this technology in teacher preparation programs, so our future educators will be confident and capable of teaching with innovative technologies that seamlessly integrate CRP.

VIRTUAL REALITY IN ENGLISH
LANGUAGE ARTS CLASSROOMS

Virtual reality can be integrated across the curriculum in K–12 schools; however, in the secondary English language arts (ELA) classroom, there is a particularly relevant space for this technology as a new text platform. The ELA classroom is a place for critical examination of texts, such as urban fiction and multicultural literature (Haddix & Price-Dennis, 2013). It is a place where culturally responsive teachers can engage students with curricular *counterstories* from voices that are often marginalized, including persons identifying as nonwhite, nonmale, and/or nonheterosexual (Bissonnette & Glazier, 2016); engagement with these critical texts can provide students with "a space in which they can express themselves, share their lived experiences, discuss their realities, and actively engage in critical reading, thinking, writing, and speaking skills" (p. 686). For generations, students have been presented with a literary canon that perpetuates dominant narratives (i.e., whiteness, masculinity, heterosexuality, Christianity, physical and mental ability), often without a critical examination of the dominant narratives in these texts (Borsheim-Black et al., 2014). However, teachers must also be cognizant and cautious of further marginalizing students of color through simplistic understandings and implementation of CRP, such as highlighting only cultural celebrations, which can continue to promote *essentializing*, or promoting "a fairly fixed and homogeneous conception of the culture of an ethnic or racial group" (Sleeter, 2012, p. 570). Moreover, Sleeter (2012) argues that teachers must understand CRP as a "paradigm for teaching and learning" (p. 569), rather than a set of steps to follow. Deeper teacher learning regarding CRP can help diversify the ELA curriculum for deeper and inclusive student learning. The use of VR as a text for seeing the world differently can help to bring a critical perspective to both canonical texts and to counternarratives present in multicultural literature.

VR brings additional learning benefits into the ELA classroom, both for teachers and for students, even within traditional canonical texts. For instance, utilizing a *critical canon pedagogy* (Dyches, 2018) can provide students with "opportunit[ies] to re-story their entirely White curriculum, and in doing so, reconsider and resist the traditional narratives and voices of the canon" (p. 538). An author such as Shakespeare could be taught within this critical pedagogy. Research indicates that while preservice teachers may feel excited about teaching Shakespeare, they also feel anxiety about how low achieving students may struggle with the texts (Elliott, 2016). VR can serve as the bridge that can increase student engagement and deepen learning (Jones & Warren, 2011) surrounding difficult texts. Through teacher scaffolding, VR technology can "foster a sense of wonder and excitement, bringing about meaningful outputs that cross both physical and virtual domains" (Marsh & Yamada-Rice, 2018, p. 49). This deep content engagement through visual and experiential learning helps scaffold prior knowledge by engaging students with virtual field trip experiences (Pilgrim & Pilgrim, 2016). Student engagement and interest in learning can also be enhanced by their direct interactions with technology, as supported by learning standards.

Digital literacy and citizenship, as defined in the International Society for Technology in Education (ISTE, 2016) standards for students, calls for active student engagement and empowerment with digital content and tools, focused on the interconnected global world. Technology competence, such as navigating through digital spaces and seeking out key data within the virtual expedition, can be taught within an interactive VR learning space also focused on a traditional ELA topic. Students and teachers alike can improve their cultural competence by visiting worlds beyond the borders of their classrooms, cities, countries, or even galaxies.

PURPOSE OF THIS STUDY

Despite the popularity of research on both CRP and the emerging research on VR for teacher and student learning, little research connects VR and CRP as a meaningful partnership for the learning of both teachers and students. Thus, the purpose of this study was to demonstrate how CRP and VR can be jointly integrated into one teacher preparation program's ELA Methods course, and then pushed out to K–12 classrooms via preservice teacher candidates.

This study describes how this VR/CRP integration occurred within one teacher preparation program at a small liberal arts university in the Pacific Northwest. The study began with an institutional grant focused on integrating innovative technologies into higher education. The $5,000 grant included the purchase of a Google Expeditions VR kit, which included: one rolling case to store the gear, one wireless router, one 10-inch Zenpad (which is a tablet resembling an iPad), ten Mattel Deluxe Master Viewers (the glasses the user holds up to their eyes), ten Magellan Devices (similar to smartphones). Three teacher educators teamed up to integrate VR into their teacher preparation courses. This chapter highlights only one aspect of this research study: the use of VR with preservice ELA teachers, including both undergraduate ($n = 5$) and master of arts in teaching (MAT) students ($n = 3$).

There were three forms of data collection for this study: quantitative pre/post-survey data from preservice teachers on their confidence using technology as teachers and students and their confidence in lesson planning; lesson plans from the methods course teaching simulation, and post-survey feedback from teacher candidates who used the VR technology in their student teaching

K–12 ELA placements. Preservice teacher candidates were required to design an ELA lesson utilizing VR technology and engage the university education methods class in a teaching simulation; students were then invited to "check out" the VR kit for use in their K–12 classrooms. Candidates completed a post-survey following the K–12 VR lessons, which included questions about their beliefs in the culturally responsive nature of VR, challenges in teaching with VR, and recommendations for other teachers. These data were all analyzed for themes, and summarized in this chapter.

INTRODUCING VR TO PRESERVICE TEACHERS WITH A CULTURAL LENS

Preservice teacher candidates were introduced to the VR technology using deliberate modeling and scaffolding with an explicit focus on CRP. For instance, in the very first introduction to the VR technology, students were taken on a virtual field trip via a Google Expedition titled *Out of Syria: Back into School* (https://www.youtube.com/watch?v=2wMqzvqRMQo). This expedition explores a Syrian Refugee Camp and the life of a 12-year-old girl living at the camp, including her school building and her home. This experience provided the preservice candidates with a lesson that allowed them to "walk in someone else's shoes," as one candidate described, and it required them to engage in written reflections and small group discussions following this VR experience to explore the connection between VR and CRP. We discussed methods for utilizing this particular expedition in an ELA classroom, such as writing from different character's perspectives and doing a character–self comparison. This introductory experience began the scaffolding of both VR and CRP knowledge. For example, one candidate said, "This experience, though short, certainly elevated empathy for refugees as I was able to see similarities and differences between my life and this specific refugee's life." Another preservice teacher described their reaction to the experience in ways they might accommodate future students who are refugees:

> I plan to accommodate my students by being sensitive to their needs and giving them time to heal and adjust to a new setting. Not only are they experiencing a culture shock, language barrier, and traumas, but they have been placed in an unfamiliar educational environment which could be incredibly intimidating.
>
> (Teacher candidate)

This reflective learning experience following a VR immersion allowed the preservice teacher candidates to make connections with students across cultures and experiences while simultaneously exposing them to a new, innovative technology in a safe, interactive space.

GOOGLE EXPEDITIONS AS A CULTURALLY RESPONSIVE LEARNING PLATFORM

The scaffolded dive into VR and CRP continued in a few key ways. After this first in-class, hands-on model of how to integrate VR in an ELA classroom using CRP, preservice teachers were then required to explore Google Expeditions with an eye for CRP and ELA, knowing they would eventually design a lesson plan utilizing VR technology. The Google Expeditions platform was chosen for VR lessons because it is a free application that can be downloaded on any handheld device, including a smartphone or a tablet, and it has a wide variety of topics.

Within the Expeditions app, there are numerous categories from which to search, which also promotes teaching across the curriculum. Current categories include Arts and Culture, Landscapes, Science, Environment, the World Today, Careers, and Colleges. Additionally, there is a search bar where key terms can be used to find relevant expeditions. For example, when "Shakespeare" is entered as a search term, six expeditions are suggested, including *The Settings of Shakespeare's Plays* and *West Side Story: The Play and the City*. Several of our preservice teachers have also thought outside the box and used expeditions such as *Geography of Europe* to teach an introduction to Shakespeare or *How Animals See the World* to teach perspective-taking. Each expedition includes numerous "scenes," which can be accessed when the user looks down to see white arrows, which can be clicked with a button on the VR headset.

An additional option the preservice teachers used when exploring Google Expeditions as the VR platform is *Guide an Expedition*, which means the teacher controls what students see on their devices (i.e., all users are on the same field trip, in the same virtual space, at the same time). This method requires all devices used for the expedition to be on the same Wi-Fi network. Then, the teacher uses a smart device, such as Google's Zenpad, a ChromeBook, or a smartphone with Expeditions, to download the desired expedition. The instructor then clicks on "Guide" within the application, which will provide the teacher with a code that will be given to the student users. The students will go to "Class" on the bottom of the Expeditions screen, which will then prompt them to join the expedition that is being led by the teacher.

A guided expedition may be warranted for younger students who may struggle navigating the digital space successfully, especially between scenes, or for students who may not be able to read the text descriptions within the expedition. Additionally, if teachers are concerned about students staying on task within the planned expedition, leading it may ensure more on-task learning. Conversely, empowering students with the freedom to explore an expedition on their own and spend more time in certain scenes also has its benefits. The teacher educator used the "Guide" platform to model for the preservice teachers this option, which they could then utilize while teaching VR lessons to both other preservice teachers and K–12 students. While there is a learning curve for using these tools to efficiently find and load the VR resources, preservice candidates quickly became used to using Google Expeditions and the headsets through the scaffolded instruction.

The VR lesson options are nearly limitless with the use of Google Expeditions; teachers can take classes to the International Space Station, visit the *Titanic*, go to a Hawaiian volcano, climb Mount Everest, visit a World War II Memorial, or explore Lesbian, Gay, Bisexual, and Transgender (LGBT) history in New York City. One preservice teacher took her middle school class to the September 11 Memorial Museum when she realized they had no conception of the 9/11 terrorist attacks, and they were going to read *Shooting Kabul* by N. H. Senzai. Students can visit Aztec and Mayan ruins, Ancient Egypt, and South Africa. A teacher planning a culturally relevant VR lesson may get lost in exciting virtual options for hours.

CULTURALLY RESPONSIVE LESSON PLANNING WITH VR

After this initial exploration of Google Expeditions, students then designed a culturally responsive lesson plan for their own ELA classroom using what they had learned utilizing the VR technology. They then engaged the university class in a teaching simulation of this lesson to help scaffold the technology, content, and pedagogical components of becoming an educator. To support the planning, preservice teachers were able to use the kit devices during class in a collaborative work space and then also used their own smartphone or tablet to access Google Expeditions outside of class to plan lessons. Students were then also invited to "check out" the VR kit for use in their own K–12 classrooms to implement the lesson in a real situation if they desired. Although there were only ten devices in the kit, preservice teachers were able to practice various strategies in our university setting for adapting to this limitation, such as partners, small groups, or stations. The authors of this chapter have secured a follow-up institutional grant to increase the capacity to thirty devices, which would provide a class set for preservice teachers to take to K–12 classrooms.

The VR/CRP lesson plans designed by preservice educators are detailed by grade level and topic in table 9.1; they spanned a large variety of topics. In a traditional secondary English literature class, for example, VR was frequently used to introduce content related to an upcoming novel. Virtual field trips to Europe, museums, or a plantation that enslaved people helped to build background knowledge and engage students in critical thinking, scaffolding academic learning. Additionally, VR was used in ELA classrooms to help reinforce literary concepts or figurative language, such as having students experience a protagonist's feeling of being *overwhelmed*, by visiting an underwater virtual scene. One teacher candidate used VR in her English Language Development class to promote student discourse in present tense by having students describe a virtual scene. In all of the lessons utilized in K–12 classrooms, there was a culturally responsive focus, typically around the content of the lesson and the way in which students were encouraged to connect with the content, such as seeing from diverse perspectives or debating challenging topics. Table 9.1 shows how each lesson was connected to at least one of the three domains of Culturally Responsive Pedagogy (Ladson-Billings, 2014), especially academic success and cultural competence.

To further scaffold their lesson planning, it was recommended to the preservice teachers that they introduce the learning targets to students and provide a guide to help students through the expedition to ensure learning targets were met. This guide could have included a critical question about each scene in the expedition or reflective questions, such as, "Which scene was your favorite and why? Whose stories are highlighted in the scene, and whose are not?" One preservice teacher candidate created a "Virtual Passport" for students to use as a guide on their virtual field trip (see figure 9.1). This experience of exploring the world and cultures beyond the classroom is another culturally responsive teaching strategy.

PRESERVICE TEACHER FEEDBACK ON IMPACT OF VR

Data from preservice teacher candidates ($n = 9$) who participated in this VR learning were collected in the form of both a pre- and post-survey regarding their confidence using technology, both as students and as teachers, and qualitative data collected via survey feedback from candidates following K–12 VR/CRP lesson implementation. Two key themes were discovered: that using VR in this scaffolded way can boost teacher confidence in teaching with technology, and that using VR can be a culturally responsive engagement strategy.

1. *Using VR boosts teacher confidence.* Preservice candidates were asked in a pre- and post-survey about their confidence in three areas: using technology as a student for learning, using technology as a teaching tool, and

Table 9.1 Virtual Reality Lessons Implemented by Preservice Teachers (Source: Rebecca Smith)

Grade Level & Class	Lesson Topic	Google Expedition Title	Learning Goal	Culturally Responsive Pedagogy Domain
Sixth-Grade ELA	*Shooting Kabul* by N. H. Senzai	9/11 Memorial & Museum	Build prior knowledge and historical context about the September 11 attack on the World Trade Center in New York City	Academic success; cultural competence
Middle School English Language Development	Practice speaking with a partner in present tense	How Animals See the World	Language development: provide engaging learning content for students to practice present tense using prompts, "What do you see?" "I see ____." "What does the animal see?" "The animal sees ____."	Academic success; cultural competence
Middle School ELA/ Science	Narrative Writing from Perspective of an Animal and Using Scientific Facts, Anatomy of Human Eye, Scientific Observations	How Animals See the World	Compare and contrast how humans and animals see the world, identify scientific facts from the VR text, and write a narrative from the perspective of an animal using one fact and at least three observations.	Academic success; cultural competence
Eighth Grade ELA	*The Skin I'm In* by Sharon Flake	Underwater Galapagos	Allow students to understand how the protagonist may have felt when she described feeling "in over [her] head."	Academic success; cultural competence

Eighth-Grade Humanities	*Chains* by Laurie Halse Anderson	Slavery in America	Create background knowledge prior to reading text; explore a slave plantation, living quarters, and fields in the South.	Academic success; cultural competence
High School ELA	*The Great Gatsby* by F. Scott Fitzgerald	The Gold Coast of Gatsby's Long Island	Build context: students can comprehend the size, scale, and opulent historical mansions from the setting of *The Great Gatsby*. Compare and contrast to their own lived experiences. Analyze how the environment of Long Island in the 1920s helped inform the idea of "The American Dream" that Fitzgerald's protagonist is chasing.	Academic success; cultural competence
Ninth-Grade ELA	*Romeo & Juliet* by William Shakespeare	The Setting of Shakespeare's Plays	Build prior knowledge by exploring diverse places about which Shakespeare wrote. Debate if virtual reality should be more prevalent in schools.	Academic success; cultural competence; sociopolitical consciousness
Ninth-Grade ELA	*Dear Martin* by Nic Stone	Martin Luther King, Jr. National Historic Site, Civil Rights Movement, & Voices of Social Justice at Smithsonian	Build background knowledge prior to reading *Dear Martin*. Students will be able to share what interested them in a classroom debrief. Make connections across time and anchor their reading in the real world.	Academic success; cultural competence; sociopolitical consciousness

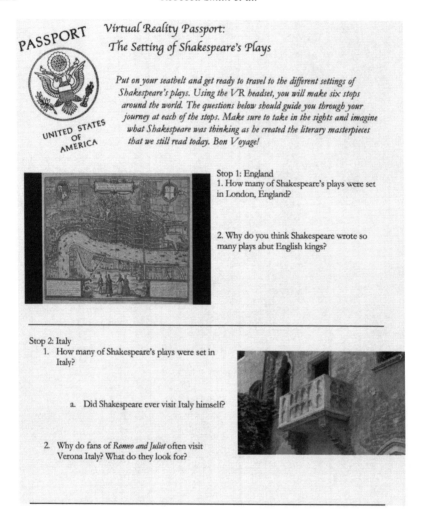

Figure 9.1   Virtual Passport for the Settings of Shakespeare's Plays Google Expedition (Created by Preservice Teacher Claire Breiholz).

lesson planning. Results of these survey data are displayed in table 9.2 and show there was statistically significant ($p < 0.05$) positive growth in all three categories after utilizing the VR in preservice education classes. These findings suggest that explicitly scaffolding student technology use positively impacted student confidence.

2. *VR can be culturally responsive.* One of the post-implementation open-ended survey items for participating preservice candidates was, *Do you see VR as a culturally responsive teaching practice? Please explain.* Overwhelmingly, preservice teachers agreed that VR allowed students

Stop 3: Ancient Britain
1.   Why might it have been easier for Shakespeare to fictionalize ancient kings and queens of Britain than rulers of his time?

Stop 4: Ancient Rome
1. Was Shakespeare's audience familiar with the tales of Ancient Rome?

Stop 5: Denmark and other locations
1. What Shakespearean play is set in Denmark?

Stop 6: Ancient Greece
1. Why might a busy city like Athens be a good location for a play?

Bon Voyage!

Figure 9.1 *(Continued).*

to be exposed to diverse perspectives and experiences that they may not otherwise be exposed to. For instance, one teacher said:

> [VR] allows students to have experiences they may not be able to have otherwise and builds their understanding of the world in unison. As all of my students have very different backgrounds and opportunities within their

own lives to travel or to understand the experiences of various communities, using VR was a way to have all my students see different parts of our country and gain an understanding of the people who live there.

Furthermore, one preservice teacher believed using VR is "an equitable teaching practice. Some of these kids haven't been anywhere away from their neighborhood and it gave them the ability to see a different environment." VR allowed K–12 students to both see and experience life beyond their classroom settings.

Additionally, utilizing technology for learning appeals to the current K–12 generation: "I think it was culturally responsive in that it really is engaging for their demographic. Just a new technology." In addition to diversity of experiences and perspectives, VR can also reach a variety of learners. One preservice teacher educator stated, "I think it's something that's very immersive, so that a lot of different types of learners can kind of profit from it." VR allowed K–12 ELA students to make cultural connections between their lives in and outside of the classroom, recognizing that technology can be used for learning.

RECOMMENDATIONS FOR TEACHERS UTILIZING VR

Several key recommendations arose for both teacher educators and in-service teachers planning to integrate VR into their instruction. The university lesson plan simulations helped to scaffold and trouble shoot many potential issues around the planning and use of VR; yet, there are inevitably challenges that arise with the use of new and innovative technologies. For example, one preservice teacher said, "I did feel like the technology, in some ways, outshone the content in this lesson." Another elaborated on this idea:

> My students were getting pretty burned out on what we had been doing for the last few weeks, and so the VR activity was great to reinvigorate them on the content and have them think about it in a new way. However, I don't think I gave students enough time to get the most learning out of the experience. I didn't properly account for the amount of time it would take them just to adjust to the VR, get the hang of using it, and actually start to do the work I expected of them. I think that if I had been able to, it would have been better to give students time to explore any of the expeditions just to get it out of their system and learn how to use it before asking them to do something specific.

Despite the benefits described and the extent to which preservice teachers experienced growth in their confidence, students did experience challenges with implementing the VR technologies, which led to several key recommendations for future teachers utilizing VR.

Table 9.2   Pre- and Post-VR Survey Results Per Item (Source: Rebecca Smith)

	Pre Mean (SD)	Post Mean (SD)	P	Pre Percent Confident	Post Percent Confident	Change
I feel confident about using technology as a student for learning.	3.04 (0.86)	3.38 (0.71)	0.043*	67%	88%	+21%
I feel confident about using technology as a teaching tool.	2.53 (0.78)	3.13 (0.80)	0.006*	50%	75%	+25%
I feel confident writing a lesson plan.	2.65 (0.71)	3.26 (0.54)	0.001*	61%	96%	+35%

Notes. * Statistically significant ($p < 0.05$) Scale 1 = not confident at all, 4 = completely confident.

Prepare the gear and the students. A consistent point of feedback from preservice teachers using VR in their classrooms was to dedicate time to preparing the gear in advance. One teacher said, "Expect the unexpected with technology implementation." However, when the preservice teachers took the time to set up, ensure the devices were charged, and plan logistics carefully, the lessons were smoother. Teachers must consider Internet connectivity and Wi-Fi network requirements, for example. It is critical that teachers plan ahead to either connect all devices to the school Wi-Fi network, which often requires a password, download expeditions in advance of the lesson, or use the Wi-Fi router provided with the VR kit. Downloading the needed expedition(s) on all devices helps to minimize implementation-day challenges around technology use. Proper planning is essential for the use of any new technology; and even with planning, there are bound to be challenges. This finding supports prior research that suggests that VR requires planning, instructor expertise, and a budget (Ferguson et al., 2014).

Use the "awe factor" purposefully. The "awe factor" of a new technology was both a pro and con in a learning environment. Preservice teachers reported high student engagement and interest in the lessons, with one K–12 student saying, "This is the coolest thing I have ever done." However, in certain classrooms, the presence of a new technology caused students to act out more than a typical day. For instance, one preservice teacher recommended: "Think about setting behavior expectations even if it seems like you don't need to." Maintaining clear behavioral expectations, including modeling usage, can help limit management challenges. Additionally, the preservice candidates recommended preparing the students for using the new technology: "I think just making sure that students are very aware of the reasons why they're doing it, how it works, and how it relates." The intrigue of using VR for student learning was contagious though; when a group of sixth-grade classes used the VR, the eighth-grade students began asking the teacher when they were going to use it. Exposing students to this new technology can increase engagement in the content. This finding is also supported by prior research on virtual learning in education (i.e., Hutchison, 2018; Jones & Warren, 2011).

Allow time to explore and play. One method for focusing student enthusiasm on learning can involve allowing them to "play" with the VR gear before using it for deliberate learning targets, so students can "get their curiosity out, so that they can commit to being focused on the desired lesson when it is time." This time for exploration can also help scaffold learning a new technology platform, such as how to navigate between scenes in an expedition, which can preserve learning time in a future lesson.

Avoid overuse. Overall, it is a good reminder for students to understand, "[Using VR] was a privilege they got to do, and it was a huge motivator, so using [the VR] sparingly is probably best." This recommendation from a preservice candidate supports prior research that VR should be used as only one instructional strategy in the midst of others (Lee, 1999; Merchant et al., 2014; Sitzmann, 2011).

Plan for cybersickness. Nausea was a consistent challenge for many users. According to researchers who study *cybersickness*, between 40 and 70 percent of users can get ill from engaging with virtual technologies (Kim, 2019). We have found that the simplest solution to this challenge is to use the screen instead of the headset. In Google Expeditions, the user can choose to view in a VR headset or to view on the screen, the latter of which will cause less dizziness. However, some users will feel queasy no matter how they view the technology, so having a back-up learning option for these students may be wise.

Plan for your VR to student ratio. Teachers must consider user capacity when using VR for student learning. We only had grant funding for a set of ten headsets and smart devices; however, preservice teachers were able to troubleshoot this limitation by having students work in partners, small groups, or stations. Preservice teachers increased student engagement by assigning students different roles to play in the groups, such as Recorder, Explorer, and Reporter. Additionally, teacher candidates utilizing the station-model were able to use the VR gear at two different stations. As is often the case for all teachers, preservice candidates in this study were innovative in their planning and implementation of VR technology, despite its challenges.

CONCLUSION

It is clear from this research that using VR in secondary ELA classrooms can be a powerful, and potentially underutilized, strategy, in two different ways. First, this explicit scaffolded learning model significantly ($p < 0.05$)

improved preservice teacher confidence and competence with the technology, and increased their confidence in writing culturally responsive lesson plans. Other research supports these findings, that perceived self-efficacy with VR and teacher beliefs and dispositions about VR impact ease of use, curriculum design, and instructional outcomes (Huang & Liaw, 2018; Han & Patterson, 2020). Throughout the methods course, students were introduced to culturally responsive pedagogy as a theoretical framework, and our class engaged in numerous readings and activities related to CRP (i.e., Christensen, 2017; Gay, 2010; Ladson-Billings, 2014). Additionally, we discussed the importance of self-reflection regarding our own implicit biases, cultural values, and racist behaviors that can cause harm to people of color (Hammond, 2015; Oluo, 2019). The integrated VR/CRP scaffolding appeared to aid preservice candidates in their planning and implementation of VR/CRP lessons.

The scaffolded strategies used in this study were key. Preservice teachers in this study were able to plan and practice virtual reality lessons in a safe learning space prior to implementing this new technology with middle and high school students. Second, it appears that VR is a culturally responsive teaching method that can expose students in K–12 and higher education to diverse perspectives and experiences in a safe, inclusive environment. Our findings support prior research indicating positive student growth in both academic and affective learning through the use of VR (i.e., Alsever, 2017; Ferguson et al., 2014; Merchant et al., 2014). However, this study explicitly highlights the capacity for VR to be used to prepare culturally responsive teachers, which is an avenue needing further research. Exploring life beyond the classroom walls enhances learning for students at all levels. The use of VR in secondary ELA classrooms promotes cultural inclusion and acceptance of new ideas, prompts students and teachers to become cognizant of their sociopolitical existence, and provides unique experiences that can expand the way our students learn.

REFERENCES

Alger, C., & Kopcha, T. (2009). eSupervision: A technology framework for the 21st century field experience in teacher education. *Issues in Teacher Education, 18*(2), 31–46.

Alsever, J. (2017). Is virtual reality the ultimate empathy machine? *Wired.* Retrieved from https://www.wired.com/brandlab/2015/11/is-virtual-reality-the-ultimate-empathy-machine/

An, Y. J., & Reigeluth, C. (2011). Creating technology-enhanced, learner-centered classrooms: K–12 teachers' beliefs, perceptions, barriers, and support needs. *Journal of Digital Learning in Teacher Education, 28*(2), 54–62. doi:10.1080/21532974.2011.10784681

Anderson, S., Griffith, R., & Crawford, L. (2017). TPACK in special education: Preservice teacher decision making while integrating iPads into instruction. *CITE: Contemporary Issues in Technology and Teacher Education, 17*(1), 97–127.

Bashir, G. (2010). Technology and medicine: The evolution of virtual reality simulation in laparoscopic training. *Medical Teacher, 32*(7), 558–561. https://doi.org/10.3109/01421590903447708

Bayne, S., & Ross, J. (2011). 'Digital native' and 'digital immigrant' discourses: A critique. In R. Land & S. Bayne (Eds)., *Digital difference* (pp. 159–169). Brill Sense.

Bissonnette, J. D., & Glazier, J. (2016). A counterstory of one's own. *Journal of Adolescent & Adult Literacy, 59*(6), 685–694. https://doi.org/10.1002/jaal.486

Borsheim-Black, C., Macaluso, M., & Petrone, R. (2014). Critical literature pedagogy: Teaching canonical literature for critical literacy. *Journal of Adolescent & Adult Literacy, 58*(2), 123–133. https://doi.org/10.1002/jaal.323

Chesley, G. M., & Jordan, J. (2012). What's missing from teacher prep. *Educational Leadership, 69*(8), 41–45.

Christensen, L. (2017). *Reading, writing, and rising up* (2nd ed.). Rethinking Schools.

Dyches, J. (2018). Critical canon pedagogy: Applying disciplinary inquiry to cultivate canonical critical consciousness. *Harvard Educational Review, 88*(4), 538–564. https://doi.org/10.17763/1943-5045-88.4.538

Elliott, V. (2016). "Study what you most affect": Beginning teachers' preparedness to teach Shakespeare. *CEA Critic, 78*(2), 199–212. https://doi.org/10.1353/cea.2016.0014

Ferguson, T. D., Howell, T. L., & Parsons, L. C. (2014). The birth experience: Learning through clinical simulation. *International Journal of Childbirth Education, 29*(3), 66–72.

Gay, G. (2010). *Culturally responsive teaching: Theory, research, and practice* (2nd ed., Multicultural education series). Teachers College.

Giroux, H., & Simon, R. (1989). Popular culture and critical pedagogy: Everyday life as a basis for curriculum knowledge. In H. Giroux & P. McLaren (Eds.). (1989). *Critical pedagogy, the state, and cultural struggle.* SUNY Press.

Haddix, M., & Price-Dennis, D. (2013). Urban fiction and multicultural literature as transformative tools for preparing English teachers for diverse classrooms. *English Education, 45*(3), 247–283.

Hammond, Z. (2015). *Culturally responsive teaching and the brain: Promoting authentic engagement and rigor among culturally and linguistically diverse students.* Corwin Press.

Hammonds, L., Matherson, L., Wilson, E., & Wright, V. (2013). Gateway tools: Five tools to allow teachers to overcome barriers to technology integration. *Delta Kappa Gamma Bulletin, 80*(1), 36–40. Retrieved from http://search.proquest.com/docview/1437196957/

Han, I., & Patterson, T. (2020). Teacher learning through technology-enhanced curriculum design using virtual reality. *Teachers College Record, 122*(7). http://search.proquest.com/docview/2422079111/

Huang, H. M., & Liaw, S. S. (2018). An analysis of learners' intentions toward virtual reality learning based on constructivist and technology acceptance approaches. *International Review of Research in Open and Distributed Learning, 19*(1).

Hutchison, A. (2018). Using virtual reality to explore science and literacy concepts. *The Reading Teacher, 72*(3), 343–353. https://doi.org/10.1002/trtr.1720

International Society for Technology in Education. (2016). *ISTE standards for students.* https://www.iste.org/standards/for-students

Jones, G., & Warren, S. (2011). Issues and concerns of K-12 educators on 3-D multi-user virtual environments in formal classroom settings. *International Journal of Gaming and Computer-Mediated Simulations, 3*(1), 1–12. doi:10.4018/jgcms.2011010101

Kennedy, K., & Archambault, L. (2012). Offering preservice teachers field experiences in K-12 online learning: A national survey of teacher education programs. *Journal of Teacher Education, 63*(3), 185–200.

Kim, M. (2019, August 14). Cybersickness: Why people experience motion sickness during virtual reality. Retrieved from https://www.insidescience.org/news/cybersickness-why-people-experience-motion-sickness-during-virtual-reality

Kirkland, D. (n.d.). *Guidance on culturally responsive-sustaining remote education: Centering equity, access, and educational justice.* Metropolitan Center for Research on Equity and the Transformation of Schools. https://www.oregon.gov/ode/educator-resources/standards/Documents/Guidance%20on%20Culturally%20Responsive-Sustaining%20Remote%20Teaching%20and%20Learning.pdf

Klemm, E. B., & Tuthill, G. (2003). Virtual field trips: Best practices. *International Journal of Instructional Media, 30*(2), 177–193.

Ladson-Billings, G. (1995). Toward a theory of culturally relevant pedagogy. *American Educational Research Journal, 32*(3), 465–491.

Ladson-Billings, G. (2014). Culturally relevant pedagogy 2.0: A.k.a. the remix. *Harvard Educational Review, 84*(1), 74–84.

Lee, J. (1999). Effectiveness of computer-based instructional simulation: A meta-analysis. *International Journal of Instructional Media, 26*(1), 71–85.

Li, Y., & Ranieri, M. (2010). Are "digital natives" really digitally competent? A study on Chinese teenagers. *British Journal of Educational Technology, 41*(6), 1029–1042. doi:10.1111/j.1467-8535.2009.01053.x

Liu, S. H. (2012). A multivariate model of factors influencing technology use by preservice teachers during practice teaching. *Journal of Educational Technology & Society, 15*(4), 137–149.

Marsh, J., & Yamada-Rice, D. (2018). Using Augmented and Virtual Reality in the Language Arts Curriculum. *Language Arts, 96*(1), 47–50.

McLean, C. (2010). A space called home: An immigrant adolescent's digital literacy practices. *Journal of Adolescent & Adult Literacy, 54*(1), 13–22. https://doi.org/10.1598/JAAL.54.1.2

Merchant, Z., Goetz, E. T., Cifuentes, L., Keeney-Kennicutt, W., & Davis, T. J. (2014). Effectiveness of virtual reality-based instruction on students' learning outcomes in K-12 and higher education: A meta-analysis. *Computers & Education, 70*, 29–40.

Mishra, P., & Koehler, M. J. (2006). Technological pedagogical content knowledge: A framework for teacher knowledge. *Teachers College Record, 108*(6), 1017–1054.

Olofson, M., Swallow, M., & Neumann, M. (2016). TPACKing: A constructivist framing of TPACK to analyze teachers' construction of knowledge. *Computers & Education, 95,* 188–201.

Oluo, I. (2019). *So you want to talk about race?* Seal Press.

Pellas, N., Kazanidis, I., Konstantinou, N., & Georgiou G. (2017). Exploring the educational potential of three-dimensional multi-user virtual worlds for STEM education: A mixed-method systematic literature review. *Education and Information Technologies, 22*(5), 2235–2279. https://doi.org/10.1007/s10639-016-9537-2

Pilgrim, J. M., & Pilgrim, J. (2016). The use of virtual reality tools in the reading-language arts classroom. *Texas Journal of Literacy Education, 4*(2), 90–97.

Rybakova, K., Rice, M., Moran, C., Zucker, L., McDermott, M., McGrail, E., …, Gibbons, T. (2019). A long arc bending toward equity: Tracing almost 20 years of ELA teaching trends in *CITE Journal*. Contemporary Issues in Technology and Teacher Education, 19(4). https://citejournal.org/volume-19/issue-4-19/english-la nguage-arts/a-long-arc-bending-toward-equity-tracing-almost-20-years-of-ela-teac hing-with-technology

Sang, G., Valcke, M., vanBraak, J., & Tondeur, J. (2010). Student teachers' thinking processes and ICT integration: Predictors of prospective teaching behaviors with educational technology. *Computers & Education, 54*(1), 103–112. https://doi.org /10.1016/j.compedu.2009.07.010

Sitzmann, T. (2011). A meta-analytic examination of the instructional effectiveness of computer-based simulation games. *Personnel Psychology, 64,* 489–528.

Sleeter, C. E. (2012). Confronting the marginalization of culturally responsive pedagogy. *Urban Education, 47*(3), 562–584. https://doi.org/10.1177 /0042085911431472

Stainfield, J., Fischer, P., Ford, B., & Solem, M. (2010). International virtual field trips: A new directions? *Journal of Geography in Higher Education, 24*(2), 255–262.

Twenge, J. M. (2017). *IGen: Why today's super-connected kids are growing up less rebellious, more tolerant, less happy—and completely unprepared for adulthood—and what that means for the rest of us.* Simon and Schuster.

Chapter 10

Empowering Language Teachers with Emerging Technologies

Augmented Reality for English Language Arts Classrooms

Babak Khoshnevisan

Emerging technologies, such as virtual reality (VR) and augmented reality (AR), have the potential to dramatically transform English language arts (ELA) education practices. Khoshnevisan and Le (2018) argue that there is no universally agreed-upon definition of emerging technologies such as AR. However, for the purpose of this chapter, I use Azuma's (1997) definition of AR, where AR is an emerging technology that blends digital information with the real environment. AR enables users to add a digital layer to the physical reality around them. Users may vary from designers to language educators who may need to superimpose a digital layer to their physical texts to both increase the motivation level and facilitate the process of knowledge acquisition (Khoshnevisan, 2019b; Park & Khoshnevisan, 2019). I make a concerted effort to both introduce AR and detail novel ways that educators can integrate AR in their practices. Beginning with a thorough explanation of AR, this chapter dives into the pertinent literature and explains the use of AR in education. I then shed light on prior AR-related studies and propose novel ways that language and ELA educators can exploit AR to facilitate students' learning process.

THEORIES USED TO CONCEPTUALIZE THE ROLE OF AR IN EDUCATION

Dunleavy and Dede (2014) stated that two prominent theories undergird augmented reality (AR): situated learning theory and constructivist learning theory. Dunleavy et al. (2009) discussed the likely connections between situated learning theory and AR. According to situated learning theory, learning occurs when people are engaged in different activities. Some AR situations allow students to use real-life experiences to facilitate learning. Learning is facilitated by a problem-solving environment where they need to contemplate and find solutions to everyday issues. Similarly, students use social interaction and collaboration to learn from one another. Dunleavy et al. (2009) argued the inextricable links between AR technology and the situated learning theory. According to Dunleavy et al. (2009), activities between learners can foster learning. In other words, learning occurs amid social activities. Situated learning theory posits that real-life knowledge acquisition has primacy over explicit instruction. If learners acquire knowledge in a real-life context, they can use the knowledge to tackle problems by the knowledge acquired (Vanderbilt, 1993). AR has gained attention, because it can create a virtual environment consistent with situated learning theories, and experiences can have additional layers of digital contextualization (Kim, 2013).

In constructivist theories of learning, meaning does not exist in the world but rather individuals impose it. Learners' prior knowledge shapes new knowledge. This knowledge formation is informed by the individuals' prior experiences, sociocultural understanding, and background (Abdoli-Sejzi & Aris, 2012; Dede, 2008; Lave & Wenger, 1991; Vygotsky, 1978). For instance, to teach a concept in history, an educator should elicit what learners already know about that event and then build upon the old knowledge with a directed activity, rather than giving a lecture. Learners interpret reality based on their previous knowledge and experiences. Constructivist learning theory sets five different conditions to enhance learning (Klopfer & Sheldon, 2010):

1. Presenting environments that are conducive to learning
2. Setting social discussions that are appropriate for a better learning experience
3. Introducing a variety of viewpoints as well as a number of methods to represent them
4. Preparing students for a self-directed learning style
5. Adopting metacognitive strategies

AR aligns with constructivist learning theory because it affords learners the social framework of the real world. Additionally, AR scaffolds learning and assists learners to participate in virtual communities. Parallel with human thoughts that are nurtured with variety, AR offers a contextualized learning environment. AR enriches the learning environment and offers quality material in a virtual world. When learners manage their learning style and pace, constructivist learning theory is being practiced. AR, thus, is in harmony with the major tenets of constructivist learning theory (Martín-Gutiérrez et al., 2010). AR has the potential to provide learners with an additional layer of information from which they can make meaning in the real world. Users have the choice to either use or ignore the added information. They can also select the required aspects of AR or digital material based on their needs. AR applications and games can create a learning environment where learners can use real-life experiences to have a unique learning experience. Students socially interact in AR-mediated situations to negotiate ideas, collaborate, and make plans for tackling complex issues.

TYPES OF AUGMENTED REALITY

There are two major types of AR: vision-based AR and location-aware AR. In vision-based AR, an image triggers a digital component superimposed on the real-world. AR learning apps such as *Reader Buddy* that help students learn the content through videos—triggered by the pictures in a text. This is an example of vision-based AR. However, for location-aware AR, no triggering picture is required, and digital information is linked with different locations in which users are placed. Location-aware AR is closely linked with the Global Positioning System (GPS). GPS is installed in most smart devices such as cellphones. GPS tracks the current location of a user and feeds the user with digital information based on the location within which he is placed. For example, *Pokémon Go* is a location-aware AR. In this AR game, users can hunt Pokémons based on their locations identified by a GPS—installed on their smartphones.

AUGMENTED REALITY AFFORDANCES

Multiple researchers have reiterated AR offers different advantages such as concretizing abstract concepts (Dori & Belcher, 2005). AR apps help learners to acquire new information in a contextualized manner (Hadid, Mannion, Khoshnevisan, 2019). AR contributes to a deeper understanding of the concepts, especially abstract concepts (Klopfer & Squire, 2008) because it helps to visualize the concepts for better understanding (Kaufmann & Schmalstieg, 2003). Besides, AR can help educators as it fosters learners' engagement (Bujak et al., 2013), helps to evolve critical thinking and problem-solving skills (Dunleavy, Dede & Mitchell, 2009), and makes learning more interesting and effective (Wojciechowski & Cellary, 2013). Having employed AR, educators can help learners enjoy the process of learning (Núñez et al., 2008) while drawing their attention to different topics (Aziz et al., 2012). An

AR environment can help educators form links with the real environment (Ternier et al., 2012) to facilitate comprehension (Ivanova & Ivanov, 2011) and increase the learners' motivation level (Di Serio et al., 2013). AR offers promises to English language art (ELA) classrooms that would be otherwise impossible. AR empowers both educators and learners by providing multimodality (Kress & Leeuwen, 2001). Khoshnevisan (2019a) reports that the use of multimodality affords educators and learners with different modalities (audio, video, and pictures) so learners with different learning styles can be benefited. Drawing on the multimodality theory, AR has the potential to supply educators with an arsenal of instructional strategies at their fingertips. Accordingly, the use of AR in language art classrooms can help learners gain insight into abstract concepts of books.

PEDAGOGICAL APPLICATIONS OF AUGMENTED REALITY

A recent body of literature indicates a disconnect between theories and the reality of technologies in educational institutions (Khoshnevisan, 2019b). The disconnect becomes apparent whenever language educators and teacher educators complain about the use of technologies and technological tools in classrooms. Even if the technology was out there, educators may be reluctant to use them. The disinterest in utilizing technologies leads to a disparity, which complicates the efficient use of technology in classrooms. According to the ELATE Commission on Digital Literacy in Teacher Education (2018), technologies supply teachers with novel ways to both understand and produce texts in ELA classrooms. The ELATE Commission recommended that ELA teachers should take new technologies into consideration only when it is clear how these technologies engage students, deepen their understanding, and expand their educational horizons. ELA teachers should make sure that the use of technology is parallel with their pedagogical instructions. On this account, efficiency and engagement should not take precedence over instructional practices. Also, the use of technology should be aligned with what we know about literacies as social practices. In and out-of-school literacies are both important. Technologies should enable teachers to help students in and out of classrooms. The use of technologies should enable students to practice what they learned in classrooms to hone their skills.

More importantly, ELA teachers should be cognizant of both advantages and limitations of AR. It is true that AR has a myriad of advantages such as increasing motivation level, enhancing understanding, and concretizing abstract concepts. However, it comes as no surprise that AR is accompanied with certain constraints that need to be taken into account before an ELA teacher steps into the class. The ELATE Commission urges ELA teachers to work with these technologies before they employ them in their practices in classrooms to be familiar with their strengths and weaknesses. Advantages and disadvantages of AR are not constant and may alter with a change in teachers' instructional practices. Accordingly, it is highly recommended that teachers familiarize themselves with these technologies before they use them in classrooms.

Aligned with the recommendations of the ELATE Commission regarding the use of technology in ELA, the use of AR needs to be detailed and delineated for ELA teachers. Khoshnevisan and Le (2018) argue that AR is not an effective technology unless it is effectively incorporated in teachers' practices. ELA teachers are then recommended to use AR whenever they feel it fits into the curriculum and daily lesson plans. While there is no one-size-fits-all prescription, ELA teachers need to tailor AR to cater to the students' needs. This may change with different audiences and their needs.

AR can be employed during a text reading session to introduce hard vocabulary in terms of pronunciation, definition, and use. Idiomatic phrases can be detailed by AR technology so students can decode the figurative meanings. This can be implemented via providing more context for learners. AR has the potential to provide us with a digital layer (context) to facilitate the process of learning. It can also serve as a novel way of glossing to aid reading comprehension and vocabulary learning. Digital glossing makes reading texts an easy task. Last but not least, abstract concepts used in texts can be digitally introduced. ELA teachers can make a video of their own, upload it on YouTube and then link it to AR. This is only one of the many ways that AR can be harnessed in literacy development in ELA classrooms. Alternatively, ELA teachers may develop AR flashcards. Flashcards can be used to learn vocabulary and idioms used in texts. Each flashcard may have a picture, definition, and example sentences of the vocabulary and idioms. These flashcards can be introduced before reading the text. Students can also use them at home to practice words, idioms, and abstract concepts. ELA teachers can link the picture of flashcards to a digital layer wherein the teacher can talk to their students or an animated pedagogical agent may explain the content (with pictures). There are many videos on YouTube that can serve as examples of how ELA teachers can use multimodal content to explain texts. These videos can be simply linked with a picture in texts or flashcards via AR applications such as *Aurasma*, *HP Reveal*, and *Metaverse*. Alternatively, ELA teachers can use QR codes in the absence of pictures in texts. The following section details AR codes as a way to link a digital layer to texts.

QUICK RESPONSE CODES

To date, researchers have exhausted positioning technologies including 802.11, IRDA, RFID, and GPS. Alongside these advanced technologies, 2D barcode technology has multiple affordances to offer. Liu, Tan, and Chu (2010) highlighted the merits of 2D barcodes including a rather "large storage capacity, high information density, strong encoding, strong error-correcting, high reliability, low cost, and ease of printing" (p. 2). Another version of 2D barcodes known as Quick Response (QR) codes were created by Japanese corporation Denso-Wave in 1994. Liu, Tan, and Chu (2010) employed QR codes printed on papers. In this study, learners used the guide map on their PDA phones to read the QR codes. Learners could talk with 3D-animated virtual learning (VLP), which popped up within a digital layer.

Liu et al. (2010) designed a course called "My Student Life" that used immersive and context-aware learning—pedagogical strategies—to encourage students to study a variety of topics through mobile game-based learning. In Liu et al.'s (2010) study, twenty students at the National Taipei University used the technology. The results of this study indicated that this technology was easy and convenient to use, increased the students' motivation, and improved four skills. The findings of the study confirmed the applicability and benefits of mobile technology in language education. Furthermore, the results implied that AR amounts to better vocabulary retention and enhances both student attention and satisfaction.

As discussed earlier, AR is a technology that provides a digital layer over reality. By the same token, QR codes have the potential to supply learners with a digital layer. The digital layer—in the case of AR—is triggered by the use of a location or a picture. In QR codes, however, the digital layer is triggered by 2D barcodes. Accordingly, if there is a picture in a book, ELA teachers can link the picture to the digital layer. In the absence of pictures, teachers can use QR codes to trigger the digital layer. In the pedagogical implications section, I list the websites that ELA teachers can use to link the digital layer to the website and create a QR code. The QR code can be either used in flashcards or added to the text. Students need to download a QR code reader on their smartphone so they can have access to the digital layer. The digital layer can be either created by teachers and stored in their computers or retrieved from a website.

PEDAGOGICAL IMPLICATIONS

Consistent with the aforementioned discussion, educators may want to use either AR or QR codes in their ELA classrooms. However, Khoshnevisan (2020a) notes there is not ample AR material in the market. Khoshnevisan

(2020a) expounds that we need to develop more AR-infused material for the current generation. To this end, ELA educators can simply create AR-infused material and use them in classrooms. Or, ELA educators who choose to use QR codes, can add the final QR codes to the page where the text is located. ELA educators can use QR codes for different purposes such as the pronunciation of words, the meaning of words, the figurative meaning of idioms, quick quizzes—to name but a few. QR codes have the potential to store or link the information and convey it to learners. Like AR, QR codes can relate the physical world to a digital world. As such, it is an interesting and intuitive way to present digital information to learners. ELA educators can have learners scan the QR codes using their smartphones or tablets and direct them to different pieces of information with different modalities (audio, video, animation, image). Unlike other proprietary tools, QR codes are available as open source. This makes this free tool a favorable technology. Educators can place QR codes in digital learning as well as physical classroom learning. To make a QR code, educators can employ one of the free QR-code creation websites. Table 10.1 details a number of QR code creation websites.

Table 10.1 Websites for Creation of QR Codes

Website	Capabilities
http://goqr.me	• Text QR Codes • URL QR Codes • Phone Number QR Codes • SMS QR Codes
http://qrmobilize.com/	• Ability to add Facebook User or Facebook Page • Ability to add Twitter • Can add over fifteen other social networks • Mobile website that works on most mobile phones
https://keremerkan.net/qr-code-and-2d-code-generator/	• Text QR Code • URL QR Codes • Phone Number QR Codes • SMS QR Codes • Google and Bing Maps QR codes • YouTube QR Codes
https://www.qrstuff.com/	• Text QR Codes • URL/Link QR Codes • Phone Number QR Codes • SMS Message QR Codes • vCard QR Codes • Google Maps QR Codes • Social Media QR Codes • iTunes Link QR Codes • YouTube QR Codes • Connect to a Wi-Fi network for Android Devices QR Code

QR Codes for Idiomatic Expressions

Sleep like a log   *Like a needle in a haystack*

Figure 10.1   QR Codes Like These Provide an Explanation of Idiomatic Expressions.

Idioms impose a challenge to nonnative language learners when they read texts (Khoshnevisan, 2018a; Khoshnevisan, 2019c; Khoshnevisan, 2020b). Providing a video to explain the figurative meaning of an idiom can facilitate the process of reading and bring up fluent readers. The QR codes shown in figure 10.1 showcase two idioms (sleep like a log, like a needle in a haystack). Scan the codes with a scan reader app to see the content. The digital information was uploaded on YouTube and can be retrieved by scanning the codes. QR codes can foster authentic language use and make learning more interesting. ELA educators do not have to create digital material themselves. They may link codes with a website or a video that already exists in cyberspace. However, I caution ELA educators against using the information in a piecemeal fashion because a large amount of information may lead to cognitive overload. AR and QR codes may fail to implement their role if cognitive load emerges during learning new information.

Another way to infuse technology in the reading of text is through the use of AR. If texts have a picture, educators can employ them to develop vision-based AR. There are many free AR apps such as *Aurasma* and *Hp Reveal* that can be used to craft AR material. *Hp Reveal* can be found in the App Store of a smartphone for free. The picture can serve as a trigger to show digital information about the text. To use AR material, learners need to install free AR apps on their smartphones so that pictures come to life and explain the content to promote deeper understanding.

CONCLUSION

AR as the technology of the future offers promises to both language educators and learners. With recent changes in education, including the prevalence of online instruction in a pandemic, one cannot ignore the vital role of technological tools in education. It, thus, behooves educators to familiarize themselves with these technological tools because their practice can be enhanced through evolving technologies.

This chapter detailed two types of AR (vision-based and location-aware) and the theories related to this technology. Additionally, the modus operandi of how best to integrate AR with the texts in ELA books was discussed. I strongly recommend teacher educators include a technology unit within their curriculum so that preservice teachers can be equipped with emerging technologies during their early stages of identity development (Khoshnevisan, 2017; Khoshnevisan 2018b; Khoshnevisan, 2018c; Rashtchi & Khoshnevisan, 2019). Similarly, in-service teachers can incorporate emerging technologies in their practice through professional development events.

REFERENCES

Abdoli-Sejzi, A., & Aris, B. (2012). Constructivist approach at virtual universities, *Journal of Procedia Social and Behavioral Science, 56*, 426–431.

Aziz, K., Aziz, N., Yusof, A., & Paul, A. (2012). Potential for providing augmented reality elements in special education via cloud computing. International Symposium on Robotics and Intelligent Sensors, *Procedia Engineering, 41*, 333–339.

Azuma, R. (1997). A survey of augmented reality. *Presence: Teleoperators and Virtual Environments, 6*(4), 355–385.

Bujak, K., Radu, I., Catrambone, C., MacIntyre, B., Zheng, R, & Golubski, G. (2013). A psychological perspective on augmented reality in the mathematics classroom. *Computers & Education, 68*, 536–544.

Dori, Y., & Belcher, J. (2005). How does technology-enabled active learning affect undergraduate students' understanding of electromagnetism concepts? *Journal of the Learning Sciences, 14*(2), 243–279.

Di Serio, A., Ibáñez, M., & Kloos, C. (2013). Impact of an augmented reality system on students' motivation for a visual art course, *Computers & Education, 68*, 586–596.

Dunleavy, M., & Dede, C. (2014). Augmented reality teaching and learning. In J. M. Spector, M. D. Merrill, J. Elen, & M. Bishop (Eds.), *Handbook of research on educational communications and technology* (pp. 735–745). Springer.

Dunleavy, M., Dede, C., & Mitchell, R. (2009). Affordances and limitations of immersive participatory augmented reality simulations for teaching and learning. *Journal of Science Education and Technology, 18*(1), 7–22.

Hadid, A., Mannion, P., & Khoshnevisan, B. (2019). Augmented reality to the rescue of language learners. *Florida Journal of Educational Research, 57*(2), 81–89.

Ivanova, M., & Ivanov, G. (2011). Enhancement of learning and teaching in computer graphics through marker augmented reality technology. *International Journal on New Computer Architectures and their Applications, 1*(1), 176–184.

Kaufmann, H., & Schmalstieg, D. (2003). Mathematics and geometry education with collaborative augmented reality. *Computers & Graphics, 27*(3), 339–345.

Khoshnevisan, B. (2017). *Developmental stages of preservice teachers: A critical analysis. TEIS Newsletter — TESOL.* Retrieved from http://newsmanager.commpa rtners.com/tesolteis/issues/2017-09-25/2.html

Khoshnevisan, B. (2018a). *Idiom Assessment: To go off the beaten path.* Proceedings of the Global Conference on Education and Research (GLOCER) Conference (Vol. 2, pp. 2–9). ANAHEI Publishing, LLC. https://scholarcommons.usf.edu/cgi/viewc ontent.cgi?article=1017&context=anaheipublishing

Khoshnevisan, B. (2018b). The developmental stages of ITAs: An introspection. *ITAIS Newsletter — TESOL International Association.* Retrieved from http://new smanager.commpartners.com/tesolitais/issues/2018-06-26/4.html

Khoshnevisan, B. (2019a). Spilling the beans on understanding English idioms using multimodality: An idiom acquisition technique for Iranian language learners. *International Journal of Language, Translation and Intercultural Communication, 8*, 128–143.

Khoshnevisan, B. (2019b). Teacher education meets emerging technologies: Augmented Reality (AR). *TEIS Newsletter — TESOL International Association.* Retrieved from http://newsmanager.commpartners.com/tesolteis/issues/2019-03-04/4.html

Khoshnevisan, B. (2019c). Idiom learning for L1 / L2 language learners: Cut from a different cloth. *ALIS Newsletter — TESOL International Association.* Retrieved from http://newsmanager.commpartners.com/tesolalis/issues/2019-08-26/5.html

Khoshnevisan, B. (2020a). Materials development for the digital native generation: Teachers as materials developers. *MWIS Newsletter — TESOL International Association.* Retrieved from http://newsmanager.commpartners.com/tesolmwis/ issues/2020-01-09/4.html

Khoshnevisan, B. (2020b). *The effects of augmented reality (AR)-infused idiom material on Iranian students' idiom achievements, motivation, and perceptions* (Unpublished doctoral dissertation). The University of South Florida, Tampa. FL.

Khoshnevisan, B., & Le, N. (2018). Augmented reality in language education: A sys-tematic literature review. *Proceedings of the Global Conference on Education and Research (GLOCER) Conference* (Vol. 2, pp. 57–71). ANAHEI Publishing, LLC. Retrieved from https://scholarcommons.usf.edu/cgi/viewcontent.cgi?article=1017 &context=anaheipublishing

Kim, J. (2013). A signboard character recognition situated learning system based on mobile Augmented reality. *Advanced Science and Technology Letters, 29*, 303–306.

Klopfer, E., & Sheldon, J. (2010). Augmenting your own reality: Student authoring of science-based augmented reality games. *New Directions for Youth Development, 128*, 85–94.

Klopfer, E., & Squire, K. (2008). Environmental detectives: the development of an augmented reality platform for environmental simulations. *Educational Technology Research and Development, 56*(2), 203–228.

Kress, G., & Van Leeuwen, T. (2001). *Multimodal discourse.* Arnold.

Lave, J., & Wenger, E. (1991). *Situated learning: Legitimate peripheral participa-tion.* Cambridge University Press.

Liu, T., Tan, T., & Chu, Y. (2010). QR code and augmented reality-supported mobile English learning system. In X. Jiang, M. Ma, & C. W. Chen (Eds.), *Mobile multimedia processing* (pp. 37–52). Springer.

Martín-Gutiérrez, J., Saorín, J. L., Contero, M., Alcañiz, M., Pérez-López, D. C., & Ortega, M. (2010). Design and validation of an augmented book for spatial abilities development in engineering students. *Computers & Graphics, 34*(1), 77–91.

Núñez, M., Quirós, R., Núñez, I., Carda, J. B., Camahort, E., & Mauri, L. (2008). Collaborative Augmented Reality for Inorganic Chemistry Education. *Proceedings of the Mathematics and Computers in Science and Engineering* (Vol. 5, pp. 271–277). WSEAS.

Park, S. & Khoshnevisan, B. (2019). Literacy meets augmented reality (AR): The use of AR in literacy. In W. B. James, & C. Cobanoglu (Eds.) *Proceedings of the Global Conference on Education and Research (GLOCER) Conference* (Vol. 3, pp. 93–99). ANAHEI Publishing, LLC. Retrieved from https://scholarcommons.us f.edu/cgi/viewcontent.cgi?article=1021&context=anaheipublishing

Rashtchi, M., & Khoshnevisan, B. (2019). The developmental stages of teachers: A critical analysis. In W. B. James, & C. Cobanoglu (Eds.) *Proceedings of the Global Conference on Education and Research (GLOCER) Conference* (Vol. 3, pp. 2–8). ANAHEI Publishing, LLC. Retrieved from https://scholarcommons.usf.edu/cgi/viewcontent.cgi?article=1021&context=anaheipublishing

Ternier, S., Klemke, R., Kalz, M., Ulzen, P., & Specht, M. (2012). AR learn augmented reality meets augmented virtuality. *Journal of Universal Computer Science, 18*(15), 2143–2164.

Vanderbilt, C. (1993). Anchored instruction and situated cognition revisited. *Educational Technology, 33*(3), 52–70.

Vygotsky, L. S. (1978). *Mind and society: The development of higher mental processes.* Harvard University Press.

Wojciechowski, R., & Cellary, W. (2013). Evaluation of learners' attitude toward learning in ARIES augmented reality environments. *Computers & Education, 68,* 570–585.

Afterword

Daydreaming of Equity and Virtual Reality

Dawn Whipple

As teachers, we dream of that magical classroom moment where student engagement and learning collide. To the untrained eye, this "magic" seemingly manifests out of nowhere. However, as most reflective educators know, these classroom moments rarely appear out of thin air. They must be planned, nurtured, and cultivated to be effective. The dream of effectively using virtual and augmented reality (VR/AR) in an English language arts (ELA) classroom is an attainable goal. As educational activists (Montaño et al., 2002), we must keep our purpose clear. In recent years, public education has felt a steady push toward having students be college-and-career ready and increased pressure to demonstrate student achievement on standardized tests. The commodification of public education transforms teachers into delivery workers and "reduces teaching to the simple and efficient delivery of the package called curriculum" (Ayers & Ayers, 2014, p. 104). Commodification dehumanizes both students and teachers, stripping them of opportunities for relationship building, empathy modeling, and mutual accountability. It contributes to an "educational hierarchy" (Ayers & Ayers, 2014, p. 104) that disintegrates the educational system into a transactional relationship (Freire, 1970). Embracing new technology, like VR/AR, must be viewed as a tool for building equity and social justice within the classroom. By building students' overall ability to excel with experiential learning, teachers build learning communities that are student-centered versus the historical teacher-centered ones. VR/AR technologies should not be used as a tool to increase test performance or prepare for a career path. Instead, these should be leveraged as tools to disrupt oppressive educational practices historically associated with formal schooling and empower students to advocate for themselves and their communities.

Audre Lorde wrote, "The learning process is something you can incite, literally incite, like a riot" (Lorde, 2007, pp. 97–98). Scholar and educator

257

bell hooks frames teaching and learning as a revolutionary act that requires "a rethinking of ways of knowing, a deconstruction of old epistemologies, and the concomitant demand that there be a transformation in our classrooms, in how we teach and what we teach, has been a necessary revolution—one that seeks to restore life to a corrupt and dying academy" (hooks, 1994, p. 30). Change is necessary and needed for the sake of our students. English educators are in a unique position to work cross-content to forge new academic innovations by combining elements of social studies, science, art, math, and technology.

A VISION OF EQUITY FOR ALL

"No justice, No peace!" These words shouted by protestors during the turbulent civil unrest in summer 2020 have resonated and taken residence in my consciousness and will not go away. The global pandemic of COVID-19 has presented educators with a unique opportunity. While we navigate the waters of virtual learning, we should use this as a time to reflect and create plans of action to drastically change and dismantle many of our face-to-face instructional practices. We must wake up to the harsh realities of what bell hooks defined as the "white supremacist capitalist patriarchy" (Jhally, 1997). If these "interlocking systems of domination" are present in government-sanctioned entities like law enforcement and the criminal justice system, then we can postulate that the public educational system mirrors these same oppressive forces.

But we should not accept oppression as humane or normal. Dr. Bettina L. Love coined the phrase *abolitionist teaching* in describing a culturally relevant pedagogy that should inform teachers integration of technology within the classroom. She wrote, "[a]bolitionist teaching is the practice of working in solidarity with communities of color while drawing on the imagination, creativity, refusal, (re)membering, visionary thinking, healing, rebellious spirit, boldness, determination, and subversiveness of abolitionists to eradicate injustice in and outside of schools" (Love, 2020, p. 3). Abolitionist teaching is rooted in the community and social justice. Instructional practices are regularly examined, questioned, constructed, and deconstructed with the underlying goals of cultivating equity and empowerment.

As English teachers, we should first consider issues of equity and empowerment. Equity and equality are not the same. Teachers should seek equitable practices when we are providing resources and opportunities to students. Our considerations should be based on what individual students need, not based on equal distribution of resources and opportunities. Equality is a teacher-centered practice that is built on the convenience, wants, and needs of the educator or the institution. Equality speaks to what is easiest for me as an educator. We recite mantras like, "Every student gets the same thing," or "I treat all of my students the same." This mentality fails to acknowledge the individual needs of every student or any of the various socioeconomic factors that are outside of the control of teachers. It also blatantly ignores the inherent bias and trauma that teachers bring into the classroom. This practice can punish students who arrive with "deficits" in academics, resources, or outside support and simultaneously reward students who enter our classrooms academically advanced, rich in resources and/or outside support.

In contrast, equity is a student-centered practice that seeks to consider the needs of individual students. In 2017, the National Board for Professional Standards (NBPS) released a series of equity standards for English educators. According to the report, "accomplished teachers use a variety of strategies and materials to address disparities among students and provide meaningful learning opportunities that meet the diverse needs of all learners" (NBPS, 2017, p. 30). Adopting equity standards, like the one prescribed, invites teachers to acknowledge disparities in student resources, personal biases, and systemic oppression that can hinder a student's growth and learning opportunities. As educators, we must take the action of allowing these standards to be a catalyst for real change in classroom practices and teacher mindset. The organization further stated that "accomplished teachers recognize their own biases and do not allow them to negatively interfere in their decisions" (NBPS, 2017, p. 31). This standard is not for the faint of heart. Are we reflecting on our own biases and how this can inflict trauma onto our students? Are we willing to engage in examining our own biases, not as a singular activity but, as an ongoing process? Will we be honest and accountable to our students, other educators, and most importantly ourselves?

WAKE UP, SHARE THE DREAM: FINAL ANALYSIS

Integrating VR/AR technology into an ELA classroom requires a mixture of practicality and imagination. Strategic planning is necessary when integrating this innovative practice in the classroom. There is no one delineated path or roadmap that teachers can follow. However, being armed with intentional guidelines for equity will help to make this dream a more attainable reality for all of our students. Like many aspects of education, this burgeoning technology will need room and time to grow. As educators, we need to embrace this new adventure with hope. As hooks (2003) says, "My hope emerges from those places of struggle where I witness individuals positively transforming their lives and the world around them. Educating is always a vocation rooted in hopefulness. As teachers, we believe that learning is possible, that nothing can keep an open mind from seeking after knowledge and finding a way to know" (p. 14).

Poet Lucille Clifton famously said, "we cannot create what we can't imagine." Before exposing students to VR/AR in the classroom, educators must reimagine how equity can be moved from the theoretical to practical. This technology has the potential of helping to decrease the digital divide instead of contributing to it. With reflective educators, VR/AR can be leveraged into a tool for social justice by exposing our students to global issues and challenges, increasing representation of forgotten and marginalized voices, establishing a broader historical context, and inspiring them to create a reality that can be seen with or without goggles.

REFERENCES

Ayers, R., & Ayers, W. (2014). *Teaching the taboo: Courage and imagination in the classroom.* Teachers College Press.

Freire, P. (1970). *The pedagogy of the oppressed.* Bloomsbury.

hooks, b. (1994). *Teaching to transgress: Education as the practice of freedom.* Routledge.

hooks, b. (2003). *Teaching Community: a pedagogy of hope.* Routledge.

Jhally, S. (director). 1997. *bell hooks—Cultural criticism & transformation.* [Video file]. Retrieved from https://www.youtube.com/watch?v=KLMVqnyTo_0.

Kibler, K., & Chapman, L. A. (2018, May/June). Six tips for using culturally relevant texts in diverse classrooms. *The Reading Teacher, 72*(6), 741–744.

Lorde, A. (2007). *Sister outsider: Essays and speeches.* Ten Speed Press.

Love, B. L. (2020). *We want to do more than survive: Abolitionist teaching and the pursuit of educational freedom.* Beacon Press.

Montaño, T., Lòpez-Torres, L., DeLissovoy, N., Pachecho, M., & Stillman, J. (2002). Teachers as activists: Teacher development and alternate sites of learning. *Equity and Excellence in Education*, 265–275.

National Board for Professional Teaching Standards. (2017). *Equity standards.* Retrieved from www.NBPTS.org.

Index

About the Editors and Contributors

ABOUT THE EDITORS

Clarice M. Moran is an assistant professor of English Education at Appalachian State University in Boone, North Carolina, and the co-chair of the Digital Literacies in Teacher Education (D-LITE) commission for the National Council of Teachers of English. She holds a PhD from North Carolina State University and is a former high school English teacher and journalist. She works with preservice and in-service English language arts (ELA) teachers in North Carolina. Her research interests include technology integration in ELA, student engagement, and teacher education. She has published several journal articles on the use of virtual reality (VR) in the K–12 classroom and enjoys using VR as a tool for writing and student engagement.

Mary F. Rice is an assistant professor of Literacy at the University of New Mexico. She teaches writing pedagogy and digital composition. Her scholarship uses interdisciplinary approaches to study the literacies and identities of online teachers and learners. Mary was a postdoctoral researcher at the University of Kansas Center on Online Learning and Students with Disabilities. She is also an Online Learning Consortium Emerging Scholar and a Michigan Virtual Learning Research Institute fellow. Mary taught junior high English language arts, ESL, and reading support classes and was a Teaching English Language Learner program instructor before becoming a professor.

ABOUT THE CONTRIBUTORS

Steven Z. Athanases is a professor and the Dolly and David Fiddyment Chair in Teacher Education at the University of California, Davis. A former Illinois high school English teacher, Athanases completed a PhD in education and a postdoctoral fellowship in English, both at Stanford University. He prepares English teachers and studies teaching and teacher education, focused on literacy, diversity, and equity. Athanases is PI/project manager (2018) for a McDonnell Foundation Teachers as Learners grant exploring how ELA teachers learn to facilitate meaningful discussions, and is the research director of the UC Davis Center for Shakespeare in Diverse Classrooms, partnering with Globe Education, Globe Theatre, London.

Christine Chang is an instructor in the Curriculum, Instruction, and the Science of Learning program at the University at Buffalo, offering graduate courses in English education. She has taught undergraduate-level courses in both online and face-to-face settings and worked on interdisciplinary research projects. Dr. Chang's research focuses on the evaluation of literacy practices in technology-supported learning environments, particularly how multimodal representation can facilitate students' learning performances and teacher preparation.

Anne Cloonan is an associate professor in Literacy Education and the Research Pathways Coordinator in the School of Education at Deakin University in Australia. Anne is known for her teaching and research in the areas of digital literacies, multimodality, intercultural understanding and teacher research. She investigates teacher learning and implications of new technologies on pedagogical design and teacher and student identities. Anne's research partners include the Australian Curriculum and Assessment and Reporting Authority; the Australian Institute for Teaching and School Leaderships; the Australian Research Council; Catholic Education Melbourne; Department of Education and Training and the Organisation for Economic Cooperation and Development.

Elisabeth Etopio is the assistant dean of Teacher Education at the University at Buffalo, Graduate School of Education. Her research examines varied factors that impact preservice teachers' professional development. Recently, she collaborated with an interdisciplinary team to create a virtual reality environment to enhance the classroom management skills of preservice teachers, implement the technology within teacher education classes, and assess the outcomes. Dr. Etopio has published multiple peer-reviewed journal articles and given presentations at national and international conferences related to the use of neuroimaging techniques to understand learning as a result of development and exposure to learning environments.

Benjamin Gallegos is an assistant professor in the School of Education at the University of Portland in Portland, Oregon. He received his PhD in Exceptional Education from the University of Central Florida (UCF). His research interests center on providing students with and without disabilities inclusive access to science content and increasing science, technology, engineering, and mathematics (STEM) career interests using virtual learning environments.

Jennifer M. Higgs is an assistant professor of Language, Literacy, and Culture and Learning and Mind Sciences at the University of California, Davis. Her research focuses on digital tool use that supports equitable learning and teaching, adolescents' digital literacies, and support structures that may help teachers facilitate consequential uses of new technologies. She investigates practices around digital tools as well as improvement of digital tool practices in partnership with educators. Prior to pursuing her PhD at the University of California, Berkeley, she was a public high school English teacher in Virginia and Illinois.

Paige Jacobson is an English teacher based in the greater Atlanta area. She has worked in special education and general education at Elkins Pointe Middle School, Alpharetta High School, and Milton High School in Fulton County, Georgia. She received her Master of Arts in Teaching Secondary English from Kennesaw State University and her Bachelor of Arts in English from Oglethorpe University. Prior to working in education, she worked in horticultural therapy at Skyland Trail, a nonprofit mental health treatment organization, and she volunteers at local farms in her community. A member of the Georgia Council of Teachers of English (GCTE), she has presented at and been a discussion leader for the "The Future Is Now" roundtable session at the GCTE annual convention. Her educational interests include media literacy, language and grammar, critical inquiry-based learning, teacher pedagogy, and fostering lifelong learning among students.

Erin Kearney is an associate professor of Second and Foreign Language Education in the Department of Learning and Instruction at the University at Buffalo. Her research focuses on multilingual education, teacher learning in initial preparations and ongoing professional development, and immersive experiences in teaching and learning. Dr. Kearney's classroom-based research and work as a teacher educator intersect in a range of publications and conference presentations as well as advocacy and professional development engagements for languages education and teachers at local, state, and national levels.

Babak Khoshnevisan has a PhD in Technology in Education and Second Language Acquisition (TESLA) from the University of South Florida (USF). He is the instructor of EAP courses at INTO USF. He is also a material developer at Teachcast with Oxford. His research interests include teacher education, idiomaticity, augmented reality, virtual reality, and computer-assisted language learning.

Rick Marlatt is an assistant professor of English Language Arts and Literacy at New Mexico State University where he received the College of Education's Emerging Scholar Award in 2018 and was nominated for NMSU's Patricia Christmore Teaching Award in 2019. His work bridges the fields of teacher education, creative writing, digital literacies, literature study, and sociocultural theory. His recent interests include the cultivation of critical digital pedagogy in secondary English language arts, incorporation of poetry into preservice teacher education, and the implementation of video games and virtual reality technologies to enhance literature study and literacy identities for adolescents. Rick is also the co-chair of the Digital Literacies in Teacher Education (D-LITE) commission for the National Council of Teachers of English.

David Mawer is a doctoral student in learning sciences and instructor in the Department of Media Study at the University at Buffalo. He has previously taught secondary-level visual arts, media, and technology courses throughout New York state. David's research interests include the implementation of GIS into educational settings and utilizing educational technology to foster student spatial thinking skills.

Christine Oughtred is a PhD candidate in the School of Education, Deakin University, Australia. Her doctoral research topic, "Emerging criteria for literary quality of interactive digital picture books" includes case studies on picture book apps, augmented reality and virtual reality for which she has interviewed young adult readers as well as specialists in the field of literature and media internationally. A previous judge and coordinator for the Children's Book Council of Australia (CBCA) Children's Book of the Year Awards, Christine currently sits on the CBCA Awards subcommittee responsible for book awards for children and young adults. She is passionate about sharing quality literature with children, young adults, and educators. Christine has also held professional positions as a primary school teacher and as a manager at both a Regional Library Service and a University Library.

Louise Paatsch is an associate professor and the associate head of school (Research) in the School of Education, Deakin University, Australia. She is also the deputy director of Deakin University's Strategic Research Centre in Education—Research for Educational Impact (REDI). Her research focuses on children's and young people's communication, language, pretend play, and literacy development, with a strong focus on metapragmatic and pragmatic language use and the link to social communication. She also investigates teachers' talk patterns and intentional teaching practices in supporting children's and young people's communication, language, and play abilities. Louise also undertakes research that focuses on the communication, spoken language, and literacy abilities of deaf and hard-of-hearing children and young people. She also works with teachers and educators to explore their own practices as reflective researchers to support positive outcomes for children, young people, and their families.

Nichole Ralston is an associate professor in the School of Education at the University of Portland in Portland, Oregon. She received her PhD in Educational Psychology with an emphasis in Measurement, Statistics, and Research Design from the University of Washington. An elementary school teacher at heart, she now teaches educational research and STEM methods courses to undergraduate and graduate students and is codirector of the Multnomah County Partnership for Education Research (MCPER). She researches in the areas of educational pedagogies, educational partnerships, and implementing educational pedagogies in engineering education.

Rebecca Smith teaches and learns from future teachers as assistant professor in the School of Education at the University of Portland in Portland, Oregon. After educating high schoolers for ten years, she earned her EdD from the University of Portland, and she now teaches methods and research courses to undergraduate and graduate students. Her research areas include teacher learning and professional development, culturally responsive practices, and innovative technologies.

Aubrey Statti is an assistant professor of Educational Psychology and Technology at the Chicago School of Professional Psychology. She has worked in higher education for fourteen years and has taught at the undergraduate, graduate, and postgraduate levels in areas of psychology, counseling, education, research, human services, and life coaching. Her research interests include educational psychology, educational technology, K–12 education, online education, early childhood education, rural education, and the impact of mentorship in educational settings.

Kelly Torres is the department chair of the Educational Psychology and Technology program at the Chicago School of Professional Psychology. She also has taught numerous university-level courses in both online and face-to-face settings in content areas such as educational psychology, foundations of education, assessment, curriculum development, linguistics, and culture. She has mentored elementary-aged learners for over a decade. Dr. Torres's research interests are focused on the implementation of technology in educational settings in order to enhance student academic outcomes and on various aspects of the motivational influences that may impact second language learning and culture.

Megan E. Welsh is an associate professor at the University of California, Davis, where she teaches graduate, undergraduate, and teacher education courses in assessment and measurement theory. She has also worked as an elementary school teacher, a school district administrator, and an educational policy researcher. She received her bachelor's degree at Wellesley College, has an MPP from the University of California, Berkeley, and earned her PhD in Measurement and Research Methods from the University of Arizona. Her research interests are in test validity and development and use of assessments.

Dawn Whipple believes in empowering students through the practice of social justice pedagogy. The year 2020 marks her eleventh-year teaching in public education. Dr. Whipple is a certified teacher leader with Cobb County School District in Georgia and serves as the department chair for the English Department at Pebblebrook High School. In 2019, Dr. Whipple was awarded an impact grant courtesy of the Cobb Schools Foundation. Through this grant, she purchased virtual reality equipment. She currently uses VR to challenge traditional pedagogy and inspire her students.

William Terrell Wright is a PhD student in the Department of Language and Literacy Education at the University of Georgia. His research spans/entangles teacher education, critical media literacy, participatory action research, and educational technology. Prior to pursuing his PhD, he was a public high school English teacher in North Carolina.